SOFTWARE DESIGN FOR MICROCOMPUTERS

CAROL ANNE OGDIN

Prentice-Hall, Inc., Englewood Cliffs, N.J. 07632

Library of Congress Cataloging in Publication Data

OGDIN, CAROL ANN, (*date*)
Software design for microcomputers.

Includes index.
1. Microcomputers—Programming. I. Title.
QA76.6038   001.6′42   78-5801
ISBN 0-13-821744-0
ISBN 0-13-821801-3 pbk.

Printed in the United States of America

10   9   8   7   6   5   4   3   2   1

PRENTICE-HALL INTERNATIONAL, INC., *London*
PRENTICE-HALL OF AUSTRALIA PTY. LIMITED, *Sydney*
PRENTICE-HALL OF CANADA, LTD., *Toronto*
PRENTICE-HALL OF INDIA PRIVATE LIMITED, *New Delhi*
PRENTICE-HALL OF JAPAN, INC., *Tokyo*
PRENTICE-HALL OF SOUTHEAST ASIA PTE. LTD., *Singapore*
WHITEHALL BOOKS LIMITED, *Wellington, New Zealand*

Software Design
for
Microcomputers

—and Brooke
…through a Pentagram.

Contents

Preface   *ix*

1 What Is Software?   *1*

2 Procedures and Data   *9*

3 Data Structures   *21*

4 Procedure Structures   *39*

5 Algorithm Design   *50*

6 Program Notations   *67*

7 Program Documentation   *85*

8 Introduction to BASIC   *96*

9 Writing and Running a BASIC Program   *119*

10 Testing and Debugging Techniques   *132*

11 Other Programming Languages   *146*

12 Real-time Programming   *164*

13 Systems Software   *179*

Index   *191*

**—and Brooke
…through a Pentagram.**

Contents

Preface   *ix*

1 What Is Software?   *1*

2 Procedures and Data   *9*

3 Data Structures   *21*

4 Procedure Structures   *39*

5 Algorithm Design   *50*

6 Program Notations   *67*

7 Program Documentation   *85*

8 Introduction to BASIC   *96*

9 Writing and Running a BASIC Program   *119*

10 Testing and Debugging Techniques   *132*

11 Other Programming Languages   *146*

12 Real-time Programming   *164*

13 Systems Software   *179*

Index   *191*

Preface

"Software Design for Microcomputers" distills much of the recent experience gained by trial-and-error in the software industry. From this sorting of the best of available techniques, I hope that you, the reader, will be spared some of the same mistakes others have made. I made the assumption that you are about to embark on a software design task (probably on a micro, but the principles work for any common digital computer), and that you want to do the best job possible. I have tried to select the best methods from all of the available literature and meld them into a cohesive methodology that experienced digital designers and engineers can apply with little fear of failure.

There are many books on programming—but few on the subject of software design. And, so far as I know, none of the available books assume that you are an intelligent, rational designer with some experience that serves as a valuable starting place. Like its companion, MICROCOMPUTER DESIGN, this book has already been "field-tested." About two-thirds of this manuscript originally appeared in *EDN* magazine's June 5, 1977, issue under the title "Software Design Course." In recognition, that issue was accorded the American Business Press' Jesse Neale Award as the best contributed series of 1977.

The purpose of SOFTWARE DESIGN is not merely to reprint a series of articles, but to add to the basis of knowledge you already have. You may be new to software, having learned the rudiments while reading MICROCOMPUTER DESIGN, or you may be experienced in digital design with a smattering of programming background, or you may have last brushed against a computer in a FORTRAN course in college. No matter what background you bring to it, "Software Design" will show you a step-by-step approach to the design, implementation and checkout of reliable and valuable software. The book is arranged in a progression of thirteen chapters, from fundamentals review to sophisticated detail.

Chapter 1 reviews the basis for software and explodes some myths. Software design is just like hardware design—no more difficult, no easier. The same design disciplines that are applied to digital systems in TTL or CMOS can be applied to programs written for a computer. The emphasis for the entire book is established with the twin premises that: 1. Literate man of the late 20th Century must know how to program; and 2. Programming is a cerebral exercise conducted by intelligent people.

Chapter 2 describes in detail the basic steps in successful software design. By intentionally drawing the distinction between designing, programming, and coding, we separate a formerly confused morass into a logical sequence. Then we show the economic consequences of doing a poor design job and expecting to recover during the debugging phase of the project.

Chapter 3 begins "Software Design's" radical departure from most introductory programming texts. Instead of showing how to write code, this chapter shows how to design data structures. *This* is one of the major keys to successful software. A set of possible variants on data structuring are shown, and some empirical rules for describing all possible data structures are outlined.

In Chapter 4, the logical "dual" of data structures—procedures—are described in equivalent detail. Parallels are constructed between data structures and procedure structures, and the power of switching from one to the other during design is emphasized.

In Chapter 5 we begin to apply these techniques to the requirements that are common to both hardware and software. By recording each step, from concept of need to final algorithm, this chapter shows how experienced designers work.

Alternative ways to describe the algorithms for implementation as a computer program are shown in Chapter 6. First, flowcharts are debunked. Next, several alternative ways of describing software during the design process are presented. Choices among these different documentation and design tools are also explained.

Chapter 7 may seem out of place in a book on software design, yet it may be the most important part of the entire work. Documentation is done *before* a program is written, not after. Chapter 7 shows a simple way to document software (and hardware) designs in a way that encourages revisions during the design stages and discourages them after the design has been settled.

Chapter 8 introduces one of the important parts of programming: coding. We have elected to use the BASIC language only because it is so easy to read. Although a powerful language, it is not the only tool in a programmer's kit. The rudimentary statements in the BASIC language are revealed in sufficient detail for subsequent chapters to show actual program implementations.

Coding a properly designed program into BASIC and onto the computer is the subject of Chapter 9. The steps, incorporating the concepts of Chapters 2 through 8, are outlined in a series of illustrations, each one a more elaborate design of the one preceding. Finally, an actual computer print-out shows all the actions taken in the testing and debugging of a simple program. Coincidentally, the application selected is unusual: the plotting of an arbitrary function on the printer or terminal of the computer.

Chapter 10 deals with the tricks and techniques of the inexact art of testing and debugging computer programs. Like design, testing is a mental activity. Most practical programs cannot be tested exhaustively, so some intelligence must be applied by the test-case designer to inspire confidence in the resulting software product.

Chapter 11 deals with several other popular languages. The discussion shows the extensions provided in advanced versions of BASIC, then illustrates programs in FORTRAN, COBOL, APL, PASCAL and Assembly Language. In each case, the advantages and disadvantages of each language are provided so you can select the best language for your own programming needs.

The special requirements of real-time programs on minis and micros are treated in detail in Chapter 12. Since most microprocessor applications involve real-time, and real-time is the bane of programming reliability, compromises are essential. Chapter 12 shows how to judge those compromises and how to design highly reliable real-time software.

Systems software, programs that aid program development, are discussed in the final chapter of the book. Monitors, supervisors and operating systems are described, as well as some of the considerations in their selection and use. Finally, principles behind language translators and program loaders are discussed, so you can understand manufacturer's software literature.

These chapters describe techniques I use every day and have taught to many other people. If you follow them carefully, you will be able to produce reliable, useful and valuable programs. Furthermore, you will have a distinct advantage over most "experienced" programmers who resist learning these new techniques because they believe they know all there is to ever know about programming, designing and coding. I do not believe that I will ever know it all—but these few techniques keep me out of the most serious kinds of troubles to which programmers seem heir.

CAROL ANNE OGDIN

1

What Is Software?

Software is no longer an avoidable subject. Although computers have been accessible to engineers and system designers for over 30 years, many of us have avoided learning the new skills required. And, of course, many of the computer experts have made a simple topic complex. Actually, as you will discover in this design course, software is not at all difficult to learn. Much of the knowledge you already have can be redirected toward the new implications of computer programs; learning how to program need not be a painful experience.

This design course will be an unconventional treatment of software. You will not find another boring introduction to binary arithmetic; if you have ever designed a digital circuit you know that already. You will not find another basic introduction to elementary computers; as an intelligent, well-read designer, you obviously already have these ideas firmly grasped. In this design course we are going to concentrate on the practical steps you must take in order to understand, use, and create software in today's electronic environment.

What Is Software?

Software is more than a collection of holes punched in cards or paper tape. It includes the whole gamut of nonelectronic support to computers. When we talk of software, we mean the computer programs (in all their various forms), the instructions for use and the user's manuals, and the necessary design documentation.

If we look at the computer itself, we can see it, feel it, even squeeze it. This part of the system is called the *hardware*. But a general-purpose computer is a useless lump of electronics until and unless it is provided with a program in the computer's store. The physical storage medium is part of the hardware; the particular binary state of each individual storage element is not something we can generally feel, see, or squeeze. This particular combination of binary states contains the program (and probably some data). Since we cannot physically handle it, we call it *software*.

There are three different kinds of software:

1. Applications programs. Software that is especially written to solve some particular problem.
2. Systems programs. Software that usually comes with the computer from the manufacturer and is designed to make the creation of applications programs easier.
3. Documentation. Software that shows us how to use the programs and how to modify them for special needs.

Sometimes, only the second kind of software (system programs) are considered to be "software." According to accepted industry standards, however, if you take

The Gutenburg Era

To be a good programmer today is as much a privilege as it was to be a literate man in the sixteenth century.

Andrei Ershov

Microprocessors have brought us all into the Gutenburg era of computing. It is almost as inexpensive to reproduce and distribute a *process* as it is to reproduce and distribute *information.* Just as Gutenburg's invention allowed the inexpensive reproduction and distribution of information in the form of printed and bound books, the microcomputer will have an astounding impact on society in the next 25 years.

The effect on electronic designers will be no less astounding. No longer need we concern ourselves with the management of vast armies of monks, secretly enscribing illuminated manuscripts of COBOL and FORTRAN, each with their own individualities and idiosyncracies. Instead, we can look forward to the creation of an elite cadre of software authors who create the major works and to the eventual acquisition of programming skills by the general populace.

Literate men of the late twentieth century must know how to program.

away the physical computer from a system, what you have left is called the software.

You will notice an emphasis on including documentation in the definition of software. That is intentional. Throughout this design course you will find a recurring theme of documentation. Good programs are characterized by good documentation. Furthermore, good documentation is written *before* the program itself is written. All too often when we think of software we imagine only the computer program as it resides in the computer's storage medium. That is the hallmark of the novice. The experienced computer user looks to the documentation, just as the experienced electronics designer looks beyond the schematic to the supporting documents. A good design document completely explains what the program does. The program is a formal restatement of the design in binary digits that the computer can understand.

Software Environments

Software exists in relation to some computer (or computers). It is important to note the differences among kinds of computers and the various environments in which software exists. The concepts of programming and software design are the same, regardless of the software's environment. However, you cannot effectively design without having some awareness of the various environments you may be called upon to exploit.

Certainly, today's designer is faced with the novel opportunity of the microprocessor and microcomputer. These devices provide the greatest impetus to learning about software only because their application domain is so pervasive. To ignore software (and therefore to ignore micros) is as foolhardy as trying to ignore integrated circuits might have been a few years ago, or transistors a decade before that. Micros represent an essentially "raw" computing capacity that is unadorned by much additional software to make using them easy. However, if history repeats itself, more and more systems programs will become available, making the use of micros easier and easier. That, in turn, will drive costs down even more and will encourage more people to use them. With more users, there will be more incentive for the development of more and better systems programs that will, of course, encourage even more use of micros.

The history of the micro is already paralleling the recent history of the minicomputer, which was originally introduced as a relatively low-cost system component (priced around $25,000; then, computers cost over $250,000). The mini was also without much software. However, today's minicomputers are augmented with a wide range of software alternatives from the simplest (not unlike the common microcomputer support available) to the most complex. Some minicomputers even have whole systems programs called *operating systems* that allow multiple simultaneous users of the same computer.

The large-scale computers of today are generally used to handle problems that require access to large files of data or massive computation. The demise of the large-scale computer has been predicted for years, but it is unlikely. The centralization of data files for an organization requires a single computer complex. And many of the problems that require high-speed computational ability need that capability for only a few seconds each day. A large centralized computer allows many, many users who have similar kinds of problems to share a single resource.

There are some subtle details in the design of software for these different environments, but the techniques are almost the same throughout. For example, if you write a program for a microcomputer, you will have to descend into a morass of details to handle the individual input/output circuits. On a minicomputer you will be able to avoid some of this detail by using some of the features of the systems programs provided by the manufacturer. On a large-scale computer you will probably be prevented from being able to get involved in the details of input/output programming. At the microcomputer end of the spectrum there is more "raw" input/output capability, but at the large-scale computer end you will find the process of implementing a program significantly easier.

The environment in which software gets written also includes other software. When you write a program, you will be using other programs to help you do your work. Instead of having to write programs in the one's and zero's of binary, you can write them in a much more readable form; a system program is used to "translate" your readable form into the computer's required binary form. In fact, as you begin to adopt the use of a large-scale computer (or, to a lesser extent, the minicomputer) you will find that you will spend less time understanding the underlying computer and more time learning about the systems programs provided as the software environment of that computer system. In this design course you will learn how to understand all of the system's software.

Uses of Computers

If you look around you will find a wealth of opportunities to exploit computer technology in the electronics industry. In this design course we will stay away from the traditional management-oriented and administrative uses of computers. Our examples will be drawn mostly from the applications for microcomputers and minicomputers with which you will most likely become involved. However, there are numerous other uses you might discover, even if you don't design around micros and minis.

For example, have you ever had to prepare a proposal for a large project? (There are two kinds of engineers: those who have and those who will.) How do you price out different alternatives for a project with lots of people and only a certain amount of time? How do you try out various alternatives, for example, making certain subsystems and buying others? To try out all of the alternatives by using a desk calculator can be terribly time-consuming. This is a natural application for a computer. You can use the organization's data processing department's computer, or an available minicomputer, or even a terminal to a remote time-sharing system. You can design and write a small program that does all of the routine math and prints out an annotated result; then, by changing the data you can produce different reports that can be compared for effectiveness.

Prewritten (*canned*) programs can be leased or bought. These programs can be used for project scheduling and analog circuit design and for solving simultaneous equations and so on. You don't necessarily have to be able to program in order to buy and use these programs, but you do have to know enough about software to be able to evaluate what you are buying.

There are even more novel applications for your new-found software skill. Have you ever needed a generator of complex digital or analog signal sequences? The experienced computer user plucks a common computer off the shelf, programs it to suit, and generates an easily changed signal sequence. It is easiest to visualize if your application is digital, but computers can also be used to synthesize analog signals. And a derivative application is the use of a computer to simulate some unavailable piece of more complex equipment. If you are designing a subsystem of an aircraft instrument panel, you can actually create all of the complex interacting signals that arrive from the various sensors to simulate an actual flight. This can be used in system testing and for important demonstrations.

The list of potential computer applications that are open to the knowledgeable user of software is virtually endless. But the most important use of your software skill is in the planning of your own career. The designer of good software is a recognized asset in almost any organization. Because of your new abilities, you may find yourself given more responsibility and presented with more interesting technical challenges. And in today's world, more and more problems are going to require the systems approach that is inherent in good software design; learning software has more to offer than just a new bag of tricks. It may be a significant step in your professional advancement.

What Is Programming?

Contrary to all the popular books on the subject, programming is *not* the writing of cryptic statements in FORTRAN, BASIC, or COBOL. Programming is the act of designing a specialized sequence of instructions for a fast and faithful clerk to carry out endlessly (and mindlessly). If you imagine a computer as an unerring clerk to whom you must provide detailed and complete instructions to carry out some task, you will begin to appreciate what has to be done in the authorship of a program. At the very minimum, you have to know more about the intended application than you would have to know if you were to do all the work yourself. The computer cannot fill in its own gaps in knowledge; it can only follow the steps in the program.

The first step in programming a computer is to understand what has to be done. It is at this point that most computer program designs fail. A clear and complete description of the intent and requirements of the software must be documented before any design is attempted. If you design any system, whether hardware or software, without understanding the needs, you are doomed to having to tear it all down and redesign over and over again. After we have introduced some of the basic concepts you need to know, we will show you how to document the requirements in a clear and consistent way.

The second step in programming is to design the software system that will be required. This generally starts by breaking the requirements down into groups, each individual group representing a semi-independent module. Each module is further broken down into individual units until a level of detail is reached at which each unit can be thoroughly understood and completely designed. These first two steps demand a significant discipline to rigorously document each important decision.

The third step in programming is to implement the program. The design is manually translated from the documented form into a form that is acceptable to the computer; this form is called a *programming language.* This phase is called *coding,* and it is the phase at which most people (erroneously) begin.

The next step in programming is generally semiautomatic and is called *translation.* Your program (in an appropriate language) is translated into an equivalent binary form that the computer will be able to execute. This translation is done under the aegis of a systems program called an *assembler* or a *compiler;* any errors you may have made in writing in the programming language are detected and reported to you by this systems software.

After you have an understood, designed, coded, and translated program, you must test it. After finding one or more faults, you must debug it to find what has to be changed in order to make it function correctly. Testing is an art of its own, as is debugging. Chapter 10 is devoted to these two topics. Testing and debugging are generally done repeatedly until the program achieves a satisfactory level of quality of behavior. The objective of testing is to find the errors that may have been made in the entire process; it should not be the point at which you attempt to make up for your lack of original understanding of the problem that you are trying to solve.

All too often neophyte programmers see the actual coded program as the only necessary object of the programming exercise. Experienced programmers know that there are many preliminary steps that must be taken. The experience level of programmers can be judged by finding out how soon they begin writing code for the computer: The novice begins almost immediately and assumes this is the right thing to do. The more experienced programmer does a lot of preliminary paper work and produces a series of design documents; actual coding doesn't begin until much later. In general, the earlier the coding is done the poorer it will be because at this stage the problem is not usually well understood.

The novice programmer typically grasps any "corner" of the intended application (often the one he "understands" best) and begins to chop away at it. If there is to be a terminal, he may start to create part of a program to read in data from that terminal. It doesn't occur to him that he doesn't know what to do with that data once it is in; it doesn't occur to him that this may not be the right way to cope with the terminal.

The experienced programmer knows that quickly rushing off to write code will produce useless software. He first sets out to understand the problem, designs the software, specifies the steps required in the solution, and finally establishes the requirements of each module and how they are to be fitted together. Eventually, he will achieve enough of an understanding of the entire system (and its partial evolution at some stage) to be able to specify the characteristics of the various components of the entire system, such as the terminal and its associated software.

Growing Complexity of Problems

All of the easy jobs have been done. From now on the applications for electronics (and for computers) will be more difficult and more challenging. The simple, sweeping solution will become more elusive and less likely to be applicable.

Engineers have tended to address problems that were easy to solve, for example, the design of radio transmitters and receivers. More difficult problems, for example, air traffic control (that may use radio transmitters and receivers as subsystems), are being tackled now. The really difficult problems, for example, designing a total transportation system from portal-to-portal, are much, much more difficult to solve and probably represent the challenges of the next 25 years.

The more complex problems do not have simple, fixed solutions. Solutions may have to be able to adapt to changing conditions, and this adaptability is most easily provided in the form of software for a computer. The earliest traffic lights, for example, had simple sequential timer control of an intersection. Later, as traffic grew, multistate controllers were created that could operate on different cycles, depending on the time of day and the instantaneous traffic. Now, with microcomputers at each corner, the traffic signal's sequencing may be the result of adaptation to the overall traffic density and flow. In the future all of the microcomputers may be linked together into a complex network that automatically optimizes the sequences of traffic lights in order to maximize the efficiency of the traffic system as a whole. Since nobody knows how to do this last step yet, it is the challenge of the future.

Coding may take a few hours to complete and debug and there will be little likelihood that it will have to be torn down and written over again as a result of design changes.

The novice is working upward from the most detailed available level of knowledge toward the eventual system. The experienced designer is working from system specifications downward toward the actual program implementation. In the novice's case, the quickly written program is produced with the assumption that it will ultimately prove useful to the whole design. This is—at best—a risky prediction. The experienced designer is betting that at some point the required functions can somehow be implemented; this is most certainly a surer kind of prediction.

Programming is just as difficult (and as easy) to do as electronics circuit design. Writing code down on paper is just a bit easier than wrapping wire or soldering, that's all. The same design and debugging steps have to be taken in either case. If you can habitually read the specs for a project and then go directly to the bench and wire up some circuitry that works, you are one of those rare people who can write correct program code "on-the-fly." If, however, you are a mere mortal like the rest of us and have to spend some time consulting books and trying different alternatives on paper before you can produce a schematic, you will find that the same methods also work best with software.

Some engineering-dominated companies relegate programmers to support and technician-level roles. There organizations are easily identified. Their programmers spend time producing programs that solve "flaps," are transient instead of steady-state, are devoid of documentation, can only be used by the programmer who originally wrote them, and are not saved as a part of the organization's software resources library. When the programmer leaves the group, any attempt to use the program again or to extend it results in paying another programmer to rewrite it, often with the same undesirable side effects. Experienced programmers know that there are no "quick-and-dirty" programs—not quick, anyway.

The objective of the rest of this design course is to show you how to specify, design, implement, and test reliable and efficient software with the least amount of fuss and bother. If we are both successful in our communication, you will learn how to avoid the pitfalls that have trapped so many budding programmers in the past. Even if you never program yourself, having the skill in reserve is a worthwhile objective. You never know when you will have to communicate with another programmer.

2

Procedures
and Data

In its raw, delivered state, just after power is applied, a computer is a pathetic piece of universal electronics. It is raw potential, but it has no purpose. A computer, as you have already learned, is capable of doing only two things:

1. Fetching an instruction from some storage medium
2. Executing that instruction

But it does so endlessly and rapidly. What we lack in our raw computer is a *program,* the group of instructions that will be sequentially executed to achieve a specific and defined objective. The combination of a raw, unadorned computer with a well-written and debugged program forms a special-purpose machine. What you do with it depends on how you program it.

Analogy of a Program

We have all had the exasperating experience of having to deal with a faithful, loyal, and dedicated employee who follows every instruction precisely as given but who uses no common sense. Well, conjure up a person like that and let him be our computer for a moment. We will supply the faithful clerk with a calculator (an arithmetic unit) and a sheet of instructions (Figure 2.1). If our clerk is unerring in following the instructions, the OUT basket will end up with a stack of papers that is a transformed version of the original IN basket contents. If the desired output from the process is the correct transformation of the input according to the instruction sheet, we have a correct and valid program.

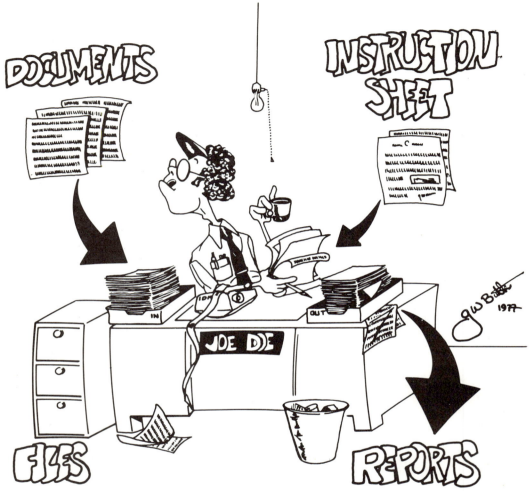

Figure 2.1 A devoted clerk can be conceived of as an analog of a digital computer; it is also a way to test your instructions.

Such a program cannot be supplied to a computer, of course. Computers are not very good at reading the English language. In Figure 2.2 you can find three distinct meanings for the sentence. (What does a computer do in that case?). Furthermore, we have not handled all of the cases for even this simple condition. For example, what if the OUT basket becomes full and overflows onto the floor? What should we do on our instruction sheet to tell the clerk to watch out for overflow and do something different? Once your computer program is underway doing useful work, you won't be able to intervene and handle all of the special cases like the overflow of the OUT basket.

Figure 2.2 There are three different potential verbs in this sentence. Can you pick them out? Could a computer pick them out?

There is another way in which this simple example differs from reality. In real problems there is nearly always a need for the Central Processor (our clerk) to keep a local "scratch pad" for intermediate results. In a digital computer the scratch pad is maintained in read-write memory (typically RAM's).

Upon modest reflection you will notice that there is more than just a program involved here. In every case there is *data*. A computer program performs transformation of data of one kind into another. If no change results between the input and output sides of the computer, there is no need for the program. The data contents of the scratch pad must also be considered. The mistake that many novice programmers make is to assume that the objective is to define a program and let the data fall where it may. As you will learn throughout this design course, you must consider both the data and the transformation of that data because programs consist of both. The transformation process is called a *procedure*.

Software is complicated (and made possible and practical) by the inherent trade-off possibilities in the procedure-data pair. For each and every problem to be solved there are virtually an infinite number of ways to do it. Some of the solutions involve the use of large amounts of data and a small procedure while other solutions require only a small amount of data and a large procedure. There is an emerging theory that suggests that there is an optimum product of space (represented by data) and time (represented by procedures) for any particular problem, but the programmer can choose either factor independently of the other.

Data takes up space in a storage medium; procedures are generally smaller, but they take more time to achieve the same result. If time is unimportant (for example, where the computer is incredibly faster than the potential data changes), we tend to opt for procedures. When time is at a premium, we elect to use more sophisticated data elements (which consume more memory space).

Consider a simple example: You have a list of five IC part numbers that require special incoming inspection because they are critical to your equipment. The receiving clerk (faithful, loyal, unerring, etc.) is directed to examine each incoming shipment. If it contains one of the important parts, the part is sent to the Inspection Department; otherwise it is sent directly to the Warehouse for storage. As we have already said, there are an infinite number of ways to solve this problem of writing instructions to the clerk, several of which are outlined in Figure 2.3.

Figure 2.3(a) is the most obvious way to express the set of instructions for this problem. However, for all of its conceptual simplicity, this is probably the single worst way to implement the instructions on a computer. Even if the part number in question is obviously not one of the important items to be inspected, we have to

If the shipment contains part number 74123, send the shipment
to the Inspection Department, otherwise
If the shipment contains part number 74181, send the shipment
to the Inspection Department, otherwise
If the shipment contains the part number 74198, send the
shipment to the Inspection Department, otherwise
If the shipment contains the part number 74298, send
shipment to the Inspection Department, otherwise
If the shipment contains the part number 74412,
send the shipment to the Inspection Department,
Otherwise, send the shipment to the Warehouse.　　　(a)

Inspection List: 74123, 74181, 74198, 74298, 74412.

If the shipment contains a part number in today's Inspection
List, send the shipment to the Inspection Department,
Otherwise, send the shipment to the Warehouse.　　　(b)

Inspection List: 74123, 74181, 74198, 74298, 74412.

Step 1. Set "i" to 1.
Step 2. If the shipment contains a part number equal to the "i"-th
item in today's Inspection List, send the
shipment to the Inspection Department,
Otherwise, go to Step 3.
Step 3. Add 1 to "i". If "i" is less than the number of
items in today's Inspection List, go to Step 2,
Otherwise, send the shipment to the Warehouse.　　　(c)

Inspection List: 74123, 74181, 74198, 74298, 74412.

Step 1. Set "i" to 1.
Step 1A. If all part numbers in this shipment are smaller
than the "i"-th number in today's Inspection
List, send the shipment to the Warehouse,
Otherwise, go to Step 2.
Step 2. If the shipment contains a part number equal to the
"i"-th item in today's Inspection List, send the
shipment to the Inspection Department,
Otherwise, go to Step 3.
Step 3. Add 1 to "i". If "i" is less than the number of
items in today's Inspection List, go to Step 1A,
Otherwise, send the shipment to the Warehouse.　　　(d)

Figure 2.3 Four different ways of expressing the very same
set of instructions, each having different desirable attributes.

compare it to five different part numbers before we finally conclude that we ought
to route the shipment to the warehouse.

Figure 2.3(b) is a different expression of the same kind of solution. In this
case, we have introduced a separate and distinct Inspection List. This data is independent of the procedure that follows, but the procedure utterly depends on the

structure and content of the data. Notice that by separating the data from the procedure, it is now significantly easier to change the Inspection List without having to modify the procedure at all. That is a common enough consideration in real computer programs to merit serious consideration during the design process.

The example in Figure 2.3(b) is in an ideal form for a human to understand because most people can easily "scan" a list to look for a particular number. Computers, however, don't usually have instructions that can "scan" automatically (although some of the newer "super computers" do). Therefore, if we replace our receiving clerk with a digital computer, it is necessary to be significantly more explicit about how to check the Inspection List. This is shown in Figure 2.3(c). An index, *i,* is used to count the *i*th item in the list; for each *i,* we examine that *i*th element to see if it matches our received-product part number. The process continues for successive values of *i* until the Inspection List is exhausted. This is called a *linear search technique,* and it requires that each item in the Inspection List be examined in turn. If the shipment contains part numbers not in the list, the entire list must be examined before we can ship the product to the warehouse.

Another strategy is shown in Figure 2.3(d). Here we take advantage of the fact that the numbers in the Inspection List are presented in ascending order. Emulating what a human might do, we insert another step (Step 1A) that allows us to avoid examining items in the Inspection List that are obviously not going to be of interest.

And the list goes on. We could add more and more examples to Figure 2.3, including dynamic tables, dichotomizing search strategies, random hashing address techniques, and on and on. But the point is made. There are more ways to implement a computer program than one. Choosing the right way will be the subject of Chapter 5.

The hallmark of the novice is the uninformed criticism of another's program without understanding the objectives. Eager novices often criticize with a remark like, "That's not the way to do it; it should've been done *this* way." But some programs are designed to be fast, others are designed to be small, and others are designed to be easy to understand. Each of these objectives contradicts the others. You can't have *all* the marbles! In Chapter 5 we will examine the different objectives you might elect to use.

Specify the Problem

The initial quality of a software system is a direct function of how well the original problem was specified. The final quality is at least what the end-user will accept. The difference between the two levels of quality is what makes most software design efforts unwieldly and difficult to predict. The way to make software projects more predictable is to design the program in such a way that the initial quality is equal to or better than the required final quality. This way you won't have to go back and redesign. If the specifications are vague, the designer is doomed to implement the wrong program, find out how it diverges from the requirements, and modify the program to suit—over and over and over again.

The importance of complete and adequate specifications cannot be overemphasized, nor can the fact that the specifications will never be complete enough to eliminate all problems. Unanticipated problems can always crop up, and in a project that takes more than a few days to complete, the needs of the end-user of the system may shift. Some downstream changes in specifications are inevitable unless the user and designer of the program are the same person. A good program design leaves room for accommodating changes to the specifications. An example of this provision is found in Figure 2.3. Separating the Inspection List from the rest of the program means that the List can be changed easily as needed without having to scrap the program and totally rewrite it.

If adequate specifications are not provided, part of your responsibility as designer is to generate them. Since the requirements have to be established before the design begins, the specification document should be readable by the eventual users of the software. If you are programming a communications system, for instance, you should be able to document the entire system performance requirements in a form that is readable and understandable by the eventual users of that system. Although there will be howls and groans about the unnecessary delays because "adequate specs have already been provided," you will save more time and money if you generate adequate specs yourself at this early stage in the project.

The form of the specifications may represent the first draft of a technical manual for the eventual users of the software. If you are creating a FORTRAN program for circuit analysis, your specifications should clearly state what inputs you will expect and what outputs are likely to result. In a communications system you will want to specify what kinds of terminals may be connected, what protocols will be used, and what kinds of input and output data streams will be processed and generated. If your new program is to be mated with a microprocessor to control a motor, you must specify not only the characteristics of the motor you can control but also the input signals that will cause this control to take place. Basically, you should specify the software/hardware complex as a black box with inputs and outputs.

Sometimes it helps to imagine that you are *not* going to implement the system in software. Instead, imagine that your "black box" will contain a huge number of little green gnomes. This technique will help you eliminate the computer jargon that so many specifications seem to be imbued with.

When you write your specifications, remember to write with a particular reader in mind. Pick out an individual who will have to approve the system and write expressly for that person's skills, abilities, and interests. This trick will help you to avoid lapsing into jargon.

When you generate specifications, you should try to put as many things as possible into tables, charts, and other graphic displays. Don't avoid using some formal notation, like finite-state machine tables, if it will help eliminate the ambiguity in specifications. Remember, each ambiguity is a potential spot where you will have to go back and redesign your software.

Many of the documentation strategies we will talk about in Chapter 7 will be directly applicable to the generation of good specifications. After you think that you have written a good spec for your software, ask somebody totally outside the project to read it and offer comments. You may find that some of the things that you think are perfectly clear are not clear at all.

Design the Program

Once you understand what has to be done, you can establish the objectives and design your program. Although the specifications can be reviewed and discussed with nontechnical users, your software design will be comprehensible only to another software designer (if it is, indeed, comprehensible at all!). Furthermore, the ways used to design software are not nearly as well known as the methods used in circuit design. Since there is no universally agreed upon set of conventions like those used for a schematic diagram, software design documents tend to be difficult to read and understand. For these (and other) reasons, about two-thirds of all errors are made during the design stage; the rest are made during the actual coding of the program. The less time you spend on design, the more time you will spend on testing, debugging, and correcting. And since you will have to redesign this part of the software anyway, why not do it right the first time?

Designing a program means setting objectives and then deciding how to achieve these objectives. Some programs are designed to be small in size, others need to execute fast, and others need to be implemented quickly. There are many, many different attributes for a good program, as you will see in Chapter 5. You must cite the attributes that your particular design should have and then go after them.

In the software design stage you should probably first look to see if anything has already been done that you can use or adapt. If you are implementing a minicomputer-based process control system, perhaps you will find that the manufacturer has already provided some software that you can use. It is best to know about this software early because it may form part of the environment in which your own applications program can operate. Similarly, each computer maker maintains a library of user-submitted programs that you should peruse to see if your needs have already been met.

If your needs can't be met "off-the-shelf," you will have to engage in your own design work. Here, the critical part of the process is choosing the right structure of the system to allow all the objectives to be met. After the overall structure is established, the choice of individual *algorithms* can be made. An algorithm is a prescribed set of well-defined rules or processes for solving a problem in a finite number of steps. The ways to design an algorithm will be outlined in Chapter 5.

Is "Bench Programming" Practical?

Some microcomputer users and vendors seriously contend that digital designers should forego all of the traditional software development steps and write their programs in a binary form right at the bench. The idea is appealing because it dispenses with the costs of designing, coding, and translating, but the costs of testing and debugging rise dramatically. When you consider the cost of the software over the entire life of the product, the loss of initial design documentation can be catastrophic.

Experienced software designers very seldom program "at the bench." Because they know that there is no such thing as "quick-and-dirty" software, they insist on the discipline of adequate, documented design and careful coding and translation (although to reduce outlay of cash, some small programs may be translated manually instead of by using an assembler).

Inexperienced software designers who may be very experienced in digital circuit design would like to believe in the fairy tale of no-cost programming. Although these designers wouldn't dream of approaching the bench with a handful of 7400 parts and a soldering pencil to implement a digital circuit, they have been led to believe that such an approach is possible with software. This is nonsense. If you consider a flowchart or other well-documented form of your program at the same level as a schematic of a digital circuit, then you will understand the need for desk work before you approach the bench. The assembly language program may be considered as the functional equivalent of a wire-list in hardware. The actual object program is the funtional equivalent of the circuit being tested.

What would you do on the bench if all you had was a circuit? How much time would you spend reconstructing the circuit diagram bit by bit? Why would software be any different?

Code and Translate

This is the most obvious part of the implementation process and although it is essential, it is not nearly so important as you might think. If the design is correct and adequate, coding is little more than the rote task of transcribing that design into a form that the computer can accept. After the design has been transcribed the *source* program can be supplied to a translator to create an *object* program in the computer's own binary language.

Coding might be done directly in the computer's own binary language, in which case the translation step has been done manually. However, the use of this approach is restricted to debugging programs on computers that have a paucity of systems software to aid the programmer. Today, only microcomputers and certain very small minicomputers fall into this category. Coding may be done in assembly language for a computer. Generally, the smaller the computer, the more likely you are to write in assembly language. Although the assembly notation (Figure 2.4)

```
            ORG    01FFH
BICVT:      LXI    H, 00H
            LXI    D, 2710H
            CALL   RNIBL
            MOV    A, B
            LXI    D, 03E8H
            CALL   LNIBL
            LXI    D, 0064H
            CALL   RNIBL
            MOV    A, C
            MOV    E, 0AH
            CALL   LNIBL
            MVI    E, 01H
RNIBL:      CPI    00H
            RZ
            DAD    D
            DCR    A
            JMP    RNIBL
LNIBL:      CPI    0AH
            RC
            DAD    D
            SUI    10H
            JMP    LNIBL
```

Figure 2.4   An example of assembly language programming.

appears forbidding, it is only a reflection of the computer's underlying architecture. If you understand the architecture, you won't find writing assembly language difficult. If you insist on programming in binary for your computer, you will find that you will have to know assembly language anyway just so that you can write down what your program is supposed to look like; the documentation utility is invaluable.

On larger computers, and now even on some microcomputers, you may elect to use a higher-level language like FORTRAN, PL/M (trademark, Intel Corp.), or BASIC (Figure 2.5). These languages permit you to state your processing needs in

```
0100    DIM B (3)

0400    LET B1 = 0
0410    LET I = 0
0420    GOSUB 440
0430    IF I < 4 THEN 420
0440    LET B1 = B1 + B (I)*10 ↑ (4-I)
0450    LET I = I + 1
0460    RETURN
```

Figure 2.5   An example of a higher-level language, BASIC.

a more problem-oriented way. Although they isolate you from the underlying architecture (with varying degrees of success), high-level languages exact a toll in the form of efficiency of the final program.

An assembly language requires that the programmer be responsible for the allocation of the computer's resources. A higher-level programming language makes the language translator responsible for resource allocation. This means that although the responsibility for efficient programs rests with the programmer in assembly language, the potential for efficiency is high. If you program in a high-level language, your final program efficiency will be reduced because you are at the mercy of the quality of the translation. Programmer productivity, however, is higher when a high-level language is used than when assembly language is used. Therefore, if your objectives are to produce a program quickly and inexpensively, you are better off with a high-level language, but if your program will be implemented in a ROM with thousands of copies, it is better to use assembly language and do all you can to reduce the program size to fit in a smaller number of ROM chips.

A computer, as a faithful and dedicated clerk, makes a good translator of restricted languages like those used in programming. Programs have been written that translate assembly language and higher-level languages into the computer's binary code form. These programs are available from the computer manufacturer and (except in the case of micros) are generally delivered with the equipment. First, you feed the translator (called an *assembler* or *compiler,* depending on whether you are writing in assembly language or a higher-level language) into your computer; it takes control and reads your *source* program, producing an equivalent *object* program (Figure 2.6). Later, after translation is done, you feed the *object* program into the computer and execute the program to achieve the result you wanted in the first place.

In Chapter 8 we will introduce BASIC, one of the popular programming languages. You will be suprised how much you can do with BASIC.

Testing and Debugging

The testing and debugging of computer software is a most neglected topic. There are important economic reasons why you must concentrate on the design and implementation of correct and reliable software; testing is designed to verify that those goals are met. If you depend on the testing phase of program development to finalize the design, you will probably create a monster program that nobody can completely understand. This leads to lurking errors that will tend to appear at the most inopportune moments. Testing only shows the presence of programming errors; it does not show the absence of them.

Once a programming error is detected through adequate testing (or through user complaints), the error is tracked down and exterminated. This is called *debugging.* It has also been called *deblunderizing.* There are some good strategies

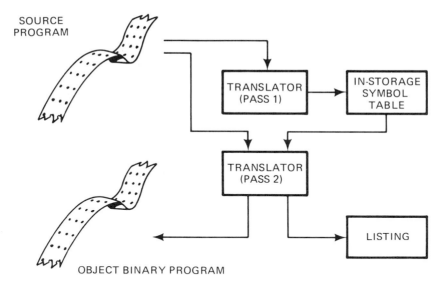

SOURCE
PROGRAM

TRANSLATOR
(PASS 1)

IN-STORAGE
SYMBOL
TABLE

TRANSLATOR
(PASS 2)

LISTING

OBJECT BINARY PROGRAM

Figure 2.6 Typical assemblers require reading the program in twice, once to define all symbols and then again to use those definitions.

for finding faulty points in a program (and then, obviously, correcting them), although your own digital circuit debugging experience will also prove useful.

We will show good testing and debugging strategies in Chapter 10.

Use and Maintenance

A program that never gets used should never have been written. If the program is of any complexity at all, it will require some post-implementation maintenance, although not the same kind required of electronics hardware.

As users become more dependent on a software system, they tend to change the way they use the system and they demand more from the system than the system was designed for. Because of the ease with which software can be changed, even major change requests can be satisfied. The result is that successful software is characterized by requirements for subtle changes in the design and implementation. Furthermore, extensive use of a successful program may uncover undesirable behavior on the part of the software that must be corrected for user satisfaction. This leads to the paradoxical conclusion that successful software is characterized by change throughout its life. Since unsuccessful software is seldom used, no changes are sought.

There is no separate chapter in this design course on use and maintenance. Instead, throughout all the chapters you will find a pervasive trend toward making sure that you design in enough flexibility to be able to change when the need arises, for change is inevitable.

The Life Cycle

All of the stages discussed in this chapter can be combined into one comprehensive view of the life of a software system (Figure 2.7). The products of each stage feed the successor stage; experience in the successor stage may feed back changes to the predecessor stage. For example, when you are way downstream in debugging, finding an error that requires propagation all the way back up to the Problem Specification stage is relatively expensive. Therefore, it is important to resolve design problems as early in the life cycle as possible because it is less expensive to correct them then.

The cost of procrastination is high: In a recent study[1] it was reported that if it cost $1 to correct an error at the *coding* stage, it would have cost only one-quarter as much to correct it in the *specification* stage, but it will cost from $2 to $5 to correct it during the testing stage and $10 to correct it when the program is in *use*. These studies were done on systems in which all the software (generally) was on one computer and was easily changed. Consider the problems if you were to ship out 1,000 copies of a product that has a bug in the masked programmed ROM's holding the program for a microprocessor! You might have to pay as much as $100,000 to correct that bug.

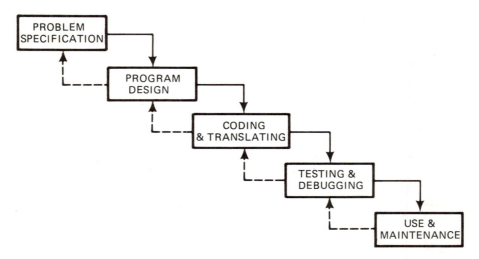

Figure 2.7 The life of a program has many phases, five of which are critical. Each phase may propagate changes back to a predecessor; each change costs money.

[1] Barry W. Boehm, Software Engineering; *IEEE Transactions on Computers,* December, 1976, pp. 1226–1241.

3

Data Structures

Before we can design any computer program, we must fully understand the nature of the *data* upon which the program will operate. All data in modern digital computers is represented as a set of integers, which is both a bane and a boon. If a word in a computer can hold sixteen bits in a register, then we can easily represent 2^{16} (65,536) different numeric values in that register. That is more than adequate for most needs, but occasionally it is not enough. In other cases, we can count two different kinds of things in the same sixteen-bit word.

Integers of a computer can be used to represent any kind of information by coding. If data is what computers process, then information is what we need to operate on. Information is data that has meaning. For example, the number 7 is *data*. When we attach meaning (say, "the number of days in a week is 7"), we have created *information*. The input *data* to a computer is some external *information* with the inherent meaning stripped off; the input value 7 might represent the number of days in a week, the current number of items in inventory, the water temperature in Celsius, or your hat size. Only the program knows.

The translation between information and data is accomplished by means of a *code*. One of the prime examples of a code is ASCII, the American Standard Code for Information Interchange. The sixteen-bit word of data in Figure 3.1 appears to contain an arbitrary binary number. If, however, we state that the *meaning* of that register's contents is "two ASCII characters," we can look up the bit patterns (in Table 3.1) and see that the register holds the letters "XL." When we store the data into this register, there is no place in the computer to mark that it contains data of the *type* "ASCII." But when we refer to that data, we must remember that it is of the

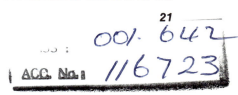

| 0 | 1 | 0 | 1 | 1 | 0 | 0 | 0 | 0 | 1 | 0 | 0 | 1 | 1 | 0 | 0 |

Figure 3.1 A simple data value in a sixteen-bit register.

type "ASCII." If we try to perform arithmetic computations on that data, we will get strange results.

Furthermore, data of different types can represent the same information. The examples in Figure 3.2 show three different forms for the same numeric value: ASCII, BCD, and binary. If our computer only has instructions for binary arithmetic, we might have data in the first two forms, but we cannot compute with it. In this computer we have to translate the ASCII and BCD data into binary before we can perform arithmetic on it. For example, add 45_{10} (binary 101101) to each of the three examples. Now, look up the ASCII results in Table 3.1 ("2P"?!); now try the BCD $(27+45=6?)$. In other words, you cannot perform operations with different types of data; if you are adding binary numbers, both numbers must be in binary form.

		b_7	b_6	b_5	b_4	b_3	b_2	b_1	

	$b_7 \rightarrow 0$ $b_6 \rightarrow 0$ $b_5 \rightarrow 0$	0 0 0	0 0 1	0 1 0	0 1 1	1 0 0	1 0 1	1 1 0	1 1 1
b_4 b_3 b_2 b_1									
0 0 0 0		NUL	DLE	SPACE	0	@	P	`	p
0 0 0 1		SOH	DC1	!	1	A	Q	a	q
0 0 1 0		STX	DC2	"	2	B	R	b	r
0 0 1 1		ETX	DC3	#	3	C	S	c	s
0 1 0 0		EOT	DC4	$	4	D	T	d	t
0 1 0 1		ENQ	NAK	%	5	E	U	e	u
0 1 1 0		ACK	SYN	&	6	F	V	f	v
0 1 1 1		BEL	ETB	'	7	G	W	g	w
1 0 0 0		BS	CAN	(	8	H	X	h	x
1 0 0 1		HT	EM	)	9	I	Y	i	y
1 0 1 0		LF	SUB	*	:	J	Z	j	z
1 0 1 1		VT	ESC	+	;	K	[	k	{
1 1 0 0		FF	FS	,	<	L	\	l	‖
1 1 0 1		CR	GS	-	=	M	]	m	}
1 1 1 0		SO	RS	.	>	N	^	n	~
1 1 1 1		SI	US	/	?	O	–	o	DEL

☐ PRINTABLE CHARACTER   ▨ AUXILIARY DEVICE CONTROL CHARACTER

▧ PRINTER CONTROL CHARACTER

Table 3.1 ASCII system and character set.

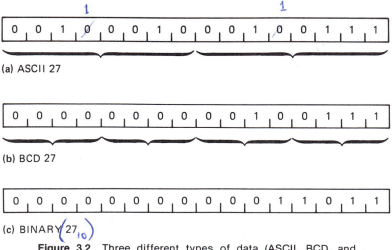

(a) ASCII 27

(b) BCD 27

(c) BINARY 27_{10}

Figure 3.2 Three different types of data (ASCII, BCD, and binary) all representing the same value.

If you will look at Figure 3.2 again, you will notice that we have variously held one value [Figure 3.2(c)], two digits of a value [Figure 3.2(a)] or four digits [Figure 3.2(b)] in one register, depending on how we coded our data. Programmers call this *packing* of data. It is not restricted to keeping all the same type in a word. The left-half of Figure 3.2(a) could hold one ASCII character while the right-half could retain a full eight-bit binary value. You will probably have to *unpack* the two mixed types of data before you can operate on either one of them. Generally, packing is done either to conserve storage space (for example, when you have hundreds of identically shaped items) or to reduce data transfer time over a communications channel.

The concept of packing illustrates a point: You can combine any two or more kinds of data into a single register.

At the other extreme, what if one register in a storage medium cannot hold a number large enough? What if we have to count 100,000 things in a computer with sixteen-bit words? We simply use more than one register. We use some part of (or all of) another register, usually an adjacent register. Two adjacent words in a sixteen-bit memory can represent 2^{32} different values, which is over 4 billion!

When we use this *multiple-precision* capability, we have to decide how to store the multiple words. Should the most-significant bits be stored in the lower- or the higher-addressed location of the space in memory allocated to hold this value? In some cases, your computer will dictate the proper order but only if it has instructions that can operate on multiple words. In smaller computers the choice is yours, and it is an arbitrary choice. You must make note of the order you choose and you must be consistent. Remember the rule about types: You can only perform operations on data of like type. If you forget and try to add the least-significant part of one number to the most significant part of another, you will likely get some strange results.

Numbers Are Not Real

When you have to write down a very large or very small number, you usually resort to exponential notation:

$$.125 \times 10^{-12}$$

In a computer we do the same kind of thing, but we rely on the natural binary radix that computers can manipulate easily:

$$.001 \times 2^{-12}$$

Since the "$\times 2$" part is understood because we are dealing with binary exponential forms of numbers, we merely have to save the fraction (.001) and exponent (-12). Of course, these two numbers represent two completely different *types* of data (-12 means one thing as a fractional part but something else as an exponent). This does not prevent their sharing a single register, however. Let us assume that we choose to allocate eight bits for the exponent and twenty-four bits for the fraction [Figure 3.3(a)]. This is an arbitrary allocation, but one we must live with once it is chosen. If our computer has special hardware instructions for adding numbers of this form, then the shape of these kinds of numbers will be dictated. However, if we must write the software to add numbers together, we may choose this particular format, or any other that suits our needs. Once we write the software, though, our format is "frozen" unless we want to rewrite our software.

A further complication is introduced when we have to handle negative numbers. For simplicity, let us assume that we adopt the *signed-magnitude* form of numbers. That is, one bit is reserved for the sign (usually, "0" implies plus and "1" implies minus), and the rest of the bits hold the absolute magnitude. The eight-bit exponent of Figure 3.3(a) is really a seven-bit value with a one-bit sign.

Now, recast as Figure 3.3(b), our number consists of four discrete data types (exponent sign, exponent magnitude, fraction sign, and fraction magnitude) all packed together in a single *item*. Depending on the word size of the computer, this item may occupy a single register, less than one register (say, in a thirty-six-bit word computer—there are still some around), or more than one register. It is important to note that the shape of the data should be dictated by the application, not the raw computer word size. Processing efficiencies may be obtained by adopting some convenient format that the hardware recognizes, but watch for the exceptions. Most often, though, you will compromise on the ideal data format so that you can take advantage of available register sizes, available and pretested software, or some special hardware feature.

We must remember that although some literature refers to these kinds of numbers as *real,* they are not. In the real world there are an infinite number of numbers between 0 and 1. Our data representation scheme can handle only a com-

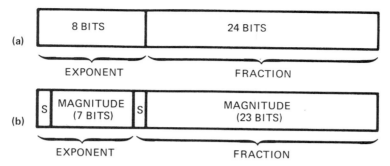

Figure 3.3 Memory registers separate a number's fraction from its exponent (a) and may also reserve a polarity bit,s, in each field (b).

paratively small number of them, for we are dealing with integers as analogies of the real numbers. Just as there is no way to exactly represent 1/3 (.333333 ...) in decimal, there are similar problems in binary. The binary equivalent of the decimal number 0.1, for example, starts out .0001100110011 ..., and it never stops. It is not unusual to accumulate numerical errors in this kind of data representation.[1]

In practice, most of the data you will deal with will not have an explicit exponent (sometimes called *floating-point* data because the exponent specifies where the binary point goes). Instead, most data will be represented as a set of integers. If you compute in dollars and cents, for example, you will invariably choose to represent the data as an integral number of pennies. If you accept data from a remote analog-to-digital converter, the input you will expect will be an integer representing the number of bits the converter can put out. Later, inside the computer, you may choose to manipulate the data in a variety of ways, but you have the option to retain the original data form or to transform it into another form.

Describing Data

In the world of electronics we have simple ways to describe all of the data that we process. We can describe our signals either as patterns of bits or as time-varying signals. Furthermore, because everybody agrees on the nomenclature and the conventions (for example, time is generally drawn as the horizontal axis, increasing to the right), it is easy to communicate with another designer.

Software designers are not nearly so lucky. Every group of designers seems to have its own way of describing things. The state of software documentation is at about the same point electronics was before the adoption of standard schematic symbols. For example, deep inside the data files of the computer at your local telephone

---

[1]For further information, see Irving Allen Dodes and Samuel L. Greitzer, *Numerical Analysis* (New York: Hayden, 1964), and Donald E. Knuth, *The Art of Computer Programming, Vol. 2, Seminumerical Algorithms* (Reading, Mass.: Addison-Wesley, 1969).

company there is a record about you and your phone bill. All of the data records for all of the subscribers are shaped alike so that a single program can process them all (imagine the chaos if each different record had a different format). You can describe record many, many different ways, all of them correct, but each way will have varying degrees of detail and precision. A simplified subscriber record is described four different ways in Figure 3.4.

Each of these different ways of describing data is appropriate to different stages of the design process. You might choose to describe the data layout in a most graphic method in early stages, but it would be hopelessly inadequate to program from. Even the detailed table of Figure 3.4(b) is inadequate because many of the conditions you must know about the data are not expressed. Although you could use the popular COBOL language, as we did in Figure 3.4(c). it has limitations of its own and cannot describe lots of kinds of data you will probably have to deal with. Finally, the "pidgin programming" approach [Figure 3.4(d)] offers enough detail, but at the expense of verbosity.

There is no one standard way of describing data in the programming business. We will now describe one that we use with the hopes that it will also prove useful to you. Remember that you can adopt any rule you want to in synthesizing your own notation for describing data, but you must be sure that whatever you write can be understood by another competent programmer (or yourself months from now). The rules we use are not hard and fast, but they seem to work.

What we need to be able to do is to describe new and complex types of data. For convenience, we attach to each type description a unique and descriptive name. For example, in Figure 3.4(d) we defined a *type* of data named "money"; that type of data is made up two individual components that we named "dollars" and "cents." Each of those items, in turn, is described as being *of* some other type.

The simplest way to describe data is to enumerate the possible members of the set. Thus, we could choose to define the type of data made up of a single bit as shown in Figure 3.5(a). We have defined a *type* of data named "Boolean," the values of which may be "true" or "false." We could also define "day" [Figure 3.5(b)] and enumerate the members of that set.

In simple definitions like these we simply state that we are defining a type of data (**type**), assign an arbitrary name (e.g., "Boolean" or "day"), and then describe what members of that data type are made up of (**of**). In some cases, the members of the enumerated set are all obvious successors of one another, such as the natural numbers. Here we explicitly state the first and last members of the set and separate them with a couple of periods to indicate that a range exists between [for example, see Figure 3.5(c)].

Types of data with disjoint members can also be described. A description like the one in Figure 3.5(d) may make perfectly good sense in some application. Also, note the use of a negative number as the lowest member of the set.

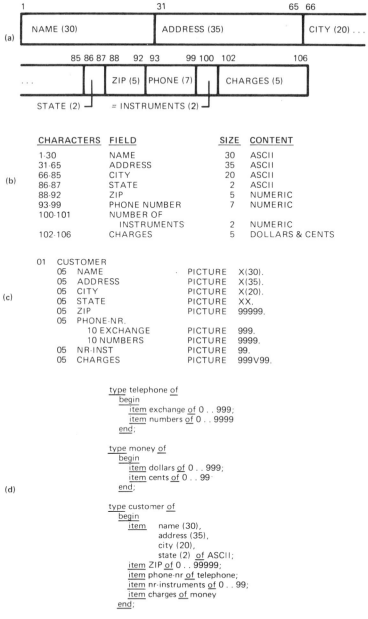

Figure 3.4 Four of the several ways data can be described. In (a) the simplest graphic means are used, but with limited precision. Better, use (b), which is more precise, but lengthier, You could use one of the programming languages like COBOL (c), or a pidgin programming language (d) to describe the data more completely to avoid misunderstandings later.

27

Numbers have their own intrinsic values. When you write 982, you and we know what that means (if we both assume decimal arithmetic!). Other objects, such as the names of the days of the week, stand for things that don't have predetermined values. Fortunately, this means that when we actually implement the program we can choose representations that are best for the design, irrespective of the meanings we attach. Whether we attach values 0 through 6 to the days Monday through Sunday, or –7 to –1, or seven arbitrary collections of bits, the meaning of "day" remains the same.

Things that have intrinsic values are called *literals*. A *literal* is enclosed in quotation marks: "A" is a literal that represents the letter A. Using this convention, then, we could define the set of letters and digits [see Figure 3.5(e)]. Then, using these definitions, we can create a new type of data named "ASCII" that includes "letters," "digits," and many other symbols. We have left the definitions of the control codes as an exercise for the reader, but any limited knowledge of ASCII will make their definitions obvious.

(a) type Boolean of true, false;

(b) type day of Monday, Tuesday, Wednesday, Thursday,
         Friday, Saturday, Sunday;

(c) type VHF of 2 . . 13;

(d) type strange of −7 . . 18, 37, 41, 57 . . 99;

(e) type letter of "A", "B", "C", "D", "E", "F", "G", "H",
         "I", "J", "K", "L", "M", "N", "O", "P", "Q",
         "R", "S", "T", "U", "V", "W", "X", "Y", "Z";
     type digit of "0", "1", "2", "3", "4",
         "5", "6", "7", "8", "9";

(f) type ASCII of NUL, SOH, STX, ETX, EOT, ENQ, ACK, BEL,
         BS, HT, LF, VT, FF, CR, SO, SI,
         DLE, DC1, DC2, DC3, DC4, NAK, SYN, ETB,
         CAN, EM, SUB, ESC, FS, GS, RS, US,
         " ", "!", """", "#", "$", "%", "&", " ' ",
         "(", ")", "*", "+", " , ", "−", " . ", "/",
         digit, ":", ";", "<", "=", ">", "?",
         "@", letter, "[", "\", "]", "^", " _ ",
         " ` ", "a", "b", "c", "d", "e", "f", "g",
         "h", "i", "j", "k", "l", "m", "n", "o",
         "p", "q", "r", "s", "t", "u", "v", "w",
         "x", "y", "z", "{", "|", "}", "~", DEL;

Figure 3.5 Examples of a textual form for describing various kinds of data. A simple enumeration of possible values (a, b) is useful for some variables, but numbers (c) can be treated more briefly. Disjount sets can be represented (d), as well as characters (e, f).

Some Language Conventions

Words that are endemic to the design notation are underlined to separate them from names of objects that you, the programmer, declare. Thus, you might define a variable named "type," which could unambiguously appear in a statement line:

<u>type</u> type . . .

Statements in the design notation are separated from one another by semicolons. Generally, the last statement in a group is *not* followed by a semicolon (notice the examples throughout this chapter and in Figure 3.7 just prior to the word **end.**

The words **begin** and **end** are best thought of as gigantic parentheses. With that as a concept, it is easy to see how they can be "nested" is used in Figure 3.7. That is, one **begin-end** pair is totally embedded within the "scope" of another **begin-end** pair.

Some abbreviation is possible by not repeating redundant elements. Thus, if several items are all of the type "Boolean," they can be declared together:

<u>type</u> a, b, c, d, **of** Boolean;

which is identical to four separate lines, each declaring one of the named objects as type Boolean.

Complex Data

Not all data can be described as easily as the data in Figure 3.5 is described. Most of the data of the world is more complex. Imagine, for example, that you must write a program that analyzes the weather in a number of cities over a long period of time. In each sample of data you might include (simplified, of course), the city, the date, the highest temperature attained, and the amount of precipitation. This quadruplet of data will be used several places throughout the software; thus, it seems appropriate to define a data **type** named "weather" (see Figure 3.6).

You could, of course, declare four different types of independent data, but in reality that is not sufficient. In each case, four data values are interrelated and should not be separated and mixed up again. The four independent declarations are shown in Figure 3.6(b).

In order to group the definitions together and name the entire complex "weather," you can recast the four individual definitions in the form shown in Figure 3.6(c). The data type for "weather" is of the complex, four-stage kind described between the words **begin** and **end** (which mark the beginning and the ending of the definition, respectively). Now, if in the implementation stages you decide that the "city" is a three-bit field in a register, "date" is a five-bit field, "temperature" is a signed seven-bit field, and precipitation is an unsigned seven-bit field, then this type declaration describes a twenty-three bit group. These

(a)

CITY	DATE	± TEMPERATURE	PRECIPITATION

(b) type city of New York, Chicago, Los Angeles,
        St. Louis, London, Tokyo;
     type date of 0 . . 31;
     type temperature of −50 . . +120;
     type precipitation of 0 . . 10;

(c) type weather of
        begin
           type city of New York, Chicago, Los Angeles,
              St. Louis, London, Tokyo;
           type date of 0 . . 31;
           type temperature of −50 . . +120;
           type precipitation of 0 . . 10
        end;

Figure 3.6 A complex data **type**, made up of four discrete parts (a), can be partially described as in (c). However, to relate the four are to be taken as a group, the complex type can be named and then defined in terms of the constitutent element's types.

twenty-three bits might be in three adjacent eight-bit bytes, the data might be stored in several different sixteen-bit words, . . . the possibilities are endless. But the clear definition of what data you are going to process is the paramount objective, and it is one that is achieved by this kind of notation.

Flexibility

Why bother with all this rudimentary detail? Why not just quickly draw a picture of the data layout and then progress to writing code? Why not skip all this design process? You can't because in most systems there is always something that crops up late in the design. Imagine, for example, that you have designed the entire software system for processing weather data and then you discover that some cities report their temperatures in Fahrenheit and others report in Celsius. Do you have to scrap all of your work?

Not if you have adequately defined the data you are working with. All you have to do is change the definition for "temperature" slightly to include the information about which scale is being used (Figure 3.7). Alternatively, you could change the definition for "city" because one city is not likely to change from scale to scale arbitrarily. Now, every part of the software that refers to "temperature" has two items of information to handle—the actual temperature and the scale in use. Therefore, when temperatures are compared or averaged in the program, conversions can be performed to make sure that they are in the same scale.

```
type weather of
    begin
        type city of New York, Chicago, Los Angeles,
            St. Louis, London, Tokyo;
        type date of 0 . . 31;
        type temperature of
            begin
                type temp-value of −75 . . +120;
                type scale of Fahrenheit, Celsius
            end;
        type precipitation of 0 . . 10
    end;
```

Figure 3.7 A revised definition of some data can be implemented during the design stages without wreaking havoc on the rest of the definitions.

Referring to Complex Data

Data within a structure may have to be referred to either in the aggregate (as in "weather") or individually (as in a reference to "city"). Sometimes it is necessary to qualify the definition. If two different types of data could be described with "city" as a constituent element, then simply referring to "city" would be ambiguous.

You can distinguish between different instances of "city" by qualifying your reference. In the case of the data type "weather," the city can be unambiguously referred to by writing "weather.city". The period between the names may be read as the possessive apostrophe (weather's city). Also notice that the larger structure is named first. This same scheme can be continued down to any necessary level in order to eliminate ambiguity from data references.

Data Structures

When we declare a **type** of data in software, we have done nothing to allocate space in memory to hold the bits that represent that data, and we have not specified anything about the valid processing that might be performed on that data. When we declare an **item** of data in a storage medium of some kind, that item

Design Your Own Language

You can freely embellish your design notation as you see fit. In the notation we use we provide for monotonically increasing integers (e.g., 2 ... 13). But what if you need some increment other than one? How would you enumerate the possible frequencies for FM radio broadcast stations? They have frequencies from 88 to 108 MHz in 0.1-MHz steps.

You could define something called "tenths" and give FM stations frequencies in tenths of megahertz (say, 880 through 1,080), but that seems unsatisfying. Alternatively, you could introduce a new notation that makes explicit the increment between members of the set; it could be written as 88 (0.1) 108, meaning "from 88 to 108 in steps of one-tenth."

Don't consider the design notation sacred. Its objective is to allow you to communicate with others (and yourself). All you need to do is describe your notation before you use it, unless the modification is obvious.

must have a **type.** The type itself does not occupy space in the store, but an item does.

Consider a simple example: Compute the resistance of two parallel resistors. As you will recall from your earliest learning, the general formula is:

$$R_p \; = \; \cfrac{1}{\dfrac{1}{R_1} + \dfrac{1}{R_2} + \ldots + \dfrac{1}{R_n}}$$

There is, of course, a simplified rule for two resistors, but we will ignore it for the moment.

Before we can write a program to compute, we have to define the data we will be using. This involves a type of data that we have named "resistance" in Figure 3.8. Now, if we use that definition for "resistance," defining "R1" and "R2" is simple. Of course, the result will also have to be stored in a variable in memory. We have named it (logically enough) "RP." These three objects, "R1," "R2," and "RP" are **item**s, all of which are of the same **type.** The **type** is an abstract idea; the **item**s are actual implementations of that abstraction in a memory of a computer somewhere.

Each **item** may, of course, be arbitrarily complex. The **item** either may be defined simply in terms of a predefined **type** or it may be defined *in situ*. The definitions in Figure 3.8, for example, could have been cast in the unrecommended form shown in Figure 3.9. The disadvantage of Figure 3.9 is the inherent lack of flexibility; if we suddenly have to use the program for data values in excess of one instances of the number 1,000,000 that mean "resistor value" and ignore all the

```
type resistance of 0 . . 1000000;
item R₁, R₂ of resistance;
item Rₚ of resistance;
```

Figure 3.8 A declaration of a type of data is separate from the establishment of a space in memory where data of that type is stored.

instances of the number 1000000 that mean "resistor value" and ignore all the instances of that number that represent something else. It is better to define useful sets of data types and use them liberally throughout the design.

megohm, we have to change much of the design. Worse, we have to find out all the

```
item R₁, R₂ of 0 . . 1000000;
item Rₚ of 0 . . 1000000;
```

Figure 3.9 The unrecommended way of defining data type, except in cases where the value's meanings are obvious. Finding all the places to change in a software design can be an error-prone process.

Arrays of Data

In nearly every computer program of any consequence the same type of data is held in storage in several places in the identical format. In the simple example of Figure 3.8 there are two resistor values that occupy space somewhere in storage. What if we must write a program that can compute the parallel resistance of up to ten legs in a network? Should we define "R1" through "R10" and then write a program to involve all of them at once in the computation?

An even more practical case arises when we choose to write a generalized program. That is, we will compute the parallel resistance of n resistors, where n may range from 2 to 10. Now, how do we handle the computations on as few as two variables ("R1" and "R2") or as many as ten? The answer is by using an *array* (Figure 3.10). In an array, each element is an *item,* and all items are identical in form. Each individual item is selected by an index, the range of which is given in the array declaration. In Figure 3.10 the index may range from 1 to 10 to refer to

```
array R (1 . . 10) of resistance;
```

Figure 3.10 A generalization of **item**s, the **array**.

the individual resistor values. Note that we have elected to retain the final value ("RP") as a separate item.

When we refer to "R(3)," we mean the third item in the "R" **array.** When we refer to "R(I)," the specific item in the array we have selected depends on the value of "I"; of course, "I" must have its value restricted to the range of indices permitted by the definition of the array (i.e., 1 . . . 10).

The item contained in each element of an array may be as complex as any data structure can be. In fact, each item in an array might even contain one or more other arrays. These kinds of multidimensional structures tend to consume large amounts of storage space, but they are necessary in some practical problems. A typical complex item uses the "weather" item defined in Figure 3.6. An array of such items is easy to declare, as in Figure 3.11(a).

Imagine, however, that our weather data contained temperature readings for each of the 24 hours in a day. Then, each individual item in the "data" array would have another 24-item array consisting of the temperature readings. Such a complex declaration of 100 items worth of information, and each item contains 24 temperature readings, the entire data structure contains at least 2,400 temperature readings; that may exhaust the storage capacity of your computer.

If there are 100 data items about weather of the type described in Figure 3.11(b) in storage, you can refer to the tenth item's noon-time temperature as "data(10).temperature(12)".

array data (1 . . 3) of weather;

	CITY	DATE	TEMPERATURE	PRECIPITATION
DATA (1):	DATA (1). CITY			
DATA (2):				
DATA (3):				

(a)

(b)   array data (1 . . 100) of
   begin
     item city of New York, Chicago, Los Angeles,
      St. Louis, London, Tokyo,
     item date of 0 . . 31;
     array temperature (0 . . 23) of −50 . . +120;
     item precipitation of 0 . . 10
   end;

Figure 3.11   Arrays may have items with inherently high complexities (a), or even other arrays (b).

Dynamic Data Structures

It is not always possible to permanently allocate memory space to individual items of an array. The total space requirement for accommodating all eventualities may just be so huge that it prevents practical implementation. In such cases, we simply generalize the **array** into a **list,** just as the **array** is made up of **item**s.

In an array, advancing from item to item is handled by implication. Since items are adjacent to one another, advancing to the next available space in the array gains access to the successor item. In a list this process is made more explicit.

Every item in storage, whether the storage medium is a shift register, RAM, or even a large disc file, has an address. In an **array**, of course, each item has a known (and probably fixed) size. To advance to the next item in sequence, we merely add the size of some item **i** to the address of that item; that produces the address of item **i + 1.** In a **list,** part of the data in item **i** holds the address of the successor item; the successor need not be adjacent to the **i**th item.

Lists are difficult to comprehend unless a clear application is at hand. So, reaching back to our example of Figure 3.4, let us embellish our data structure with more reality. In your monthly telephone bill you receive a list of all the long-distance (toll) calls you made during the month. Each call must be kept in your file between billing cycles so that the detailed statement can be printed.

Now, we could create an array for each and every subscriber in which we store the long-distance call information. But that would lead to a very practical problem: How much space should be left in that array for calls so that we won't run out of space? Won't that space be wasted on the vast majority of callers who make few long-distance calls?

When novice programmers are faced with a problem like this, they are all too often tempted to impose severe restrictions and constraints on the number of long-distance calls that are allowed to be made. Experienced programmers, however,

Life-cycle Costing

For years programmers have had the implicit objective of generating "efficient" software. That is, programs that were compact and executed in the smallest amount of time were prized over others that were not so efficient. However, the price paid to attain this efficiency has often been the future maintainability and flexibility of the software. In recent years, with the dramatic reduction in actual costs of computer time, more and more emphasis has been placed on the total life-cycle costs of software.

As computers become even more pervasive and achieve cost levels approaching books, there is an even larger incentive to create programs that are designed to be flexible and maintainable. This implies that "neat tricks" must be avoided in the programming process and that data structures must be well defined, but with contents left undefined until the very last moment. Old-time programmers look askance at these new ideas, but the economics weighs against the old-time practices.

Throughout this design course we will emphasize the concern about life-cycle costs by encouraging practices that will minimize the future costs of maintenance and modification.

resort to the **list** form of data structures. In a **list,** all of the unused space in storage is *linked* together in a *free-space list.* It doesn't matter whether the free space is in semiconductor storage, core storage, or even on a large disc file. The items in the free-space list contain nothing but addresses to other items in the free-space list; the rest of the item is not used (yet).

When a data record, for example, a subscriber record, has to have some information appended to it, one of the items is removed from the free-space list and appended to the list of items in the record that needs more space (see Figure 3.12).

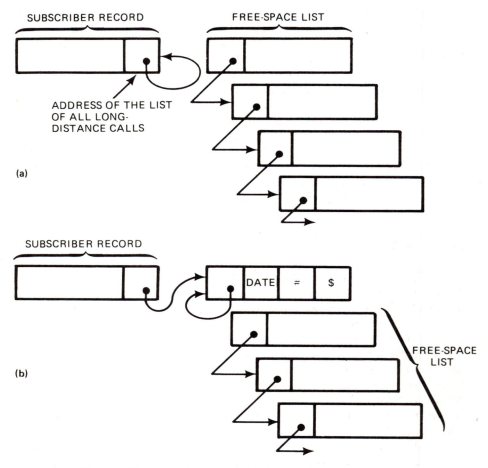

Figure 3.12   A list of free-space items can be the source for data storage space. One of several subscriber records in a telephone billing system can have a record of no long-distance calls (a), or a long-distance call can be recorded by appending a list item to the basic record (b).

By carefully keeping track of where all of the data is stored, we can easily provide more storage space just where it is needed. The only limitation is that the free-space list must initially be large enough to be able to satisfy all of the future requests. Of course, as the information is utilized and is no longer needed, list items can be restored to the free-space list. Thus, free-space lists are pools of resources that can be allocated wherever they are needed and whenever they are needed. As our design course unfolds we will see more and more applications for lists.

Several important features of lists should be noted. First of all, they are among the most generalized data structures, but they can be abused if they are used when arrays would be more efficient. But, like arrays, each member of a list may be made up of an arbitrarily complex item structure. You will also note in Figure 3.12 that only addresses of data references are changed. The data itself is not moved in the process of extending the basic record.

Lists can be described in a nongraphic (textual) form, as in Figure 3.13. Like arrays, lists are assigned names as convenient handles. However, since lists are not linearly arranged like arrays, we cannot directly refer to the ith item of a list as "list(i)." Instead, we must find each list item's successor until we locate the particular item we want. This means that we must have a scheme for designating particular data types as pointers to list elements. In defining numbers we let the numbers stand for themselves; we enclose characters in quotation marks; for pointers (which are, after all, addresses) we use the "@" sign because it implies "at." Therefore, we can define "pointer **of** @free-space" which clearly means that the pointer is the name of a register that contains the address of some item in the "free-space" list.

```
list free-space (0 . . 100) of
        begin
            item pointer of @ free-space;
            item number of telephone;
            item date of 0 . . 31;
            item charge of money
        end;

array customer (1 . . 1000) of
        begin
            array name (1 . . 25) of . . .
                        .
                        .
                        .
            item LD-calls of @ free-space
        end;
```

Figure 3.13 A list of potential long-distance calls can be defined; this example provides for up to 100 calls to be recorded. In data records, pointers such as "LD-calls" can be made to point to the list of items. Such items are said to be detached from the free-space list and attached to the LD-calls list.

A Review of the Rules

Every datum must have a *type,* whether simple or complex. The simplest kind of data are:

1. Enumerated possibilities (like **of** true, false)
2. Numbers (**of** 0 . .99)
3. Encoded characters (**of** "A", "B", "C")
4. Addresses of other data items (**of** @ list).

Complex data structures can be made up by surrounding more primitive compositions with the **begin-end** pair of brackets.

Once data types are defined, there are only three data structures that can be allocated to occupy storage media:

1. **Item**s are single instances of some simple or complex data type.
2. **Array**s provide for large numbers of repeated items, all of the same general shape, to be efficiently stored and referred to.
3. **List**s are generalized arrangements of items that allow different **item**s to have effectively different sizes as required by the requirements of the application.

TOKEN TYPE	DISTINCTION	EXAMPLE	IN-STORAGE REPRESENTATION
SYMBOLIC NAMES	START WITH LETTER	XYZ	XYZ: [?]
LITERAL CHARACTERS	ENCLOSE IN QUOTATION MARKS	"XYZ"	"XYZ": [X,Y,Z] XYZ:
POINTERS TO MEMORY	START WITH "AT-SIGN"	@XYZ	@XYZ: [XYZ •]→[?]
DECIMAL	START WITH 1 . . 9	123	123: 01111011_2
BINARY	START WITH %	%101	%101: 00000101_2
OCTAL	START WITH 0	0123	0123: 01010011_2
HEXADECIMAL	START WITH =	=123	≠123: 000100100011_2

4

Procedure Structures

Now that we have agreed upon ways of describing data, we can embark on a treatment of various ways we can describe how to transform data. It is this part of programming that generally gets more treatment in the conventional texts, but it is no more important (or less, for that matter) than the data structures. We do have an advantage, though, since you understand how data structures are defined. So, in the program segments that appear in the rest of this book the necessary data will be described.

Procedural Elements

Programming is little more than composing sequential register transfers, that is, moving data from one register to another. In the design of procedures for practical implementation, we choose to avoid limiting the number of registers we can manipulate and to separate the classes of registers into two types: data and control. The data registers are those items, arrays, and lists that are defined in the program and that are to be operated upon. The control registers are the program counters and stacks that exist in the computer that will be used to implement this program. In the description of procedures we need to take cognizance of the differences between these two registers. We will deal with the data registers very explicitly and the control registers only implicitly.

Registers transfers are specified by an *assignment* statement. The source and destination registers are identified, and an arrow specifies in which direction the data transfer is to take place [Figure 4.1(a)]. In general, you should only transfer data from a source to a destination that is compatible in **type.** That is, it is probably meaningless to transfer data from, say, a "money" item into a "resistance" item [Figure 4.1(b)]. We use type declarations to avoid such meaningless transfers because they are the source of the majority of programming errors.

For convenience, we allow entire **item**s to be transferred from one place to another with a single assignment. Both Figures 4.1(c) and 4.1(d) are equivalent, but the shorter example is preferred. We are concerned, remember, with the design of the algorithm and technique, not the specific coding tricks to be used on a particular computer.

(a)　type byte of 0 . . 255;
　　　item a, b of byte;
　　　　a ← b;

(b)　type money of 0 . . 99999;
　　　type resistance of 0 . . 1000000;
　　　item charges of money;
　　　item R_p of resistance;
　　　　R_p ← charges;

(c)　type weather of
　　　　begin
　　　　　　type city of New York, Chicago, Los Angeles,
　　　　　　　　St. Louis, London, Tokyo;
　　　　　　type date of 0 . . 31
　　　　　　type temperature of −50 . . 120;
　　　　　　type precipitation of 0 . . 10
　　　　end;
　　　item oldwx, newwx of weather;
　　　　oldwx ← newwx;

(d)　　　oldwx. city ← newwx. city;
　　　　oldwx. date ← newwx. date;
　　　　oldwx. temperature ← newwx. temperature;
　　　　oldwx. precipitation ← newwx. precipitation;

Figure 4.1　Four different register transfer specifications.

Data Manipulation

By separating the data and procedural descriptions of a computer program, we allow the data to be described without regard to the kind of modifications that are likely to be undertaken; these modifications are reserved for the procedure descriptions. We specify these operations in the assignment statement; the assignment operator (the arrow) shows where to put the result. To add two values together and store the result somewhere else, an assignment statement of the kind in Figure 4.2(a) is used. The " + " sign is called an *operator,* as is the assignment arrow. Other operators commonly required are provided in Figure 4.2(b). Each operator specifies one operation to be performed on two operands; the assignment operator is, of course, somewhat unique in this scheme yet it conforms to our basic rules.

The operators of Figure 4.2(b) are by no means exhaustive. You can add to the suite of operators almost endlessly, but these basic few remain the most popular.

An example of the application of this kind of operation on data is the calculation of parallel resistances (Figure 4.3). Because the reciprocals of resistances must be calculated, we define the *type* of data to range from the very large to the very

(a)   item a, b, c of 0 . . 255;
$$a \leftarrow b + c;$$

(b) $a \leftarrow b - c;$ subtract c from b
           $a \leftarrow b * c;$ multiply b by c
           $a \leftarrow b/c;$ divide b by c, save quotient
           $a \leftarrow b \bmod c;$ divide b by c, save remainder
           $a \leftarrow b \ll c;$ shift b left c bits
           $a \leftarrow b \gg c;$ shift b right c bits

Figure 4.2   A simple addition operation (a) and other popular operators used in programming (b).

small. The four sequential steps in Figure 4.3(b) describe precisely how the computations should be performed. Given initial values for "R_1" and "R_2," the equivalent value, "R_P" will be computed. We can also introduce another simplification [Figure 4.3(C)] if we observe the mathematical rule that expressions within parentheses are evaluated first, and then multiplications and additions are evaluated. A complete but brief sample of a program to compute the resistance of parallel values of 100 and 200Ω appears in Figure 4.3(d).

(a)   item R_1, R_2, R_P of 10^{-6} . . 10^6;

(b) $R_1 \leftarrow 1/R_1;$
           $R_2 \leftarrow 1/R_2;$
           $R_P \leftarrow R_1 + R_2;$
           $R_P \leftarrow 1/R_P$

(c) $R_P \leftarrow 1/(1/R_1 + 1/R_2);$

(d)   item R_1, R_2, R_P of 0 . . 10^6;
           $R_1 \leftarrow 100;$
           $R_2 \leftarrow 200;$
           $R_P \leftarrow 1/(1/R_1 + 1/R_2);$

Figure 4.3   The genesis of a whole program to compute parallel resistance values, starting from some simple data definitions (a), a detailed algorithm (b), an abbreviated form of the algorithm (c), and finally, a practical application.

Functional Notation

Functions are the heart of the expandable nature of mathematics. Similarly, in software design the ability to define and implement functions is central to the power of computer programming. For example, we might make up a function that implements the computation of parallel resistances. In a form not unlike mathematics, then, we can invoke that function and produce the following result:

$$R_P \quad P(100,200);$$

where "P" is the name of the function, "100" and "200" are the *arguments,* and "R_P" is the conventional destination of the result of applying that function over those arguments.

We define a function in programming by calling it a **procedure.** A procedure has a name (the function's name), a description of the arguments that are used, and a body that describes how to transform those arguments into a result. In mathematics, of course, we assume that the entire range of real numbers may be used in a function; in a computer we have to be more explicit about the shapes of the arguments and the results. An example is shown in Figure 4.4(a) (the definition) and Figure 4.4(b) (the invocation). Since a procedural definition may consist of a few or many, many statements, we bound them with the now familiar **begin-end** pair to define which statements belong to this particular procedure.

(a) procedure parallel (R_X, R_Y);
 begin
 type resistance of $0 .. 10^6$;
 item R_X, R_Y, parallel of resistance;
 parallel $\leftarrow 1/(1/R_X + 1/R_Y)$
 end;

(b) type resistance of $0 .. 10^6$;
 item R_1, R_2, R_P of resistance;
 $R_P \leftarrow$ parallel (R_1, R_2);

Figure 4.4 A simple definition of a function for computing parallel resistance (a), and a use of that function (b).

There are two very important points about this way of defining new capabilities in a computer program: From the viewpoint of the procedure, it doesn't matter from how many different places the procedure is invoked. From the viewpoint of the invocation in the larger program, the internal complexity of the function is unknown. In other words, the program has been partitioned into two independent modules, the only communication between them being the arguments and the types of data that have been defined. This is important for several reasons, and it will be discussed in more detail in Chapter 5. For the moment let us just cite two reasons why this principle of separation of procedures is important.

First, a procedure may be used many different places in a larger program to accomplish some goal, but it occupies only one small part of the computer's memory. Regardless of how many different places it can be invoked from, the procedure occupies a relatively small amount of space. Of course, each time it is invoked, the procedure takes time to execute. Hence, procedures offer an inherent space–time trade off; they minimize space consumed, but at the expense of the additional time it takes to prepare the data and "pass" it from the invoking program down into the procedure.

Second, a procedure can be used (conceptually) before it is defined. If our computer program must have the ability to compute the resistance of two parallel resistors, we can define "parallel" as a procedure without defining the algorithm. We then write the larger, dependent program in such a way that we adhere to whatever conventions we may have established for communicating with that procedure without regard to the internal complexity of the procedure. Later, when we must fulfill it in order to complete the program we can address the internal complexity of the procedure without regard to the complexity of the rest of the software system. In other words, a procedure is a device for preserving the programmer's sanity! Because it permits us to concentrate on one thing at a time, a procedure is one of the most powerful tools in the programmer's arsenal.

Controlling Flow

We have already introduced, by implication, one major kind of program flow: sequential execution of successive statements or instructions. However, if computers were limited to performing one set of instructions (linearly), they would not be of much use. We need the ability to handle both alternation and iteration. *Alternation* is the choice of one of two possible paths to follow; *iteration* allows the same path to be followed time after time. Only after we understand how these flow-control options work can we design truly interesting programs.

Before we address the more complex forms of control, we should review what we have said so far about sequential execution. When two statements appear sequentially, separated by a semicolon, the first statement and then the second statement are executed. Any number of statements or instructions can be arranged linearly and executed one after another. For convenience, we often write a **begin-end** pair around the sequence; this defines a *basic block*. A basic block of program is a segment of instructions that has only one entry point and only one exit point. As we shall see, the basic block becomes an important tool in the rest of this chapter.

In terms of the computer's registers, each new statement or instruction represents an incrementation of the program location counter. To *enter* a basic block, we set the program location counter to the address of the first instruction. Eventually, the program counter will be set to the instruction immediately following the last instruction in the block; we say that this is the block's *exit point*. The internal complexity of the basic block makes no matter to us; it may be one instruction or thousands. It may execute purely sequentially or invoke the out-of-line procedures that may have been defined earlier. But from an organizational point of view, the basic block performs a function and is structured into a simple entity that has known behavioral characteristics.

If we use the basic block approach, the **procedure** is nothing more than an out-of-line basic block that has a name. Wherever the name appears, it is functionally identical to having the actual body of the procedure in-line in the program at that point. Except for execution time and space consumption requirements, the program segments of Figure 4.5(a) and 4.5(b) are identical. The first example uses an out-of-line procedure; the second uses the same procedure in-line. Although the simpler in-line approach may appear more appealing in this example, in general the out-of-line approach will be more attractive as your programs grow larger and larger.

<u>type</u> resistance <u>of</u> $0 .. 10^6$;
<u>item</u> R_1, R_2, R_p <u>of</u> resistance;
<u>procedure</u> parallel (R_X, R_Y);
<u>begin</u>
    <u>item</u> R_X, R_Y, parallel <u>of</u> resistance;
        parallel $\leftarrow 1/(1/R_X + 1/R_Y)$
<u>end</u>;
    $R_p \leftarrow$ parallel (R_1, R_2);

(a)

<u>type</u> resistance <u>of</u> $0 .. 10^6$
<u>item</u> R_1, R_2, R_p <u>of</u> resistance;

$R_p \leftarrow 1/(1/R_1 + 1/R_2)$;

(b)

Figure 4.5 Two equivalent programs, one using a generalized "out-of-line" procedure (a), and the other having the procedure inserted in-line as needed.

Simple linear programs are nice introductory devices, but they hardly occur in real programming problems. Almost invariably you have to make a choice among two or more alternatives: **If** some statement is true, **then** do this, **else** do that. The truth or falsity of a statement can be reduced in computers to setting or clearing a bit somewhere in a register. Some typical alternation examples are shown in Figure 4.6. Note that sometimes the second option is "do nothing." Here we delete the **else** clause from the statement.

Alternation, in the form of the **if** statement, is designed to allow some condition(s) in storage to determine the future course of events in the program. If data

(a)   <u>item</u> switch <u>of</u> true, false;
      <u>if</u> switch
      <u>then</u> $R_p \leftarrow$ parallel $(100, 200)$
      <u>else</u> $R_p \leftarrow$ parallel $(100, 250)$;

(b)   <u>item</u> a, b <u>of</u> $0 .. 16383$;
      <u>if</u> a = b <u>then</u> b $\leftarrow$ 1900;

(c)   <u>item</u> keyboard <u>of</u> ASCII;
      <u>if</u> keyboard $\neq$ NUL
      <u>then</u> process-key (keyboard)
      <u>else</u> wait-for-activity;

Figure 4.6 Three different examples of how to use the **if** statement to choose alternate paths for execution.

is being accepted from a terminal or from some remote data acquisition device, it is common to include an "input-and-edit" procedure in the program. The necessary input instructions are issued to acquire the data in some register. The **if** statements are then used to validate that data to be certain that it lies within acceptable extremes.

Similarly, when processing depends on some other related events or recent history, we use **if** statements to select which program path to execute. Complex programs generally contain large numbers of **if** statements, which is why they are complex. But experienced designers can easily expand the functions of a particular program by implementing options that are selected by setting a variable that is subsequently tested by an **if** statement.

It is difficult to write a program that does not liberally use **if** statements.

The condition in an **if** statement that selects among the alternatives is any statement that can have a binary outcome. Thus, a Boolean variable that can take on the values "true" or "false" can choose between the two paths. Similarly, any statement of inequality or equality that can have only a Boolean outcome (such as "**if** a is less than b") can be used to select. Remember, however, that comparisons of this sort may only be made between items of like **type;** it is not meaningful to compare apples and oranges, even in a computer.

Each of the two alternatives in an **if** statement is a basic block. That is, a block may consist of single statements or complex sequences of statements bounded by **begin** and **end.**

Iteration is similar, but not identical, to alternation. In iteration we continue to execute the same basic block over and over until some condition is no longer satisfied. This means that the same program (or basic block) can be used with different values of data without having to replicate the program. Again, remembering the notion of the procedure, you can conceive of the basic block in an iteration group as having one point in space but many points in time.

To control iteration, we write a **while** statement, as shown in Figure 4.7. The logical condition of continued iteration is identical to the alternate selection con-

```
(a)    while i ≠ 0
       do begin
                   process-data (i);
                   i ← i − 1
       end;


(b)    i ← 1;
       while i less than 10
       do begin
                   process-data (i);
                   i ← i + 1
       end;
```

Figure 4.7   Some examples of iteration, or "looping," described for simple program segments.

dition of an **if** statement. That is, it must have a true or false outcome. If the condition is true, the basic block is executed and the condition is tested again. The process repeats until the condition test fails.

The last example of iteration, Figure 4.7(b), is so common in programming that a special variant of it is provided for convenience. The date value "i" is called an induction variable; it is used to select the *i*th item out of a group of items for processing, especially if the items are in an array. The first statement in Figure 4.7(b) is called the *initialization of the variable;* the condition within the **while** statement is the termination test, and the first statement in the **while's** basic block is the *increment*. It can be written more compactly as shown in Figure 4.8. The **for** statement declares the initial and terminal values for the induction variable, and it declares the increment (or step) to take in between.

for i ← 0 <u>to</u> 10 <u>step</u> 1
<u>do</u> process - data (i);

Figure 4.8   An abbreviated form for the most common kind of iteration in programming, the loop counter.

A Review of the Rules

There are statements that deal with data and there are statements that deal with control. All of these statements are executed sequentially. A sequential group of statements that has one entry point and one exit point is called a *basic block*. When the programmer is in doubt, he bounds sequential statements by **begin** and **end** in order to delimit the scope of the basic block.

Procedures may be in-line or out-of-line. An in-line procedure is a basic block that appears precisely where it is needed in the program. An out-of-line procedure is a basic block that appears elsewhere in storage and is invoked by name when it is needed. In-line procedures occupy more space than out-of-line procedures if they are required in more than one place in the program. Out-of-line procedures require slightly more execution time to set up the conditions to "pass" the necessary data to the procedure.

In addition to the simple kinds of data manipulation statements, programmers need to have **if-then-else** and **while-do** statements to implement alternation and iteration, respectively. Each of these statements may contain other basic blocks so that programs of arbitrarily large complexity can be constructed.

Program Structure

How do data structures and procedure structures fit together in the final working design of a computer program? Most software designers adopt some general conventions based on elementary rules that are fair and easy to remember.

First of all, in a software system we are defining a kind of a language that describes how to process some particular kind of data to achieve a particular result. As

Parallels Between Data and Procedures

There are five basic rules for describing data and five basic rules for describing procedures. Are they somehow "duals" of one another? Decide for yourself.

ATTRIBUTE	DATA	PROCEDURES
Three basic structures	items, arrays, lists	sequence, alternation, iteration
One fundamental objective	to define the type of data to be processed	to define the statements that process the data
In- and out-of-line options	type declarations	procedure statements
Recursive application of rules	begin-end pair	begin-end pair

Figure A

with any language, we must define our terms before we use them. In human communication, if we slip and use a novel term before defining it, the listener can be smart enough to ask for clarification. Generally, computers are not that smart. Therefore, we must design all of our data structures first, define all of the procedures, and then describe how they are all interfaced together.

A computer program exists in both space and time. In space, the way the program is laid out on paper bears some resemblance (usually) to the way the program is to be laid out in memory. There is no rigid correlation, however, and it is important to remember this. During the design stages our paper copy of the design should be arranged for easy comprehension by humans. Later, as the program becomes computer-readable, its spatial orientation may be shifted to take advantage of one or another feature of the computer or the language we are programming with.

The organization of a program in time may be completely different from the arrangement in time. As different procedures are invoked, they occupy sequential time. Since the order of the procedures on the printed page does not bear any necessary relationship to the order in which they are invoked, it may take considerable study and effort to uncover the time-sequence invocations of the procedures. Yet, this one facet of programs, the time–order, is most important in understanding how a program works and what it does.

To simplify the programmer's task, and to aid those who may follow us in reading this program, we adopt some rules of practice. First of all, we divide all data structures into two classes, global and local. *Global data* is used throughout the entire program by many of the procedures. It is defined once, and this definition "sticks" throughout the entire program. *Local data* "belongs" to a particular procedure. The data values are defined and are used only inside that procedure; they cannot be referred to by any other procedure. In other words, local data is private and does not affect the interrelationships among procedures. Global data is public and is the means by which procedures are interfaced.

Next, we define the program as being made up of a few major global procedures that perform the majority of the work. These procedures have names like "read input data" and "process the data." Each procedure may refer to the global data, and each may have private (local) data structures for intermediate results. Each procedure may also have other local procedures. A global procedure named "read input data," for example, may have several local procedures (Figure 4.9), each one performing a small part of the job. The local procedure "prepare input" may initialize the input operation, "accept" may acquire the data, "validate" probably makes certain that accepted data is valid for processing, and "error" is a procedure that handles the data that is not valid. Each of these local procedures considers all of the data defined in the next larger procedure global data; the local procedure may also have its own privately defined local data.

```
procedure read input data;
begin

        procedure prepare input;
        begin
            . . .
        end;

        procedure accept;
        begin
            . . .
        end;

        procedure valid;
        begin
            . . .
        end;

        procedure error;
        begin
            . . .
        end;

        prepare input;
        accept;
        while not valid do
        begin
            error;
            accept
        end;

end;
```

Figure 4.9 The structure of a procedure with internal procedures as part of its makeup.

To simplify the structure and make it easy to understand, each procedure is written so that it is small enough to fit on a single page. This is an ideal that is not always met. However, if the design can be partitioned down to the point that each procedure occupies a single page and the global data can be documented on a single page, you will find that your design will have an inherent understandability. There are programming staffs in the country that *insist* on one-page procedures and they contend that any procedure larger than that would probably be so poorly understood that it should be partitioned anyway.

Each procedure in the program has the basic structure outlined in Figure 4.10. Since every procedure is a basic block, it is bounded by a **begin-end** pair. The data that is local to this basic block is then defined; that data is, of course, global data to any procedures that may be defined in this basic block. After the data is defined, all of the subordinate procedures are defined. Finally, once all of the terms (i.e., data and procedure structures) are defined, we can write down all of the statements that perform the work of this procedure. These statements are called the *body* of the procedure.

An entire program is nothing more than a basic block like the one that makes up a procedure. Therefore, an entire program consists of all of the global data structures, followed by all of the subordinate procedures, and then the main program statements that use those data structures and procedure structures to accomplish the work of the program.

```
begin

        (item, array and list declarations for all the
        data accessible to the following procedures and
        the main program statements);

        (procedure declarations for all suborainate pro-
        cedures required by the main program statements);

        (all of the main program statements)

end
```

Figure 4.10 A general model for the composition of every procedure, including the main program itself.

5

Algorithm Design

Now that you have trudged through two chapters of what looks a lot like pure theory, we are going to show you how to put this theory into practice. Just as a drafting template is used to design a digital circuit, we are going to use the "templates" of the past two chapters to describe the data structures and procedures of a software system.

Much of what follows will be rehash to you. Since you already have experience in designing digital systems, many of the steps will seem familiar—and they are. But there are some subtle differences. The scope of the problems that you might be tempted to challenge with a new logic design is significantly smaller than the scope of the problems you can potentially solve with a computer. Often there is a temptation to add in a new capability to a computer program, just because "software is so inexpensive." Software is deceptively inexpensive and simple, and all of the easy problems have been solved by mankind. From now on even though the problems will become bigger and more intractable, you don't have to make your job any more complex than is really necessary. Restraint and discipline, especially on the first few programs you tackle, are very important.

Requirements

The first step in any successful design is to understand the requirements—and to separate them from the "wish list." Requirements are most often easily stated in terms of objectives to be achieved instead of in terms of some attributes of the final product. At this early stage it is better to state that the objective of a particular program is "to implement a system to analyze and display wave forms of less than 1 MHz that can be sold (profitably) at under \$1,000" instead of establishing at the outset that the objective is "to program an 8080 to do Fourier transforms." An example is shown in Figure 5.1.

SOFTWARE REQUIREMENT

COMPUTE THE CYCLIC REDUNDANCY CHECK (CRC) WORD
ON A DATA WORD OF SPECIFIED LENGTH USING THE
POLYNOMIAL

$$X^{16} + X^{12} + X^5 + 1$$

TO SIMULATE THE FOLLOWING HARDWARE EQUIVALENT:

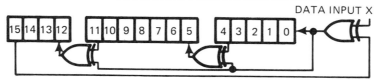

Figure 5.1 A sample (overly simplified) software requirement statement for one procedure within a larger software system.

Ideally, these requirements come from outside the design organization. They originate from someone who has a need or from someone who perceives a need that can be filled (the marketing or product planning department). The form of the requirements may be verbal. You should document the requirements, analyze them, and be sure that you understand what they imply.

Always look beyond the requirements. A favorite question that good systems designers like to ask of a potential user of the system is, "If you *had* the data, what would you do with it?" Often, the user wants to use the results of some computer processing to do something that ought to be properly considered part of the computer system. If somebody wants some large mass of data processed and reduced, ask, "What would you do with it if you *had* the reduced data?" His answer might be, "Plot it on graph paper for analysis." Your response to this would be, "Let me produce the graphs on the computer and save you all that effort."

Similarly, you should ask where the inputs from the system come from. If you are designing an instrument, must the data be entered by hand through a keyboard? How about adding an interface to one of the now-standard buses, like the IEEE 488, so that data can be acquired automatically. Often, that kind of contribution to a shift in the requirements of a design may become more valuable than the original.

In the requirements analysis stage it is also important to grade the objectives into an ordered list. Is it more important to get some particular feature or to get the product into use sooner? The program that has all the features asked for but too late to be of any use is probably less valuable than the program that works on time but has a few of the "bells and whistles" missing.

Cyclic Redundancy Checking

In data communications and magnetic media (tapes and discs) there are several error-detecting schemes in vogue. One of the most effective is called the Cyclic Redundancy Check (CRC). Because the CRC is well formulated, this particular problem of calculating the CRC will be used for some of the examples to follow in this design course.

In effect, the entire bit stream that is the data to be transmitted, stored, retrieved, and/or received is divided by a constant bit pattern called the *generating polynomial*. The remainder after that division is the *CRC word*. It is appended to data transmitted or stored and it is compared to the previously computed value when the data is retrieved or received. Both versions, of course, should result in the very same bit pattern result if the data was received (or retrieved) without error.

There are many generating polynomials, and one of the most common divisors for this algorithm is

$$10001000000100001$$

Since this bit pattern has seventeen bits, it results in a sixteen-bit remainder. Instead of expressing the generating polynomial as a bit pattern, it is common to express it in algebraic notation:

$$x^{16} + x^{12} + x^5 + x^0$$

where x may be either zero or one.

Long binary division is not practical on most computers. Therefore, simpler sequential algorithms that operate on each bit (or on each byte) have been developed. A division by the most-significant bit is equivalent, for example, to left-shifting the entire CRC word and then feeding the shifted-out bit back around into the low-order position. This leaves the remaining bits in the polynomial to worry about. If the incoming data bit (x) is zero, then no further changes to the CRC word are necessary. If the incoming data bit is one, then the generating polynomial is exclusive-or'd with the CRC word. Graphically, this process can be represented as a sixteen-bit shift register with exclusive-or's and taps at each of the generating polynomial's significant bit points (see Figure A).

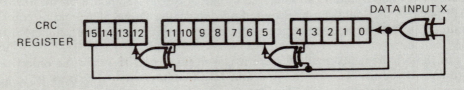

There are other objectives you should establish in the requirements phase that don't directly relate to the job to be done. For example, what are the reliability requirements? If the program is delivered with a latent bug (one that exists but hasn't been encountered yet), what is the impact on the entire program? A latent bug in a circuit design program that can be rerun after the problem is fixed is certainly less critical than a bug in a process control program that handles explosive materials. In each case, the bugs may be trivial, but the penalties for finding them *after* delivery are vastly different.

Other objectives that should be considered in the requirements analysis phase include the following:

1. Flexibility, the ease with which the design can be changed as future needs and requirements change
2. Durability, the extent to which the program can be applied to similar but not identical applications
3. Portability, the ease with which the program may be changed from one computer to another as users change computers

The list of potential requirements considerations is probably endless. But you should thoroughly establish at the outset and get agreement from the end-user or his proxy that these really are the requirements. In fact, in formal requirements analysis for large-scale software systems it is now fashionable to attach relative costs and benefits to each of these objectives so that subsequent analyses can be performed. However, projects like these usually involve large numbers of highly experienced software designers who have had lots of large-system experience.

Environment

The environment that any computer program operates in includes the computer, of course, but just as important and often neglected are the inputs and outputs. The definition of these inputs and outputs is critically important to the design of the software—remember our caveat about designing the data structures first (see Chapter 3).

The medium of input and output data is highly dependent on the kind of computer for which you are going to write your software. In a large-scale computer or commercial time-sharing system your input and output data will take on the form of certain allowable "strings" of characters, usually in the form of punched-card images or lines of print on a terminal or high-speed line printer. For a minicomputer, you will probably have to specify the input and output data more precisely and consider the limitations of the media more carefully. You may have to accept the input from an external piece of electronics equipment that generates sequential words of data. For a microcomputer, you will probably have to get down to the details of how fast the data is arriving and how it is buffered internally or externally. You might even have to be concerned with details like clock timing and rise and fall times of signals. A typical project's input and output description are shown in Figure 5.2.

INPUT DATA

THE FIRST PARAMETER IN THIS PROCEDURE'S INVOCATION GIVES
THE ADDRESS OF AN ARRAY OF BITS FOR WHICH TO CALCULATE
THE CRC.
THE SECOND PARAMETER, TAKEN FROM A 16-BIT REGISTER,
SPECIFIES THE NUMBER OF BITS IN THE ARRAY.

OUTPUT DATA

THE PROCEDURE PRODUCES A VALUE IN A 16-BIT REGISTER
CORRESPONDING TO THE COMPUTED CRC.

Figure 5.2   A description of the inputs and outputs for the software required in Figure 5.1.

Defining data at the abstract structural level for a large-scale computer usually requires little else than using the **item**s, **array**s, and **list**s defined in Chapter 3. For a minicomputer, though, you may have to introduce one or more procedures to control the acceptance and emission of data. When you have to provide software for the primitive input/output operations of a microcomputer, you will most certainly find that you will have relatively primitive data structures but elaborate sets of interacting procedures to service the external peripheral devices.

Reading data from a terminal is a good example of the differences. In a large-scale computer your program will be provided data from the terminal one entire line at a time; until an entire line is accumulated by the operating system, the computer is used to handle other programs that must run along with yours. When an entire line is available, your program is reactivated until you again ask for more input data.

In a minicomputer you may have the same high-level control through an operating system, although more likely you will be responsible for reading in one character at a time. Your software will have to test some input bit to see if a new character has arrived yet and then read the character in when it has arrived. Your program may process each character as it is received or the characters may be buffered in memory until an entire line is completed.

In a microcomputer you may have the ability to interface to the terminal like the minicomputer or you may have to do considerably more work. In many microcomputers you must examine the incoming serial data from a terminal on a single bit; as that bit changes, your software must decode the changes in time to create the received character. Again, the applications program you write may process each of those characters individually or you might buffer them in memory and let the application program process the entire received data line at once.

Design-in-the-whole Versus Partial Implementation

Today there are two schools of thought on software and system design. Traditionalists sincerely believe that full and complete requirements analysis can be performed and should be performed for each system. Their objective is to design the entire required system or program at once. There is a new school, however, that holds that a minimal subset of the intended system should be implemented, that users should take advantage of it, and that improvements for the next iteration of design should be fed back.

Sometimes there is no choice. You may have a commercial product to produce, but there may be no opportunity to "test market" or it may require a full-scale design at the outset. Or you may have to implement a system to which users may immediately begin making requests for changes as a result, you may implement an expanded second generation whether you intended to or not.

In most cases, however, you can take a middle ground. If you are developing a product, for instance, it is a good idea to implement a "stripped" version of the software without the defensive programming features of carefully diagnosed input. This breadboard of the eventual product can be used for (limited) demonstrations to in-house and marketing staff. These demonstrations can be effective in teaching the marketing personnel how to exploit the product and they may provide you with valuable feedback about various features.

When you lay out a project, consider the interim product versions that you can implement and how they can be exploited. You will end up with a better product. It may take a little longer over the entire project cycle, but management will be a little less worried about invisible progress because they will see something working earlier than they expected to.

It is the complexity and potential sophistication in input/output that separate micros, minis, and maxis from one another. Microcomputers permit highly flexible input/output arrangements, but at the cost of considerable additional effort in programming for even the simplest of interfaces. Minis permit the development of simpler software, but it is at the expense of the range of possible designs that could be undertaken. Finally, maxis do most of the work for you, but you are left with little flexibility in case you need to something truly unique.

If your program is to take advantage of external storage media, such as tape or disc, for storing intermediate results or data files, you must treat these as input/output devices as well. Most microcomputer applications won't have this problem, but almost all minicomputers and maxicomputers use the extra storage.

Remember, most input and output data to and from computers is a complex structure, especially over time. For example, you may have to interface to a single data communications channel from your computer. Since that channel could be deceptively simple, you should investigate the *protocol* or message format convention used on that channel. You may be receiving eight-bit characters at a relatively slow rate of, say, 2,400 bits per second. Yet, the program that processes that data, accounts for missing data, and handles errors that creep into the messages through the communications channel may be larger than the entire rest of the application! In this admittedly extreme case, the potential sequences of messages that can occur are huge and lots of special cases need to be handled in your software.

There are several methods for describing data, including finite-state machine (FSM) models and Backus-Naur Form (BNF). Many of the now popular software engineering texts show alternative ways of formally describing input and output data. But whether you adopt one of the popular methods or derive your own, you must define the inputs and outputs thoroughly enough that your software design can be considered a "black box" with just these inputs and outputs. To the extent you have left the input and output data formats undefined, you will have difficulties in the implementation, testing, and debugging stages.

Formalization of Requirements

Once the requirements and the input/output data descriptions are in hand, a more formal definition of the program to be implemented can be constructed. A typical example appears in Figure 5.3. Most programs you are likely to write are going to have complex sequential inputs, typically from other electronic devices (we don't expect that you will be writing very many conventional data processing packages). The large number of complex sequences can be difficult to sort out, especially if many of the inputs are read into the computer asynchronously. One of the most popular methods, and one that serves the novice and pro equally well, is the finite-state machine (FSM) model.

This technique works for almost any program, but it is especially useful for real-time programs on minis and micros.

Decision tables are also helpful in the early design stages. A *decision table* allows you to describe all of the conditions that might exist from inputs (or in memory cells as history) and all of the outputs to be generated and then to interrelate the two.

The left half of a decision table is called the *stub* (Figure 5.4), and the right half is called the *entry*. The top half of the table contains the *conditions* and the bottom half contains the *actions*. All of the relevant conditions are listed in the condition stub, and all of the potential actions are listed in the action stub. The entries are divided into columns called *rules*. A rule consists of a column of Y (for "yes"), N (for "no"), or—(for "don't care") entries; when all of the conditions satisfy some rule, then all of the actions marked in the rule are taken. It is common to number the actions in the order in which they are to be performed.

Input Data Description

item length of 1 .. 65535;
array message (1 .. length) of 0 .. 1;

Remarks: "length" is the number of bits in "message," the bit list for which the CRC is required.

Output Data Description

item CRC of 0 .. 65535;

Remarks: "CRC" is 16 bits long

Algorithm

1. Preserve the most significant bit in CRC
2. Shift CRC one place to left, leaving the least significant bit ZERO
3. Exclusive-OR the previously saved most significant CRC bit with the next message bit and install in the least-significant-bit position of CRC
4. Repeat steps 1 through 3 until all bits in message have been processed.

Figure 5.3 A more formalized, yet not final, description of the inputs, outputs and processing required of the CRC-calculation program.

The decision table helps us organize thinking. If they are properly used, decision tables can prevent forgetting some important combination of conditions. For n conditions, there must be a total of 2^n "pure" rules made up of simple Y and N

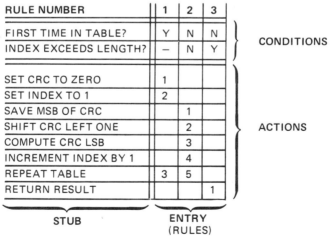

RULE NUMBER	1	2	3	
FIRST TIME IN TABLE?	Y	N	N	CONDITIONS
INDEX EXCEEDS LENGTH?	—	N	Y	
SET CRC TO ZERO	1			
SET INDEX TO 1	2			
SAVE MSB OF CRC		1		
SHIFT CRC LEFT ONE		2		ACTIONS
COMPUTE CRC LSB		3		
INCREMENT INDEX BY 1		4		
REPEAT TABLE	3	5		
RETURN RESULT			1	

STUB   ENTRY
              (RULES)

Figure 5.4 A decision table with three rules for computing the CRC.

entries. However, a particular column represents 2^d rules, where d is the number of dashes ("don't cares") in that column's condition entry. If there are too few or too many rules, errors will have to be corrected before the formalization of the requirements is finished. Other operations that can be performed on decision tables can be found in the literature on programming. Generally, decision tables will be useful in nonreal-time applications in which all of the relevant conditions can be resolved from tests on data values already in storage.

Review

After the requirements have been formalized, the input/output data descriptions and the formal requirements should be reviewed independently. Certainly, the end-user or another interested party should become involved in this review, especially if the program requirements are complicated. The formal documentation method should be readable by a knowledgeable user who has had no software design experience. By enforcing its readability, this document can be the pivotal document in the review. Once the formal description has been approved by the user/customer, there should be little need to change it in the future. It will also prevent squabbles later about undocumented requirements.

At this stage the design should also be reviewed by someone competent in software design, for an experienced software designer can often spot weaknesses that the user might not catch. Especially when you are just starting out, you should try to learn from more experienced designers. One way of learning is to have them review work you know well (since you did it).

Program Design

So far, what you have designed could be implemented in hardware, in software, or with an army of clerks. Now we must get down to describing the actual program we are going to implement to satisfy the requirements. But before we begin we must settle our objectives.

In software we can generally write a program that is small or fast, but not both. Or we can quickly write a program, but it will not likely be durable or robust. There are dozens of competing demands upon our resources in each program design. The software experts are still trying to come up with a comprehensive list of all the important variables in program design, but the list keeps growing. One version of such a list of potential objectives is provided in Table 5.1.

These objectives are self-explanatory and are generally competing. We cannot, for instance, minimize both the time required to design a program and the time required to debug it. Generally, the longer we spend in design, the less debugging we will have to do. But if we short the design process we will invariably have to spend time debugging the faults we have designed into our software.

At this point we will probably have to choose a language or computer that our program will operate on. If our goal is portability of the program, we will have to

Table 5.1 Some possible objectives you might wish to impose on a program design.

MINIMUM COST
MINIMUM TESTING TIME
MINIMUM EXTERNAL HARDWARE
MINIMUM PROGRAM SIZE
MINIMUM DATA STORAGE SIZE
MINIMUM EXECUTION TIME
MINIMUM DEBUGGING TIME
MAXIMUM RELIABILITY
MAXIMUM FLEXIBILITY
MAXIMUM EASE OF MAINTENANCE
MAXIMUM ERROR RECOVERY
MAXIMUM MODULARITY
MAXIMUM READABILITY OF CODE

choose a programming language that can be recognized by many computers. But this means that we must sacrifice something in the way of efficiency. There are novel tricks that each computer is capable of performing (that's what makes different models sell). If we choose to use a high-level language for portability, we must forego the use of these time and space savers because use of them on one computer would make the program importable to another. It is obvious that the program objectives are an important part of the design process.

And we must not forget to assign these objectives lest we get something we don't want. In days gone by programmers were permitted to set their own objectives. Generally, programmers developed habits early in their careers and blindly stuck to these habits. Thus, some programmers charged with the responsibility of writing a program quickly could never seem to produce because they were so involved in trying to produce code that always executed in the smallest amount of time. Writing programs in the smallest available space was also in vogue for some programmers, especially those who started out on small computers that had limited resources.

Yet, studies have shown that when programmers are provided with reasonable sets of objectives, programmers can perform. When they are formally directed in writing to produce programs that are small, programmers can produce small programs—although the programs may execute slowly, be almost unreadable, and totally importable. If programmers are requested to write readable programs to make life-cycle maintenance easier over time, programmers can produce readable programs. In this case, however, the problem is somewhat more difficult, since measures for readability are not as well defined as program size. But, remember, if the objective is readability, you should not expect small "tight" programs as a consequence.

Because of these variations in objectives, it is easy to criticize someone else's programs. If the reader's objectives are not the same as those of the original author's, criticism is not warranted. Nevertheless, novice programmers who have

Top-Down Versus Bottom-Up Design

When we design by defining the largest set of requirements and progress downward to the finest details of implementation, we are practicing *top-down design*. *Bottom-up design* means defining all of the details first and then interfacing them together to create the whole. Actually, few designs progress strictly top-down or bottom-up, but the general trend (and intent) is what we are interested in.

Bottom-up design, building the elementary bricks first and then cementing them together with interface mortar, is the classical approach and the one you probably learned in school. However, it has its inherent disadvantages. Because we jump down to some very low level of detail, we may lose sight of the overall objective. Or, in one module of software we may not consider some special case that will crop up later in the design as the requirements are refined. Bottom-up design encourages an early appearance of progress, but it can also cause drastic delays later when the primitive modules won't work because of inadequately defined interface conventions.

Top-down design is the preferred approach to software design today. In top-down design we attempt to define all of the requirements of the program before we attempt to implement it. Once the requirements are known, we can devise a program structure that is made up of the main procedure and skeletal subordinate procedures (sometimes called *stubs*). Then, each of the subordinate procedures is treated in turn.

In top-down design we are expressing our confidence in our ability to satisfy each requirement posed at each level of the design by somehow implementing procedures and data structures at the next detailed level. Since the interfaces are defined before the internal details, interface conventions are assured from the outset. In bottom-up design we are expressing our confidence in our ability to predict the utility of what we write before we have designed the rest of the system. That is more difficult to do. Because the interfaces between some detailed piece of code and some as yet undefined higher-level module are not defined before both parts are constructed, we are doomed to tear down and rewrite large parts of our detailed program over and over again.

no knowledge of these competing demands often, in their own ignorance, criticize programs written by another because the programs do not adhere to some (unspecified) set of performance criteria.

For your program, you should make an ordered list of the important items to remember during implementation. A typical list is shown in Figure 5.5. If you are writing on a large-scale time-sharing system, you might make "Minimum Testing

	OBJECTIVE	REASON	IMPLICATION
1.	MAXIMUM READABILITY	CODE TO BE PUBLISHED IN PRENTICE-HALL BOOK	DON'T USE ABBREVIATIONS IN SYMBOL NAMES DO INDENT THE SOURCE PROGRAM DON'T INTRODUCE NEW PROGRAM-DESCRIPTION STRUCTURES
2.	MINIMUM PROGRAM SIZE	PROGRAM USED ONLY INFREQUENTLY	DON'T TRY CLEVER BYTE-BY-BYTE ALGORITHMS DO PROCESS EACH INDIVIDUAL BIT AT A TIME DO COMPRESS PROGRAM INTO LOOPS
3.	MAXIMUM MODULARITY	FUTURE UTILITY	DON'T USE GLOBAL DATA STRUCTURES DO USE PARAMETERS TO PASS INPUT AND OUTPUT DATA

Figure 5.5 A list of the objectives to be achieved for the example CRC-calculation program.

Time'' your top-priority item in order to minimize the costs of development of the program. That decision would influence your design so that it would allow you to do more ''desk checking'' and to use smaller test cases to test more of the program. On a minicomputer you might want to assign top priority to ''Maximum Modularity'' so that the programs you develop will have utility in the next design you undertake. The decision would influence the design of your procedures so that they are highly parameterized; all data would be passed to the procedure through the arguments, never through global data. And, if you are implementing a program on a micro that has a limited memory, you should probably choose to set either ''Minimum Program Size'' or ''Minimum Data Storage Size'' as the top priority (with the other one as the second priority).

Binding Time

One of the major impacts that the proper selection of program objectives will have is on settling the issue of *binding time.* Each variable in a computer program has a binding time, the time at which the variable is assigned a value that can be used in other parts of the program. Some variables **item**s, **array**s, and **list**s alike can only be bound at execution time. That is, since the actual data content will be the consequence of some input data or computation process, it cannot be specified in advance. However, there are earlier binding times that can be used for some variables.

The size of an array of data is an example of a variable that can be bound at many, many different points in time. If in the initial design we declare that some array must be large enough to hold one value for every day in the week, we can confidently bind the size of the array to seven in the design stage. In fact, if there is no reason for this array to ever change size, it is best to bind the variable at this point. If, however, the program is to process data from a terminal and if the number of items are specified by the user when the data is submitted, we may wish to defer binding the array size until later. It could be bound at design time, for instance, but it would have to be restricted to an arbitrarily low number, low enough to encompass all of the environments that this program might ever have to encounter. For some users the array size might, then, be too small.

The size of the array could be bound at translation time so that the final program would have a particular array size. This would defer the decision to a later point. If we had a new environment, we could reassemble or recompile the program in order to get a larger array size.

The size of the array could be deferred to loading time, that is, when the program is loaded, we could define how big to make the array. Then, each time the program is loaded into the computer for execution a different array size could be selected.

The size of the array could be bound as late as actual execution time of the program. Upon detecting how much storage is actually required, the program may "appeal" to the operating system for enough additional storage to make up that array, and then data can be installed.

Why is one binding time better than another? In general, the earlier things are bound, the more efficient (and therefore less generalized) the program will be. If the array size is bound during design, all the parts of the program that refer to that array can depend on the fixed size; smaller and faster programs generally result. If the array size is not bound until execution time, the ultimate in generality results, but at some expense in terms of efficiency. A large and cumbersome software system may be required to maintain records of available storage and to parcel pieces of that storage out as required to different programs.

The choice between **array**s and **list**s is often related to the binding time issue. A small number of fixed-size arrays can be very efficient; data can be accessed in storage by simple indexing. The list structure allows many, many lists of widely varying length to be created, but at the expense of additional data storage (for maintenance of pointers) and additional program storage (for the list-manipulating procedures).

Ready-Made Programs

Before you invest a lot of time and money in the design and implementation of a program, you owe it to yourself to see if they have already been done. There are many sources of prewritten algorithms and programs, some of which you might find useful.

If your problem is largely mathematical (especially if it contains matrices), consult the Association for Computing Machinery's *Collected Algorithms*. This series (updated bimonthly) contains programs in highly readable form from algorithms that have been published in the *Communications of the ACM* and the ACM's new *Transactions on Mathematical Software*.

Another good source of algorithms is in the Art of Computer Programming series by Donald Knuth. There are three volumes published so far: *Fundamental Algorithms, Seminumerical Algorithms,* and *Sorting and Searching.* The first volume contains many of the fundamental kinds of data manipulation algorithms you might need, such as multidimensional array computation, handling of sparse matrices, and general list manipulation. The second volume provides a good foundation in fixed- and floating-point arithmetic, the trig functions, and random number generators (among other topics). The third volume describes most of the conceivable ways to sort out or search among data.

Knuth's books are written in a pidgin-English-cum-math algorithmic language, as well as assembly language for a hypothetical computer, to describe all the algorithms. This series is on every programmer's bookshelf as a ready reference.

You should also consider the library maintained by the manufacturer of your computer. Most minicomputers and large-scale computers are represented by User's Groups. These groups trade information about services and features. Most importantly, they trade programs. Usually, the library is maintained by the manufacturer and a catalog of contents is available for the asking.

Remember, however, that the programs you find in a User's Library may not meet your needs. The program may have been designed to conform to a totally different set of program objectives from yours. And even if the program does meet your objectives, treat it as though it were totally undebugged. Usually, since a very early version of the program is submitted to the library, it may still have some rather obnoxious errors to plague you.

Designing the Program

By now your program is represented by a rather impressive array of supporting paper work. If you have been executing all these steps, your documentation is almost done. Now you need a program that proves that the documentation is correct.

Design should proceed from the requirements down toward the implementation details. First, describe all of the global data structures you are sure to need. If you are going to read data into an array in one procedure and then process that data in another, the array should be defined as a global data structure. Generally, our initial set of global data structures will be brief. Don't worry. It will grow.

Next, using these data structures, write the main procedure for the programs. Decide how each major element is to be accomplished. If it is too complicated to write down in a line or two, define a procedure for it. At this level of the program you should probably have from ten to twenty lines of program statements, and you may have named anywhere from a six to twenty procedures.

Reading of Programs

Because programs are made up of familiar letters and digits on a page, novices are misled into believing that they can "read" a program. It is much more realistic to consider the program listing or description as an analog of an electronic schematic. Only after many years of experience will you be able to pick out major areas of familiar territory.

You should attempt to understand a program completely, in the same sense that you must completely understand a schematic. Read all of the statements first to see if there are especially unfamiliar (or unusually familiar) sequences or statements. Then study the data structures. Later, as you read the executable statements, you will need to have a firm grasp on the data structures they manipulate. If the data structure contents are not clear, make marginal notes to clarify them during the rest of the learning process. Next, understand each of the subordinate procedures. To understand an entire program, work your way up from the most primitive level. When you see an invocation of some procedure, be sure that you know what data it transforms and how it transforms that data.

Finally read the main program, sequentially executing each statement in your head. Simulate the computer. If the program (or some procedure) still isn't clear, start with some simple test data and work through the program step by step. For each important data variable, set up a column on a work sheet. At the top of the column write down the value (or a question mark if the value is not yet defined) that variable had at the start of the program. Each time you simulate a statement, make all of the relevant changes in data variables by writing a new value at the bottom of the column.

Reading programs is hard work. Just as you would trace schematics and follow signal flows in digital electronics, you should trace the program logic and document data changes as they occur in order to fully understand the program.

As you name a procedure in the main program, define the procedure exclusively in terms of the data that it accesses and the work that it is to perform. Don't try to write the procedure yet. After you have the entire program written and all of the procedures defined, assure yourself that you have completely defined how the procedures communicate with the main program. In addition, reassure yourself that all of the necessary data structures have been defined.

After you have defined the data structures and the main procedure and have verified your design, examine each procedure in turn. Repeat the design process for each procedure, defining the data structures and then the procedure itself—defining ("spawning") new procedures within this one as necessary. You can generally repeat this process over and over for successive procedures.

You can expect this process to take up lots of time and consume large amounts of paper. The design of a large-scale operating system may take several man–years of this effort before a line of code is written. A small microcomputer program that eventually requires 1,000 or 2,000 bytes of storage may require an experienced programmer to spend 10 working days on the program design.

Designing the program this way is much like drawing a rough schematic in pencil. You can expect to erase a lot, to make different trade offs, and to redraft. But since you have a design notation to help you do that, you can easily arrive at the final solution without unnecessary extra effort.

An example of the successive stages of refinement of a typical applications program is illustrated in the sequence of Figures 5.6, 5.7 and 5.8. Some study will show how the design becomes more detailed at each step.

```
(a)    item output message of
            begin
                       array text (1 . . 150) of 0 . . 1;
                       item checkword of 0 . . 65535
            end;


(b)    procedure CRC ("address of buffer", "length of buffer");
            stub;



       . . .
       "set up output message";
       checkword ← CRC (text, 150);
       "issue output message to terminal";
       . . . .
```

Figure 5.6 A first-cut design of a communications program showing how the CRC procedure is initially defined. The notation **stub** alerts the reader the fact that this procedure has yet to be defined completely enough to warrant coding in some programming language.

```
       procedure CRC (message, length);
       begin
                  array message (1 . . length) of 0 . . 1:
                  item length, CRC of 0 . . 65535;

                  "compute the CRC of message"
                  stub
       end;
```

Figure 5.7 The first-draft of the CRC procedure in which the communications conventions with the invoking main program are clearly and formally defined, but the actual internal workings are still a mystery.

```
procedure CRC (message, length);
begin
        array message (1 . . length) of 0 . . 1;
        item length, CRC of 0 . . 65535;


        item MSB of 0 . . 1;
        item index of 0 . . 65535;

        CRC ← 0;
        for index ←  1 to length step 1 do
        begin
                MSB ← CRC ≫ 15;
                CRC ← CRC ≪  1;
                CRC ← CRC + (MSB xor message (index) )
        end
end;
```

Figure 5.8   The final definition of the CRC calculation routine, within the requirements and sequential design process of this chapter.

6

Program Notations

There are many ways, and many reasons, to represent programs and program segments in a readable form before they are prepared on manuscript for a computer. Although these early (often incomplete) forms of the program are not in a form that can be accepted by the computer for which they are intended, they are critically important to the successful production of good, efficient programs.

Much of the effort expended on quality programs is in the form of documentation of design alternatives. And, although the "pidgin" programming notation of the past several chapters can be used exclusively, there are times when other schemes are possible and even preferable. In fact, you may find the "pidgin" notation new because you have heard so much about *flowcharting* as the preferred program design tool. Flowcharts are useful but only in a certain way, as we will see later in this chapter.

Since the reason for precoding design has already been emphasized in earlier chapters, it will not be repeated here. But design documentation can take on many different forms. Brief English-language statements, flowcharts, finite-state machine (FSM) models, and other schemes that you may or may not be familiar with all have their strong points. Knowing when to use each one can make your tool kit of software design larger than if you limit yourself to a single "hammer."

Design clarification is the real goal of these program design tools. Poorly understood problems (and poorly understood solutions) lead to poorly understood programs. And, if your final coded program (suitable for the computer, but incorrect) is poorly understood, how can you hope to debug it and demonstrate to your own satisfaction that it will work correctly for the rest of its life? A design notation allows you to keep refining the *design* until it matches your understanding of the problem and its solutions. A good design notation helps you discover parts of the problem that you hadn't imagined existed at the outset and then it offers solutions that are meaningful.

Even when the most competent of programmers are faced with a problem in which they have had little experience they find that their program designs become successively better as a result of solving the problem. Most of these programmers, for example, would really like to hide some of their first-cut designs as embarrassingly naive. They use one or more of these design notations to help in the iterative improvement of the design until they are satisfied with the results. As in any research and development effort, false starts are often fruitful experiences that lead to better ultimate solutions.

No designer works in a vacuum. There are other designers with whom he must communicate, and this communication demands a common, concise language. The more closely the design notation resembles the natural notation of the application area, the easier it will be to communicate, especially with the nontechnical community. If you are designing a product that communicates, for example, using one of the techniques like that in Figure 6.9 (see later) for describing communications protocols will be much more valuable than presenting the end customer with a "pidgin" program or an overly redundant flowchart. Consider the qualifications of the intended audience when you choose a notation. If you are using the notation as a design tool for yourself, you can adopt whatever conventions you wish—just remember what they are because you may be faced with them a year or more later and may have to try to understand what you did so that you can modify the program to do something new. If, however, your intended reader or readers have experience and skills similar to your own, you may wish to use one of the detailed forms like flowcharts to describe your design. If you intend to present the design for review to a community of users who don't have your software skills, you will probably want to use a notation that is as close to English as possible. In this case, you might use the English narrative approach or a wordy form of the finite-state machine model.

English as a Design Notation

Suprisingly, many novice designers forget that most of their colleagues use a language that can be exploited. This language is English. Unfortunately, English has its problems because it is imprecise and ambiguous. However, if you are careful, you can describe data structures and procedures in pictures and words that can survive careful scrutiny and still serve as a useful documentation and review tool.

In writing English language descriptions of intended programmatic solutions, write as carefully as possible and imagine that your reader is the faithful clerk we introduced in Chapter 2. Don't leave anything to chance or to the imagination. If you leave out certain definitions, you may find that you will get lots of questions like: "What does your program do if *this* happens?" Worse, your reader may *assume* that something happens when you actually intended something very different. Since you both appear to agree on what has been written, you will end up wrangling over the scope of those agreements in the future.

In the English narrative approach to initial program design, you should describe *what* is to be done, not *how*. As an example, let us imagine that you have been charged with creating a program that will compute the Cyclic Redundancy Check as described in Chapter 5. Another group of programmers and system designers is constructing a communications system and it has called upon your expertise to solve this one nagging problem. So that you may proceed independently, you all agree that the external interface to your program will involve the passing of three data objects or structures:

1. A contiguous array of bytes of some length, the address of which is specified
2. The length of that array, as a number
3. The sixteen-bit computed result, using the CRC generating polynomial $x^{16} + x^{12} + x^5 + 1$

The first two data structures are supplied to you from a dependent program (and should generally remain unmodified); the third is your computed result.

This is an ideal example that can make use of the English-language narrative form. Without getting into the detailed mathematics involved, you can describe to a data communications specialist (who may have no personal software experience) just how you intend to solve his problem. In fact, in the example narrative of Figure 6.1 you have offered two distinct alternatives. The user may select from an algorithm that is small and slow or from one that is larger but faster. Both algorithms, of course, produce the same mathematical result.

This particular algorithm, involving the sequential execution of instructions to transform data from one format to another, is easily represented by English narrative. Of course, a flowchart could also be used, but for this program in which there are only a few decision points ("are there more bytes or bits to process"; "was the result **1** or **0**"), a flowchart would reduce a little more than boxes drawn around these English statements. The additional pictoral redundancy would add little to the overall value of the program description. A familiar form like this is especially valuable when you have to communicate to old-liners who may be still "afraid" of the computer.

Flowcharting As An Option

Flowcharts are the most common program design and documentation tool in use today. Flowcharts graphically present the fine structure of a moderately complex program so that related parts can be easily comprehended without having

INPUTS: 1. Array of 8-bit bytes, the address of
the lowest addressed of which is supplied
2. The length of the array; a number in the
range 1 to 65535

OUTPUTS: 1. A 16-bit CRC calculated from the data
supplied in the array, using the generating
polynomial $X^{16} + X^{12} + X^5 + 1$

RESTRICTIONS: 1. No inputs should be modified by this program

ALGORITHM:
Alternate # 1 (bit-by-bit approach; slow but simple):
1. Set initial CRC to 0
2. For each byte in the array
   a. For each bit in the byte
      i. Shift the CRC left one place;
      save the shifted-out most
      significant bit; set LSB to 0
      ii. Exclusive-OR the MSB and the next
      bit of the data byte; call
      the result t
      iii. If t = 1
      exclusive-OR the bit pattern
      $2^{12} + 2^5 + 1$ into the CRC
3. Return the value of the computed CRC

Alternate # 2 (byte-by-byte approach; fast but longer):
1. Set initial CRC to 0
2. For each byte in the array
   a. Exclusive-OR input with most significant
   eight bits of CRC that have been shifted
   right eight places; call the result t
   b. Shift t right four places, exclusive-OR
   with t; call the result t
   c. Shift t left five places, exclusive-OR
   with t, exclusive-OR with the least
   significant eight bits of CRC which have
   been shifted left eight places; call
   that result t
   d. Shift t left twelve places, exclusive-OR
   with t; call the result CRC
3. Return the value of the computed CRC

Figure 6.1   An English-language narrative description of a particular program to be developed to compute the Cyclic Redundancy Character.

to worry about more distant parts. Programs that are more complex than those for which English narrative descriptions are effective are often described with flowcharts, especially if the decision logic is reasonably complex.

Relevant parts of a flowchart are the distinctively shaped boxes containing words. The interconnecting lines are called *flow lines.* The different shapes of the boxes offer a quick means for the reader to pinpoint the relevant decision and change-of-flow points. Some of the basic flowchart symbols are shown in Figure 6.2. There is a formal standard (ANSI X3.5) that goes to great lengths to specify height and width ratios for the various shapes, but it totally ignores the central issue of readability. The fine details of that standard can generally be safely ignored in practice.

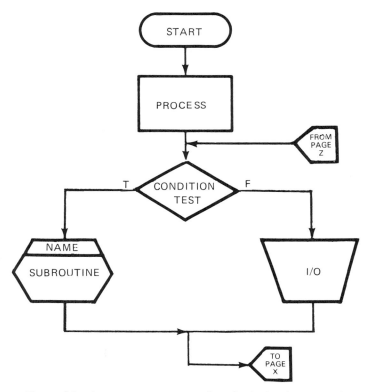

Figure 6.2 A nonsense program flowchart showing several different flowchart symbols connected by flowlines, and two off-page connectors.

Flowcharts are drawn on paper, but paper has physical boundaries (regardless of the shape or complexity óf *your* program). Therefore, it is often necessary to partition a flowchart into many pages. Since much page turning is necessary to follow a flowchart, it is good practice to label the off-page connectors with page numbers. If very large pages are used, you might even include the coordinates of the specific flowchart symbol to which that imaginary flow line is connected.

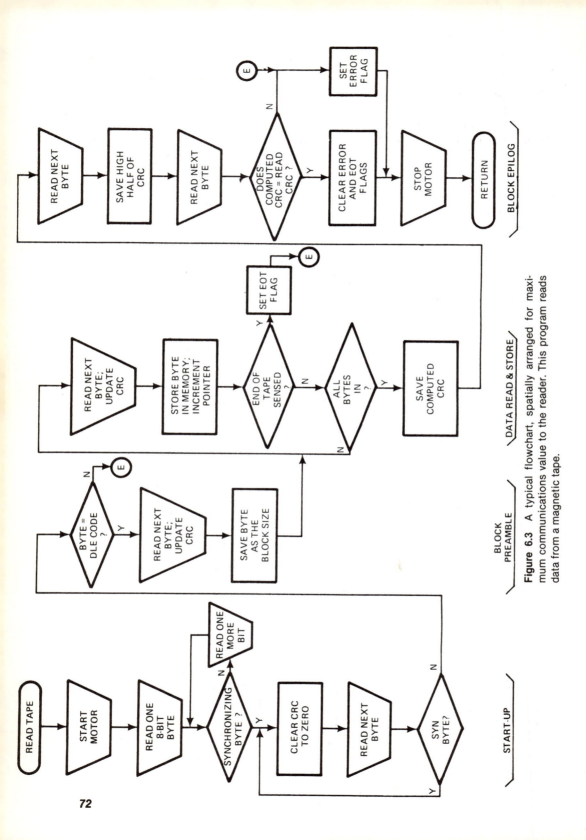

Figure 6.3 A typical flowchart, spatially arranged for maximum communications value to the reader. This program reads data from a magnetic tape.

Similarly, for the connector on the destination page, the source (or sources, if more than one) should be consistently identified.

There are many pragmatic rules that you should follow when you develop a flowchart, most of which fly in the face of officially imposed flowchart standards. For example, the flowchart example of Figure 6.3 is arranged to communicate information, not fill up the page with symbols. Such a flowchart will not conveniently fit on a single page, but the relevant divisions flow into logical entities so that the reader can understand the program's intent.

This particular example is a good one to illustrate where flowcharts are most effectively used. In general, when the flow of control is complicated by many alternative paths that are the consequences of many interlocking decisions, a good flowchart can help sort things out both during the design stage and later when someone else has to understand the program. Peripheral device control (of which this is one example) is a classical case of when flowcharts may help.

Is Flowcharting Important?

Virtually every introductory text in programming exhorts budding programmers to flowchart, flowchart, flowchart. But are flowcharts really useful? It is doubtful.

Flowcharting is graphic representation of a computer program in a form that allows the programmer to understand his work better and allows another programmer to understand the processes. In most cases, however, the flowchart neither adequately models the program nor supplies any information not found in the program itself. The flowchart can most often be useful as an informal "thinking-out" tool; it is more useful when it is drawn on a chalkboard than paper.

Each basic function required of a computer program can be implemented as a relatively large data structure with a comparatively small procedure, or conversely as a large procedure with a small data structure. Since flowcharts describe only procedures (not data structures), use of a flowchart practically guarantees procedure-oriented solutions. The examples from Chapter 2 (Figure 2.3) can serve to illustrate. If you have to design a program that processes a list of important numbers (such as the part numbers in that incoming inspection example), it is difficult to do it with a flowchart without resorting to other documentation (Figure 6.4). There is a definite incentive to imbed the data values in the midst of the procedure (Figure 6.5), thus making the entire program much more difficult to modify in the future. A more flexible design notation (one that provides for the description of data as well as procedures) encourages the designer to consider alternative solutions to the problem.

Probably the worst aspect of the flowchart is the sheer physical effort required to change it when the programmer sees a better solution to the problem (or as design flaws are detected). Most programmers, weary of drawing boxes and lines all day, are reluctant to start all over from scratch to introduce some significant refinement. Thus, instead of encouraging the programmer to experiment with design alternatives, flowcharts actually can discourage efficiency and improvement.

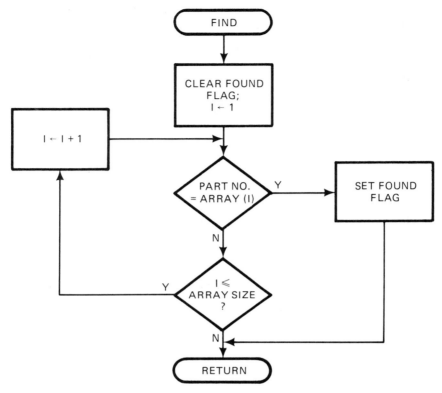

Figure 6.4 A flowchart of the incoming inspection problem (Chapter 2). The shape, size and contents of the array holding the part numbers of interest are all unknown in this description.

When a flowchart is used for program design, the contents of the various boxes tend to be annotated in terms associated with the eventual programming language. Although this is not desirable, it is the current practice. When programming language notations are used within the boxes of a flowchart, it is a sure bet that the programmer has not considered many alternatives in the design. Familiar patterns from recently completed programs are reflected in the new program, whether they are appropriate or not. And, of course, if the boxes contain programming language statements, why bother with the boxes in the first place?

The design of a program requires the program to be a mental juggler; the terms of reference must be constantly refocused from the largest generality to the finest detail. One instant the programmer must consider the impact of the system design as a whole. The next instant he must consider some primitive detail about the processing of a specific number. The flowchart, by its very nature, restricts useful and documented thinking to one level—that of the utmost detail. Efforts at the development of several flowcharts, each at a different level of detail, usually meet with spectacular failure as the design proceeds. At different levels, the flowcharts take off in different directions, seldom to converge again.

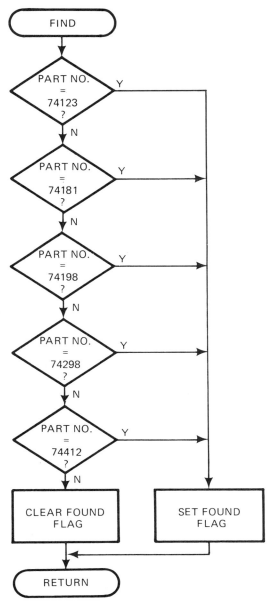

Figure 6.5 A complete flowchart includes all the data, but prevents description of flexible software.

Ex Post Facto Flowcharts

There are many commercially available software packages that will produce flow-charts from programs written in popular languages like COBOL and FORTRAN. The value of these programs is probably significantly less than the cost of the computer time required to execute them. All these programs can do is draw appropriately shaped boxes around the programmer's own source statements. Since most programmers already know that an "IF" statement corresponds to a diamond-shaped box, the pictures add no useful information.

Some software contracts even require the production of these kinds of flow-charts after the programs are finished. They are seldom, if ever, read. If automatically produced flowcharts are not worth the cost, what can be said for the cost of having each one manually drawn by a skilled draftsman?

Use of Flowcharts

There are two occasions that demand flowcharting: when the programmer is initially thinking out a complex program segment and when the contract demands it. When you are initially designing a brief segment of complex code, it is often useful to lay out the sequences in a graphic form on the chalkboard. This is especially true when two or more designers are collaborating on a solution. Since the mind comprehends pictures more readily than sequential instructions written out in longhand, this is a good time to resort to the flowchart.

In general, when a flowchart has lots of messy crossing lines, it is ample evidence of messy thinking. As you refine the flowchart, eliminating unnecessary complexities, you are simultaneously making your eventual program clearer, easier to write, and significantly easier to test and debug.

When flowcharts are required under the terms of a contract (often from the federal government), you will have to produce them. In lieu of requiring adequate documentation, most procurements merely call for conformance with the American National Standard (X3.5). Generally, what gets delivered (and worse, accepted) in such circumstances is carefully close to the standard—and totally devoid of any meaningful content. Since nobody ever uses the flowcharts anyway (because of their inherent reputation for meaninglessness), there's little harm done! If this is your problem, use one of the postprogramming automatic flowcharters because their outputs are usually acceptable for the purpose.

Flowcharts and English narratives are good complements of one another. When a flowchart consists of strings of boxes and narrative inside, a narrative form would probably have been better. When a narrative form becomes so complex that it rivals the "pidgin" programming notation in depth, a flowchart (or other design notation) should have been used.

The boxes of a flowchart should have English-like narrative inside. We want to describe *what* is to be done, not how it is to be accomplished. Of course, there are some programming conventions that we usually adopt, such as supplying the name of invoked subroutines to coordinate separate design efforts, but these are in addition to the basic logical content. If the boxes contain programming language instead of English, the flowchart serves no useful purpose except to artificially impose graphics on the program code itself.

Structured Programming

Just as engineering emerged into a rigorous discipline, programming is on the verge of maturation. The name of the discipline is not yet firm. It is variously called *top-down design, systematic programming,* and *GO TO-less programming,* although the term *structured programming* seems to be most prevalent. Actually, the entire discipline contains elements of each of the labels that have been applied. There is no single comprehensive theory of programming technique that covers them all. And, to confuse the issue, the provocative term *software engineering* is gaining currency; this will probably be the ultimate label the field will use.

You have heard lots about structured programming. To allay your fears and suspicions, let us first dispense with what structured programming is *not:*

1. It is not coding without the GO TO statement in some language.
2. It is not a new compiler or language.
3. It is not a panacea.

Controversy still rages over how to define structured programming, but there is no compelling reason to define it precisely, so long as the working definition is useful. For this design course, structured programming is a set of conventions and rules that, when followed, yield programs that are easy to write, easy to test, easy to modify, and easy to read. In short, structured programming is the very thread that has held the first five chapters together. If you have understood the principles outlined so far, you already have a good working grasp of the concepts of structured programming that lead to good programs.

Instead of defining instructions willy-nilly to accomplish some task in machine code, the careful and selective use of the power of the design notation we have introduced means that you can start out with structured programming as a habit. With these few simple control and data description structures, you can effectively "program the world," although you may wish to augment the notation in special circumstances.

Finite-State Machines

A finite-state machine (FSM) is a variant of the flowchart. When used to describe the potential ordering of sequential data processing in a software system, a finite-state machine is a powerful tool. Used to describe sequential computations with little decisional control, it is vacuous. Carried to extremes, the FSM can actually be used to describe programs formally in notations that the computer can accept.

A finite-state machine has nodes that describe the potential states the software may reside in and the edges (or lines) that connect the states. When a node has several lines leaving it, there is some implied decision about which path to take (and, therefore, the resulting byproduct actions and the next state to be assumed). FSM descriptions can be turned into flowcharts, although some flowcharts are difficult to turn into FSM descriptions. If your program has many complex input data sequences to be recognized and processed, you will find the FSM an easier way to describe the process.

The details of how FSM's are created and refined are covered in some detail in Chapter 6 of *Microcomputer Design*[1]. You should refer to that book to learn how to use FSM's. As a brief review, an example of a small FSM is summarized in Figure 6.6. In this small example there are only three states; but in most practical designs there may be upward of 50 or 100 states. This example is a classical case because it simplified an otherwise intractable problem.

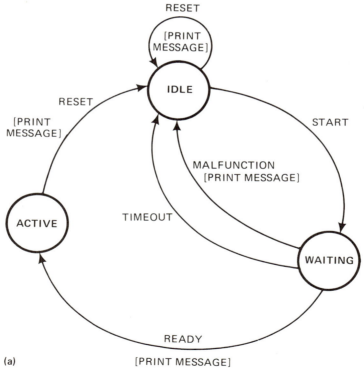

(a)

Figure 6.6(a)   A simple finite-state machine graph that reduces 560 inputs down to a simple few,

[1]Carol Anne Ogdin, *Microcomputer Design* (Englewood Cliffs, N.J.: Prentice-Hall, 1978).

The problem posed was to monitor 40 different machines, each of which had 14 wires coming from it. That meant, at first blush, we had to cope with 560 inputs! Under certain conditions a message (including the time of day) was to be printed on a terminal. At first we thought of bringing all 560 wires into a computer and then scanning them all. That was clearly too onerous. Instead, we examined the actual sequential needs of the system and created the FSM of Figure 6.6(a) for one machine.

The machine being monitored is in an IDLE state; if the operator depresses the RESET or START switches, something happens; all other inputs can be ignored in this state. Similarly, the inputs READY, MALFUNCTION, and RESET are examined from the other states only when they are relevant.

```
array state (1 . . 40) of (idle, waiting, active);
array timer (1 . . 40) of 0 . . 10;

procedure print; stub;          (print out message)
procedure reset; stub;          (true if RESET switch depressed)
procedure start; stub;          (true if START switch depressed)
procedure malfunction; stub;    (true if MALFUNCTION signal true)
procedure timeout; stub;        (true if timer (i) decrements to 0)

(the following is only one iteration of the FSM)
for i ← 1 to 40 do
if state (i) = idle
then begin
            if reset
            then print
            else if start
                    then begin
                                timer (i) ← 10;
                                state (i) ← waiting
                        end
        end
else if state (i) = waiting
        then if malfunction
                    then begin
                                print;
                                state (i) ← idle
                        end
            else if ready
                    then begin
                                print;
                                state (i) ← active
                        end
                else begin if timeout
                            then state (i) ← idle end
        else if state (i) = active
                then if reset
                            then begin
                                        print;
                                        state (i) ← idle
(b)                             end;
```

(b) the program resulting from applying the FSM over 40 input sources.

This FSM is extended into the handling of forty machines by writing a "pidgin" program description, shown in Figure 6.6(b). Here, a single loop is traversed forty times; the innards of the loop represent the finite-state machine for the *i*th machine being monitored. As you can see, translating from a state machine model to program code is very easy.

The FSM approach is useful when the control flow of the program is input driven. If there are many exceptional error handling and recovery routines, then the FSM will get exceptionally messy. In those cases, like the one shown in Figure 6.3, it is probably better to use a flowchart.

Linguistic Notations

Sometimes you have to describe data and sometimes you have to describe the procedures that will be used to process this data. Line drawings of data structures are often used in the former case, except when the variety of possible data structures is too large for effective graphic presentation. Similarly, describing the acceptable data forms by describing the procedures that are used to "crack" this complex data into manageable pieces can actually obscure the underlying structure of the data.

Using yet another notational scheme, one drawn from the field of linguistics, we can do *both.* By describing the data structures in a certain way, we can provide a *de facto* description of the major control flow of a program that operates on that data. This notation has been used to describe computer programming languages (in what is called *Backus-Naur Form,* or BNF). But all orderly input to computer (and all input must have some order, or we can't distinguish one kind from another) is, in effect, a special-purpose language.

Again, imagine a real and practical problem: You have been asked to analyze several magnetic tapes full of data from some instruments in the field. Since nobody is sure just what format the tapes are in (or even if someone does know, the format descriptions don't match what you find when you look), you have to dope out the structure all by yourself. The tapes (and there are several of them) appear to look like the examples in Figure 6.7.

Although this graphic representation may be sufficient, it is not very formalized and it could be interpreted several different ways. To formalize it, you should use a linguistic description like the one shown in Figure 6.8.

Each item in quotation marks is called a *terminal symbol;* items not in quotation marks are called *nonterminal symbols.* Each nonterminal symbol is linguistically defined and is made up of one or more terminal symbols or other (elsewhere defined) nonterminal symbols. Any symbol followed by an asterisk is an item that may be repeated any arbitrary number of times (including zero). The square brackets can surround things that are optional, that is, may occur zero or one times (unless followed by an asterisk, of course).

As an example of reading, you can see that a data-file is made up of a volume-label, a header-label, and an arbitrary amount of data. This data may appear on

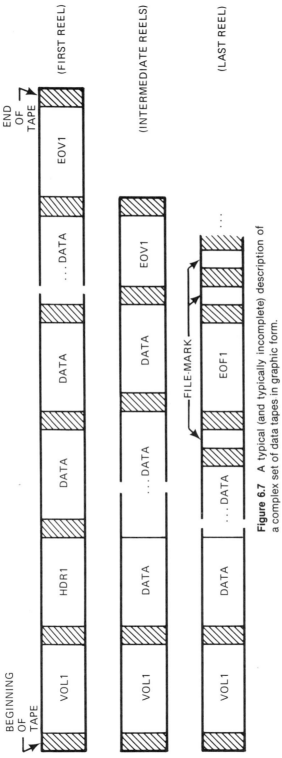

Figure 6.7 A typical (and typically incomplete) description of a complex set of data tapes in graphic form.

```
data-file:                          volume-label    header-label    data*
                                    [end-volume    volume-label    data*] *
                                    end-file
volume-label:                       "VOL1"
header-label:                       "HDR1"    file-mark
data:                               id-record
                                    [instrument-calibration-record]
                                    reading*
end-volume:                         "EOV1"
end-file                            file-mark "EOF1" file-mark    file-mark
file-mark:                          . . .
id-record:                          . . .
instrument-calibration-record:              . . .
reading:                            . . .
```

Figure 6.8 A linguistic description of a complex data file with multiple options for data structure and content. This is a formalization of the informal diagram in Figure 6.7.

second and successive tape reels, as evidenced by the end-volume (for the first reel), a new volume-label, and another arbitrary amount of data. There may be an arbitrary number of reels, but the entire data file ends with an end-file.

This scheme obviously describes data. How does it describe the procedure that operates on data? Well, imagine each nonterminal symbol as the name of a procedure and each terminal symbol as an argument to a procedure that compares the input to the terminal symbol. Thus, the definition of header-label implies a procedure of that name that compared the input to "HDR1" and then invokes the file-mark procedure. If the input matches *and* the file-mark procedure finds the necessary terminal symbol present in *its* definition, then you can categorically state that you have found a header-label (i.e., the header-label procedure returns true).

Sometimes alternative definitions are permitted and can be linked together with the "or." If any one of the alternatives is true, then the entire nonterminal symbol is declared to have been found.

We have left the definitions for id-record, instrument calibration record, and reading out because they tend to be highly complex and not germane to our example. However, in practice, you would continue the definition process until everything you could possibly encounter is defined in terms of terminal symbols. In this case, you might wish to add the object "number" as one of your terminal symbols, in addition to the individual characters; "number" would be the name of a procedure that identifies one single number, regardless of the number of digits it might contain.

Data Sequence Charts

Many of the input and output structures of a system are serial in nature. Although a linguistic notation like that used in Figure 6.8 might be used to describe them, it is often more valuable to provide for some "sequence" model. This practice is especially prevalent in the field of data communications in which sequential transmission and reception of character strings can be very complicated. This technique is used in the American Standard for Use of Communication Characters (X3.28) to good advantage.

In a data sequence chart each significant input is presented as a sequence of words or symbols. Thin and thick lines show the order in which these inputs may appear (or outputs generated). Thick lines are the most common sequences; thin lines represent the special cases and error-recovery paths. In most cases of data communications, a data sequence chart has two procedural interpretations, one for the originator of the traffic and one for the receiver. The numbers in parentheses (Figure 6.9) allow the associated text or English narrative form to be keyed.

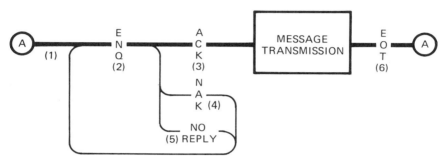

Figure 6.9 A data sequence chart shows the primary flow with a heavy line, and infrequent (or undesirable) alternatives with light lines.

From the vantage point of the originator, we start at point A. A bid for permission to send is initiated by sending the ENQ (Enquiry; enquiring about the status of the intended receiver) character. In this particular chart there are three possible responses: The positive acknowledgment (ACK) is the most common, but the receiving station can also restrain the sending station with a negative acknowledgment (NAK). If a NAK is received, or if no response at all is received within a specific period of time, the originator of the traffic repeats the ENQ. After a positive acknowledgment is received, a subroutine named "Message Transmission" is invoked to actually send a message out. At the end of the transmission (6) the originator sends an EOT character (End of Transmission) to free the channel for other uses. The flow of control then reverts to point A for the next sequence when required.

As you can readily see, this diagram is especially suited for time-sequential transactions. By convention, time flows from left to right in the diagram, although not exclusively. Although a flowchart could be used, as could a finite-state model, they would not lend themselves as well to the sequential representation. This same scheme can be used in the sequential control of a machine tool or in other process controls.

Mixing Notations

There is little justification for picking just one design notation and slavishly sticking to it. Different parts of a design may require different tools. The more tools you have, the better equipped you will be to deal with novel problems. In many of the cases we have cited we have recommended that other parts of the design be represented in another notational scheme.

There are many, many other kinds of notations that we could describe. All of those defined here, for example, are procedural. There are nonprocedural notations that are used to describe only inputs and outputs because the transformation is well known for certain classes of applications. However, these schemes are more likely to be of use in a more traditional data processing environment than in the dynamic world of programming that the system designer is likely to encounter.

Why Bother?

Why can't we step directly to code and skip the preliminaries? Can't correct code be designed in the source language in which we intend to program? Well, yes, but only in very limited cases. There are a few trivial cases when an experienced programmer has already handled similar kinds of programs many times and the new program of the same kind can be developed directly in the programming language. However, these kinds of programs are seldom longer than a couple of hundred statements.

In practice, most programs are written with very little investment in design—sad to say. Of course, this means that the designer may completely misunderstand the problem. The convergence of the program product and the understanding of the problem usually takes place at debugging time. Since there is no way of knowing how far off the programmer's understanding is from reality, there is no way to predict how long it will take for the debugging phase to end. That is what causes programs to be 90% done for months on end.

7

Program
Documentation

"There are more opportunities for improving software productivity and quality in the area of management than anywhere else."[1] If management depends on information to make successful decisions, then one of the major detriments to good software management has always been *documentation*. All too often documentation is a subtask of a software job that get left to the end, that is, after the basic system is operating and it is about to be delivered for use by the customer.

Until coding begins documentation *is* the specification and *is* the design.[2] If documentation is bad, the design is bad.[3] After all, the rationale of any computer program is to satisfy human needs, not the computing system's. How can we organize the software to encourage good management and good design? By organizing the documentation scheme and proceeding with documentation in parallel with all of the individual design activities.

Concurrent, Incremental Documentation

Documentation of a design is difficult for most of us because we imagine the need to sit down for several days (or weeks) at a time and *write*. Since that is traditionally how documentation has been done, it is a well-founded fear. In

[1] Barry W. Boehm, *Software Engineering* IEEE Transactions on Computers, Vol. C-25, No. 12, December, 1976, pp. 1126–1241.
[2] W. W. Royce, *Managing the Development of Large Software Systems: Concepts and Techniques* (Wescon, 1970).
[3] Robert C. Tausworthe: *Standardized Development of Computer Software,* (Englewood Cliffs, N.J., Prentice-Hall, 1976).

Why Talk About Documentation at a Time Like This?

Documentation is a difficult subject. Everybody purports to do it, but few actually do. Recent studies have all shown that most errors are made in the design stages of projects—not in coding. Since documentation *is* the design (until code is produced later), the quality of the documentation determines the quality of the design.

Even when only one person comprises the design team, documentation is important. There are too many tiny details that must be mastered, even in the simplest of programs. They should not be left to memory. Only the most competent and experienced programmers who are writing trivially simple programs do so without adequate documentation first.

Therefore, before we leave the design phase and proceed to coding and checkout in succeeding chapters, it is important to know what constitutes good program documentation and how to generate it.

practice, though, massive writing efforts can be avoided by documenting incrementally. As soon as something happens, it is documented—on one page, or two pages, but seldom more than ten. Then, properly filed, these individual documents form a complete finished document at the end of the project. Since the documentation is done at the time important decisions are made, they are not doomed to be remade and rejustified everytime the subject comes up again. And at any point in the project the progress to date can be immediately shown by referring to the partially completed file of documentation.

We call this concept the *working design manual.* Although it may be difficult to get used to because it differs from current practice so much, converts to the concept never seem to ever go back to any other scheme.

WDM Structure

The working design manual (WDM) is usually maintained in a three-ring binder (or more than one if the size of the project warrants). Most software projects that are completed by one person can be documented in a single 1-in. binder. Complex hardware/software design projects may require a 2-in. binder. Projects in which many people are involved may require different WDM's for different subprojects and one master WDM for the entire system (and even a special WDM for standards and practices that evolve during the design stages).

The binder is divided into indexed sections, the names of which are chosen to be relevant to the particular project. Although a totally generalized set of index tabs could conceivably be designed, the notion of the informality of the WDM is best served if index tabs are created *ad hoc.*

The first index tab is always named "ADMIN" and identifies the section of the WDM that is concerned with the rules for administration of this WDM (and, by implication, the design effort). This is *not* the place for administrative memos and other normal interoffice traffic. The "ADMIN" section contains a description of the WDM, its purpose and content, and how it is to be maintained. In fact, you might use an edited version of this chapter as your first-draft WDM "ADMIN" section.

The administrative section of the WDM also contains several tables, usually as appendices to the basic WDM description document. These tables include the list of project participants, the identification of holders of copies of the WDM, and the fine structure of the WDM in terms of the index tabs to be incorporated. Examples of these three appendices are illustrated in Figures 7.1, 7.2 and 7.3.

The WDM distribution list (Figure 7.1) is no more than a list of relevant names and addresses. However, to be certain that all WDM copies are identical, it is necessary to maintain a list of recipients. In some organizations in which there are multiple small projects it is not uncommon to have several *dozen* WDM's in various stages of completion at one time. It is essential, then, for the secretarial staff to know who has copies of which WDM's so that the update pages can be posted to the right people.

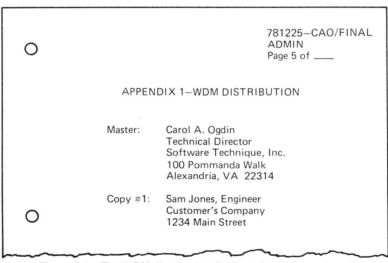

Figure 7.1   The WDM distribution list is maintained so that all copies of the WDM can be maintained with identical contents.

The design team membership list (Figure 7.2) relates initials to names and telephone numbers. Since all items posted in the WDM will be identified by the originator's initials, it may be necessary to be able to "decode" them. This is especially true if the parts of the design team are geographically separated (it proved invaluable when one successful design team had active members in Con-

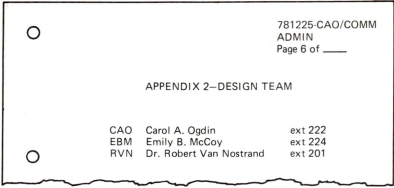

APPENDIX 2—DESIGN TEAM

CAO	Carol A. Ogdin	ext 222
EBM	Emily B. McCoy	ext 224
RVN	Dr. Robert Van Nostrand	ext 201

Figure 7.2 The design team membership, which may be added to at any time, is maintained so initials can be "decoded."

necticut, Arizona, Virginia, and Illinois, all of whom made daily contributions). Even if there is only one designer, it is wise to initial all entries. You will find after time that you will reach back into your own past to fetch copies of relevant WDM items for new projects.

The WDM subject index (Figure 7.3) defines the index tabs under which information is filed. The objective, of course, is to choose subjects that are logically consistent with the structure of the system. If the structure changes, so should the WDM. You may find a need to change the index tabs in order to coalesce certain subjects and break others into constituent parts. Remember, the goal is to make it easy to *find* data when you need it.

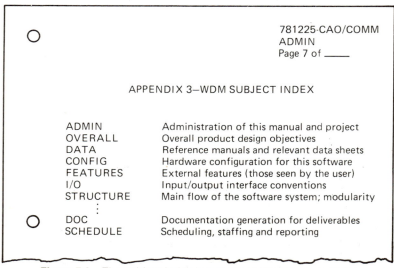

APPENDIX 3—WDM SUBJECT INDEX

ADMIN	Administration of this manual and project
OVERALL	Overall product design objectives
DATA	Reference manuals and relevant data sheets
CONFIG	Hardware configuration for this software
FEATURES	External features (those seen by the user)
I/O	Input/output interface conventions
STRUCTURE	Main flow of the software system; modularity
DOC	Documentation generation for deliverables
SCHEDULE	Scheduling, staffing and reporting

Figure 7.3 The subject index is a guide to the structure of the project.

In the subject index the OVERALL section usually contains the management-stated objectives and a nontechnical discussion of the product and its design. This is usually a relatively thin section. The DATA tab is the place where all unusual data sheets or other background documentation derived from other sources is filed. The DOC section relates to the documentation standards to be used for final manuals derived from the WDM later in the project. The SCHEDULE section is where the actual day-to-day management is documented with personnel allocations and resource estimates and actual consumption records.

Identifying Contributions

Each and every page is identified in the upper right-hand corner with six items:

1. Date of origination
2. Originator's initials
3. Status indication
4. Revision identification (if necessary)
5. Subject index for filing
6. Page number

Although the day might be written in any one of several acceptable ways, we prefer the now standard "YYMMDD" form. The first two digits cite the year, the next two (01 through 12) the month, and the last two the day. In this dating scheme the ambiguities of the form "3/4/77" can be avoided (April 3rd or March 4th?).

The author's initials follow the date and can be "decoded" through the use of Appendix 2 (Figure 7.2).

Each document should have its status clearly identified. We have found that the following five categories are usually sufficient:

1. COMM (for Communique)
2. TENT (Tentative)
3. PROB (Probable)
4. FIRM
5. FINAL

A communique is usually a simple informational document. It may raise a broad issue or general question to be considered by the design team, or it may be nothing more than an informal report of a meeting with a prospective vendor. WDM contributions that are marked "COMM" usually do not directly affect the progress of the project, although they might. If you learn that some potentially useful piece of software may be made available from an outside source, now would be a good time to write a one- or two-page communique for the WDM.

Tentative contributions are initial proposals for design that can be freely modified. They are intended to communicate the trend of current thinking. If you are considering a particular kind of algorithm, you might make that a tentative decision; other team members are then alerted to your action and can make contributions appropriately. If you are the sole WDM recipient, you probably won't write very many tentative contributions because they are primarily intended for interpersonal dialog.

Probable contributions are those from which implementation documents may be drawn, and they should be changed if really necessary. They alert other team members that the time for contributions on this subject may be drawing to a close.

Firm documents describe essentially finished designs or subsystems that have already been implemented in a prototype form. Changes can probably be made to design elements described in FIRM documents, but at large expense and with wide (and perhaps unknowable) consequences.

When WDM contributions are marked FINAL, they describe fixed and unchangeable parts of the design. Change is always possible, of course, but it should be avoided if at all practical.

The second line of the page heading should contain the name of the index tab under which this WDM contribution should be filed. Generally, additions are made at the *back* of a section (except for pages being changed) so that there is a chronological ordering to the data.

The third line contains page numbering, which is especially useful when certain pages within a document have to be changed individually.

Making Revisions

All of the WDM contributions described so far have been added to the manual. Certainly, some means for changing erroneous pages and contributions must be provided. There is no easy way to delete data from the WDM *by design!*

Additions to the WDM are easy to spot because they have dates that are later in time than any other items already filed in the relevant indexed section. The new items are added to the end of the named section.

Revisions are noted by identifying the document that is being replaced. The prior document's date, originator, and status are repeated (in parentheses) underneath the date, originator, and status. A change to the subject index of Figure 7.3, for example, might look like Figure 7.4. If many, many changes are made in a WDM, it might be worth putting a clear mark in the left margin next to the changed data to draw attention to the changes.

What to Document

In the initial stages of design of new software you will mostly document the intended external characteristics of the system you are developing. It usually starts with a copy of the original program specifications (if any), which are placed into

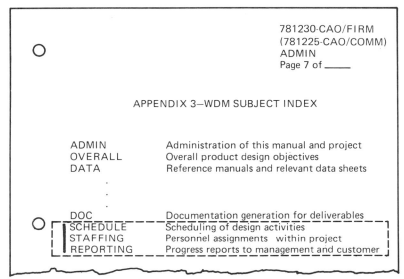

APPENDIX 3—WDM SUBJECT INDEX

ADMIN	Administration of this manual and project
OVERALL	Overall product design objectives
DATA	Reference manuals and relevant data sheets
.	
.	
DOC	Documentation generation for deliverables
SCHEDULE	Scheduling of design activities
STAFFING	Personnel assignments within project
REPORTING	Progress reports to management and customer

Figure 7.4 A revised subject index with the changes noted. The identity of the previous page is shown in the upper right hand corner in parentheses.

the WDM, *in toto*. Next, you will probably generate a single rather lengthy document that outlines what the software is to do and how it is to be done.

At this stage the most important kinds of things that you can document are the very things most documentation schemes leave out: Document the unclear, unknown or yet-to-be-decided items. Outline what is known (and, to the limits of your knowledge, what is not known). These documents will alert you to look further. Since errors of omission are the most difficult to detect, this can be the most valuble contribution you can make to useful and reliable software.

After the initial external design is completed (by external design we mean the features that the user will see), you can begin partitioning the design into constituent elements. This is the point at which you are most likely to change the structure and index tabs of your WDM. Logically separated elements ought to be separated at this early stage (although you may find later that you need to merge some of them together again). At this stage of the design process you will probably find yourself adding several tables and charts to the WDM. Much of the information lends itself to tabular arrangement, such as lists of input/output devices and assignments, general diagrams of data layout, computer printout mock-ups, and the like.

The third stage is characterized by the inclusion in the WDM of successively improved versions of your "pidgin" program. Don't be afraid to "publish" your earliest efforts. They will be vague and incomplete, but hopefully they will be accurate. It is easier for other team members to follow your reasoning if it is

A Typical Success Story

In one recent case the working design manual concept proved its worth in a way that was dramatic and worth repeating. The original designer created the WDM up through the program descriptions in "pidgin" form. The program was then estimated to require about 2K (2048) bytes on the computer and should have taken about 25 days to write and test. The labor estimate was based on the designer's vast experience with programming.

Then the designer unexpectedly had to go to the hospital for surgery. The finished WDM—ink still wet—was handed to another programmer who had less than two year's experience. No means of communication with the programmer beyond the WDM was provided since the original designer was totally unavailable. Of course, the new programmer had the opportunity to ask questions of the engineers who participated in the design, but few questions were necessary.

The estimates proved to be in error—by two bytes and 3 days! The final program occupied 2046 bytes and was delivered on the 28th day. Both the customer and the programmer were amazed.

I wasn't.

presented with incremental pieces of program description (say, in three- to five-page chunks) than if you hit them all at once.

If you have done all of this correctly, you will find that your software is completely documented before you have actually written a line of code for the computer. In the next chapter we will show you how to turn this design into the final computer program.

At each of these documentation stages you should have your work reviewed by an interested but objective person. Another designer who has similar skills would be a good reviewer. If your project is a major one for your employer, you should subject it to an entire committee to review at each of these three stages. Since other people bring different experience sets to the solution of your problem, you may receive some novel inputs that will aid your implementation.

How Much Is Enough?

How much documentation is enough? One guiding rule is judgment by peers. You shouldn't move from the specification phase until you have defined the system clearly enough that any other designer of equivalent competence could carry on with it. Similarly, you shouldn't consider the program design complete unless you feel confident that you could turn over the documents to somebody else and he could implement the program successfully.

Intraprogram Documentation

After you have begun writing your program in one of the acceptable programming languages, you aren't finished documenting. Every programming language offers a way to introduce comments into the program. These comments are reproduced in printed listings of the program; they never affect the object program.

It is important to document *why* the instructions exist, not *what* they do. If your comments are only English expansions of the mnemonic instructions, you have missed the point. Compare the two programs in Figure 7.5. The program on the left is readable and understandable even if you don't understand the 8080's assembly language. The program on the right doesn't offer you much help.

A good guideline is to ask youself if you could suppress printing all of the source code and then fill it in again by hand using only the commentary as a guide. If you can't, perhaps you are shortchanging yourself. You will invariably have to inherit this program someday in the future. Will you be able to figure out how it works then?

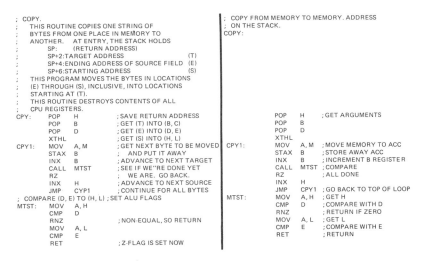

Figure 7.5 (a) Adequate intraprogram documentation; (b) Inadequate documentation.

Configuration Control

Software is so easy to modify and copy that you will inevitably one day have two different copies of a program—and no way to tell which one is the more recent. Some means of configuration control is imperative in order to avoid confusing different versions of the same software.

Once you control the generation of copies of your software and log the existence of each discrete version, you will find that you spend a lot less time "reinventing the wheel." By using your growing library of documented programs, you will find subsequent programs easier and easier to generate.

A simple configuration control scheme is to apply labels to everything of potential interest to the software system you are generating. A typical label is shown in Figure 7.6. This is called a *component identification*. If the medium (say, a cassette tape) doesn't have a writable surface, you can use a small label. No component should remain unlabeled, even in the partially developed state.

The five elements of a component identification are:

1. Component name
2. Medium
3. Version and revision level
4. Date (optional)
5. Originator's initials (optional)

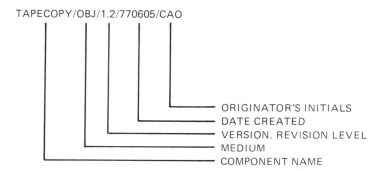

TAPECOPY/OBJ/1.2/770605/CAO

ORIGINATOR'S INITIALS
DATE CREATED
VERSION. REVISION LEVEL
MEDIUM
COMPONENT NAME

Figure 7.6   A simple but standardized labelling scheme for items of software development.

The component name should clearly identify the particular software system. It should be brief and it might include a particular customer's name. Names should, of course, be unique. In a large orgaization names may have to be centrally controlled and allocated. Of course, if you have job numbers, they would be an ideal part of the component name.

The medium is important. If you have a magnetic tape, you'd like to know whether it holds the source code or object code for your program. Some common media abbreviations include:

DWG	Drawings and other finished artwork for assemblies, cards, printer formats, etc., but not including schematics
LST	Listings of the software, preferably showing both source and object code
OBJ	Object code on machine-readable media
ROM	ROM, PROM, or EPROM versions of some object (OBJ) program
SRC	Source code for the software in machine-readable form
WDM	Working design manual

When you write a program, you should remember that you are really writing one in a family of programs that will exist over time. This program may have to be modified, new features may have to be added, or, heaven forbid, a bug may have to be corrected. Therefore, it is imporant to maintain accountability for the various versions and revision levels of the system. Revisions and versions differ by degree; they have similar genesis but different effects. A new version of software is called for when the users may have to change the way they use the program. A new revision is called for when a simple "transparent" change has been introduced.

For example, if you have changed a program to operate with a different arrangement of input/output devices (and that required changes in your program), you have created a new version of the software. Similarly, if you have changed the required order of input of data, this necessitates a change on the part of the users and must be accompanied by a change in the version number. If you have loosened up some restrictions to make the program more useful without *requiring* the users to change their habits, all you have to do is change the revision level number.

If you have more than nine revision levels, you may have to consider a redesign of the software. Usually, when revision levels get too high it means that the software was poorly designed for the intended application in the first place.

When a program is in the initial development stage, the revision level is always cited as zero. This alerts prospective users of partially completed software that there may be bugs lurking within. However, when the program leaves the hands of the originator, it should be assigned a nonzero revision level.

In printed listings it is common to leave the revision level number (and the date) blank so that they can be written by hand as required.

The date and originator's initials are optional. If you maintain no other data file for configuration control, you should probably mark these on every item. However, if you maintain a configuration control card file, you can note the originator's initials and the date each version/revision level was put into service on the appropriate card.

8

Introduction to BASIC

You have finally reached the point in the development of your new software at which you may generate instructions for a computer to follow, but to do this you need a common language that both you and the computer can understand. You may choose to program in a language that is very close to the underlying architecture of the computer (an *assembly* language) or a language that is more oriented toward the problem you want to solve and is independent of the computer (a *procedure-oriented* or *higher-level* language). Since in this design course it is our intention to present readable programs without burdening you with the idiosyncratic features of some host computer, we opt to use one of the most popular high-level languages, *BASIC*.

BASIC stands for Beginner's All-Purpose Symbolic Instruction Code. Don't let that word "beginner's" throw you; BASIC is a full-fledged language for a certain class of applications and is used daily by hundreds (perhaps thousands) of engineers and designers. Because it lacks the most sophisticated features, it isn't needlessly complex.

The Look of a BASIC Program

A BASIC program (Figure 8.1) is made up of *statements* written on *lines*. The purpose of this particular program is to accept some factors from the user and then compute the value of the function $ax^2 + bx + c$. A typical execution of the program is shown in Figure 8.2.

```
1000   PRINT "WHAT ARE VALUES FOR X, A, B, AND C?"
1010   INPUT X, A, B, C
1020   LET Y = A*X*X + B*X + C
1030   PRINT "THE FUNCTION VALUE IS "; Y
1040   END
```

Figure 8.1 A small BASIC program, to show the "look" of a program.

The program itself is made up of five lines, each of which contains a single statement in the BASIC language. In BASIC every line must be numbered, and all lines are automatically maintained in ascending numerical order. Execution starts with the lowest-numbered line and proceeds according to the program's structure; in the absence of any other program statements, each statement is executed in sequential order.

Every statement begins with a "key word." This word is the programmer's way of specifying to the computer the particular action wanted. "PRINT," for example, specifies that something is to be printed out on the user's terminal device; "INPUT" specifies that some input is to be accepted from the user (via the terminal); "LET" is notification that we are going to specify some computation step.

```
RUN

WHAT ARE VALUES FOR X, A, B, AND C?
?2,3,9,2.5
THE FUNCTION VALUE IS 32.5
```

Figure 8.2 A simple example of execution of the program in Figure 8.1. "RUN" is what you type to cause the program to be executed; user-typed information is underscored.

The last line in every BASIC program contains the single key word "END" to alert the BASIC compiler or interpreter that there are no more statements to be processed.

A line number consists of from one to five contiguous decimal digits. No spaces are allowed to appear in a line number. The order in which lines of a BASIC program are typed in makes no difference because the system will automatically place the lines in ascending order. This makes it easy to change programs. Each BASIC system is supported by an *editor* program of some kind so that you can add, delete, or change lines by number.

A BASIC program is written in upper case (capital) letters only. Also, in order to distinguish between a zero and the letter "O," a stroke is written through the letter, like this: "Ø." Many computer terminals have this distinction built into the printed character set.

It is not apparent in the example, but spaces in a BASIC statement are usually ignored. Of course, spaces may not appear in a line number. Otherwise, spaces are significant only when they appear in quotation marks (as in the PRINT statements). It is customary to use spacing to enhance the readability of programs.

Why Basic?

The computer industry resembles nothing so much as the Biblical town of Babel. Languages abound. Almost every new issue of a computer periodical announces a new and outstanding improvement in languages. Most of these languages have few adherents.

There are popular languages, for example, FORTRAN, COBOL, PL/I. There are others that you have probably heard of, for example, ALGOL or APL. There is one that you will probably hear more about: PASCAL. But for most desk-side programming chores, BASIC is the popular language.

BASIC differs from other computer programming languages because it was designed and implemented by users who had problems to solve. John Kemeny and Thomas Kurtz, at Dartmouth in the early 1960's, decided that existing languages were too tough for students to learn quickly. Therefore, they developed their own language. Somewhat inelegant, it is still one of the most powerful and easy to learn tools at the engineer's disposal.

BASIC is not the most complete programming language in the world, however. You will find concepts that are unique to the language and that are nontransferable to other languages you might have to use. Because of the limitations in the language, you may find that it just can't solve some of the kinds of problems you might have. But once you have some experience in programming in BASIC, you will have acquired skills that you *can* transfer to other languages. Skills like learning the computer's intolerance for mistakes, how to track down a bug, and how to test a program are all useful—and since they are acquired with your first language, they make that language an easy one.

For our examples (especially the worked-through example in Chapter 9), we have chosen practical problems that engineers face frequently enough to be worth the effort and that are uniquely suited to BASIC's math orientation. Had we chosen a problem that had lots of external data files, or one that required lots of external data files, or one that required lots of detailed peripheral device control, or one that required many list structures, BASIC would not have been as good a choice.

Statement Structure

Each kind of statement in BASIC (PRINT, INPUT, LET, etc.) has standard rules, although each statement has a different detailed format. The rules for the statements are called the *rules of syntax* of the language; the interpretation of the meaning of the statement is called the *rule of semantics*. We will discuss the proper syntax for some of the most common BASIC statements and some of the simpler semantics. Since different BASIC compilers and interpreters treat some of the semantics differently, detailed treatment should come from the reference manual for the system you intend to use.

Elements of BASIC

Statements of the BASIC language can be separated into just a few elementary parts. Knowing all these components facilitates discussion of all facets of the language. Statements combine the following elements:

1. Constants
2. Symbolically named variables
3. Operators
4. Statement numbers

Constants and variables are often called *operands,* especially when they are combined together with one or more *operators*. BASIC has only two data types, real (floating-point) numbers and alphanumeric character text.

Numbers in BASIC are similar to the numeric quantities of arithmetic. They may be given as integers (the natural numbers) or real quantities (numbers with fractional parts supplied after a decimal point). Some of the typical numbers that may appear in a BASIC program are illustrated in Figure 8.3.

−4.08	1.951632614	.000001
48	147.2	0.090
50.5	−3029741	+302.598

Figure 8.3 Some typical numbers that can be written (and recognized) in BASIC programs.

Any number may be preceded by a minus sign to mark it as negative. If there is no minus sign, the number is positive. The number may be preceded by a plus sign, but this form is seldom used.

BASIC symbolic names may be a letter of the alphabet. It is common practice to use symbolic names with some resemblance ("mnemonic value") to the quantity represented. To represent velocity, for example, a useful symbol might be "V." Because only twenty-six numeric variables could be presented by the single letters of the alphabet, it is necessary to provide a way to create more. These additional permissible symbols have a single digit after the letter. BASIC assumes absolutely no connection between a symbol that consists of a letter and one that consists of that same letter and a digit. In your program, however, you may make some tenuous link. For example, you might call the variable that represents minimum velocity "V1" (or "V0") and the variable that represents maximum velocity "V9."

In most BASIC systems each variable is initially set to zero just prior to commencing execution. However, since not all systems consistently do this, it is good practice not to use any variable until it has been set to a known value.

Notice especially that numbers may not contain commas to mark off thousands, millions, etc. Furthermore, a number is simply a number. A number may be used to represent the peas in a pod, or dollars, or a ratio. It is not possible to indicate its meaning. For example, the string of characters "$5.00" cannot constitute a number because the dollar sign "gets in the way."

In BASIC an integer is fully equivalent to a real number that has a fractional part of zero. Below are alternative, fully equivalent ways to represent the value "five":

$$5 \qquad 5.0 \qquad 5.00$$

Leading zeros to the left of the decimal point and trailing zeros to the right are ignored.

Extremely large and small numbers can be represented in BASIC. Scientific and engineering applications often require this capability. To represent the number one hundred billion requires twelve digits (100,000,000,000). However, ten billion also can be represented as:

$$1.0 \times 10^{11}$$

In BASIC the letter "E" is placed before the superscript 10 (the exponent). Then, the number one hundred billion, written so that BASIC can interpret it, is:

$$1.0E11$$

where "E" is the abbreviation for "exponent." The number to the left of "E" must be present, but it need not even be near the value 1. In BASIC the part to the left of "E" must conform to the same rules as any real or integer number. The exponent must be an integer, although it may be signed.

From the user's point of view, not all computing deals with numbers. Many applications deal with collections of letters and digits, as in names, part numbers, and the like. In BASIC most alphanumeric text is enclosed in quotation marks in order to set it off from the rest of the program. This alphanumeric text is called *quoted text*. Almost any character that can be sent from and received by a terminal device can be represented with quotation marks. This includes letters (both upper case and lower case), digits, special printing characters, and blank spaces. Quoted text may extend from one line to another. The final quotation mark must be on the same line as the initial quotation mark. Quoted text can be used to represent an "empty" alphanumeric text item. This occurs when there are no characters between the first and last quotation marks in the quoted text.

Variables

A symbolic name stands for a value. The value may be constant or it may change from time to time depending on its use by this program, but the name is fixed. Since the value may change, a symbol is also called the name of a variable.

Many statements in BASIC use arithmetic expressions. An arithmetic expression consists of a number or a symbolic name (i.e., an operand) or groups of operands linked together by appropriate BASIC operators. BASIC contains many kinds of operators. Certain types are admitted only to certain statements. Operators are often called *special characters* in order to distinguish them from letters and digits. The following operators may be applied in BASIC:

−	Subtraction	+	Addition
/	Division	*	Multiplication
↑	Exponentiation	=	Assignment or equal
(	Grouping	)	Grouping
>	Greater than	<	Less than
,	Separation		

BASIC operators are most used often to link two or more operands (constant or symbolic names) together.

An arithmetic expression may contain other arithmetic subexpressions. An arithmetic subexpression is any arithmetic expression that is enclosed in parentheses and it is included as part of another arithmetic expression.

A subexpression may contain other subexpressions. A subexpression is an operand, just as a number or numeric variable name is an operand. The essential difference is that a number is a value, a numeric symbolic name names a value, and a subexpression must be evaluated to get an intermediate value to be used as the operand.

Addition and subtraction operators are "+" and "−," respectively. These operators are used to link two operands together. Subtraction takes place by subtracting the second (rightmost) operand from the first operand.

The sum or difference created by the two operands and associated operator constitute a new operand in some other addition and subtraction. In this way, an arbitrary number of operands can be added and subtracted in any arithmetic expression. For example,

$$A + B + C + D - E - F + G$$

An operand in an arithmetic expression does not have its value changed by performing the addition or subtraction.

Multiplication and division operators are "*" and "/", respectively. The asterisk indicates multiplication and it avoids conflicts that might arise if "X" were used, for a variable name might begin with an "X." Similarly, the symbol "/" indicates division because the symbol "÷" doesn't exist on most terminal devices and because BASIC statements must be written straight across lines. Division takes place by dividing the first operand by the second operand. No operand in an arithmetic expression has its value changed by multiplication or division.

The product or quotient value created by the two operands and associated operator also constitutes a new operand. When an operand of addition or substraction is made up of multiplication and/or division operators, all the multiplication and division is performed before the addition or subtraction is performed. That is, the arithmetic expression $A + B*C$ is evaluated by multiplying B and C and then using this intermediate value as one of the addition operands.

When a product or quotient is linked to another operand by multiplication or division operators, the operations are performed from left to right. This becomes important when one of the operations is division. The BASIC arithmetic expression

$$A/B*C$$

is equivalent to the algebraic expression

$$\frac{A}{B} \cdot C \text{ not } \frac{A}{B \cdot C}$$

because of the left-to-right rule. If the latter form is the calculation to be performed, parentheses must be used. For example, in $A/(B*C)$ the parentheses force evaluation of the subexpression before division is done.

Exponentiation (raising to powers) is indicated by the "↑" operator. This operator links two operands. The operand on the left is the base value. The operand on the right is the power to which that value is to be raised.

Extraction of roots can also be performed with the exponentiation operator. In BASIC the exponent need not be an integer. Therefore, it is possible to raise values to powers less than one. Mathematically, the nth root of a value is identical to the value raised to the $1/n$th power. For example, to take the square root of $R5$, that value can be raised to the 1/2 (i.e., .5) power. This is written as

$$R5\uparrow.5$$

When the exponentiation operator occurs in one of the operands of multiplication, division, addition, or subtraction, exponentiation is performed first.

When the system evaluates an expression, the order in which it performs operations depends on the BASIC hierarchy of operators. It performs operations within an expression in descending order within the hierarchy. For example, in the expression $A + (B*C)\uparrow D,$ the system first "removes" the parentheses by evaluating the product $B*C$, then performs exponentiation, and finally adds the operands.

If an expression involves operations at the same level in the hierarchy, the system performs the operations from left to right. It treats an expression within parentheses as a single operand. The system must evaluate the subexpression before it can perform the indicated operation. Therefore, parentheses can be used to modify the normal rules of hierarchy. Table 8.1 illustrates the BASIC hierarchy of operators in descending order.

TABLE 8.1 Hierarchy of BASIC operators in descending order

LEVEL	OPERATOR	OPERATION
4	( )	GROUPING
3	↑	EXPONENTIATION
2	*	MULTIPLICATION
2	/	DIVISION
1	+	ADDITION
1	−	SUBTRACTION

BASIC also offers a predefined set of functions for computing common kinds of values (see Table 8.2). You can use these functions to avoid having to create your own programs for these common needs. For example, the arithmetic expression to compute the square root of $T2$ would be written:

$$SQR(T2)$$

The ''x'' in parentheses in the list of functions in Table 8.2 represents the argument of the function. In BASIC the argument of an arithmetic function may be any expression, no matter how complicated. Several novel uses can be found for some of BASIC's functions, and the following rules must be observed.

TABLE 8.2 Some of the standard functions provided in BASIC for your computational needs.

TABLE 2—STANDARD BASIC FUNCTIONS		
BASIC FUNCTION	MATHEMATICAL NOTATION	DESCRIPTION
ABS(x)	$\|x\|$	Absolute value of x
ATN(x)	$\tan^{-1} x$	Arctangent of x (radians)
COS(x)	$\cos x$	Cosine of x (radians)
EXP(x)	e^x	Natural exponential of x
INT(x)	$[x]$	Integer part of x
LOG(x)	$\ln x$	Natural logarithm of x
RND(x)		Random number between 0 and 1
SIN(x)	$\sin x$	Sine of x (radians)
SQR(x)	$\sqrt{x}$	Square root of x
TAN(x)	$\tan x$	Tangent of x (radians)

ABS This function changes a minus sign of the value of the argument to a plus sign. This new value is the value of the ABS function. The original value is unchanged.

COS, SIN, TAN These trigonometric functions operate on arguments that are angles expressed in radians. The ATN trigonometric function returns a result expressed in radians.

EXP The natural exponent (EXP) can be computed only for arguments in a certain range, depending on the particular BASIC system.

INT This function returns the integer part of a value that might not be a whole number. INT always operates by taking the next lower (i.e, more negative) integer, whether the value is positive or negative. Therefore, although the INT (7.8) is 7, the value of the expression INT (-7.8) is -8. One use of INT is to round off values to the nearest whole integer. This is done by adding one-half to the argument, as in

$$\text{INT } (T\,3 + .5)$$

$T\,3$ may be negative or positive. For values of 7.8 and -7.8 for $T\,3$, the result of INT $(T\,3 + .5)$ would be 8.0 and -8.0, respectively. INT can be used to round off to any specific number of decimal places. The arithmetic expression

$$\text{INT}(100 * X + .5)/100$$

will round off X to the nearest value and leave it with two decimal places.

LOG The logarithmic function computes results only for positive, nonzero arguments.

RND This function is used to generate random numbers during execution of a program. Numbers generated are supposed to be distributed rectangularly in the range from 0 through 1. The argument of the RND function is not used in most systems. Also, in most systems, you get the same *sequence* of random numbers each time you use the program. If this is troublesome, you can read in an arbitrary integer from the terminal and then ignore that many random values before continuing. The value returned by the RND function is always positive. It is possible to generate random values in any chosen range. For example, to generate values from 7 through 85 randomly, write the arithmetic expression

$$7 + 78 * \text{RND}(0)$$

The subexpression 78 * RND(0) yields random values distributed rectangularly in the range 0 through 78. Then, by adding the 7, the range is shifted to 7 to 85. For example, the expression RND(0)* $2 - 1$ will generate random values distributed from -1 to 1, and the sign will be chosen at random.

SQR This function might seem redundant since the square root of a number may be expressed as $X\uparrow.5$. However, the SQR function is more efficient because it has a single purpose. If the exponent of X will always be .5, it is more economical of computer time to express it as SQR(X). Similarly, when calculating the square of a number, it speeds execution to write $X * X$, instead of the more general form $X\uparrow2$.

Statement Types

BASIC has ten elementary types of statements that are the building blocks for programs. Even novice programmers can write practical and useful programs with them. They are as follows:

1. LET (arithmetic assignment)
2. PRINT (printing of results)
3. GO TO (transfer of control)
4. INPUT (acceptance of input data)
5. STOP (termination of execution)
6. IF (conditional execution)
7. FOR (loop control)
8. NEXT (loop termination)
9. GOSUB (procedure invocation)
10. RETURN (procedure termination)

When you read the brief descriptions of these ten statements in the following pages, you should refer to Figure 8.4. This illustration is a "nonsense" program that carries many pertinent examples of the eight elementary statement types. In our discussions we will not dwell on the advanced features of the language, such as subtle uses of certain statements types, and we will not address many of the other powerful BASIC statements. You should gain some experience with this limited set of statements first and then consult the BASIC language reference guide published for the computer that you are actually using.

Intraprogram Documentation

Any line that starts with "REM" is called a *remark* statement. The line is ignored by the BASIC system, but it will be printed out in listings of your program so that you can add commentary. It is wise to include many REM lines so that you can aid your own debugging and future sanity (see Chapter 7).

LET Statement

The LET, or assignment, statement occurs frequently since it assigns values to named variables. It contains the following:

1. Symbolic name
2. Equal sign
3. Expression

```
1010    REM EXAMPLES OF THE 'LET' STATEMENT
1020
1030    LET X = 0
1040    LET D = A1* A −A3* A3
1050    LET X4 = (B2 * A2) / D
1060    LET R8 = 17 + SQR(R8) − R8
1070
1080
1090
2010    REM EXAMPLES OF THE 'PRINT' STATEMENT
2020
2030    PRINT A, B−5, 72
2040    PRINT "ANSWER =", Y
2050
2060
2070
3010    REM AN EXAMPLE OF THE 'GO TO' STATEMENT
3020
3030    GO TO 1030
3040
3050
3060
4010    REM EXAMPLES OF THE 'INPUT' STATEMENT
4020
4030    INPUT A
4040    INPUT A, B, C
4050
4060
4070
5010    REM EXAMPLE OF THE 'GOSUB' STATEMENT
5020
5030    GOSUB 7010
5040
5050
5060
6010    REM EXAMPLE OF THE 'STOP' STATEMENT
6020
6030    STOP
6040
6050
6060
7010    REM EXAMPLES OF THE 'IF' STATEMENT
7020
7030    IF N8 = 5 THEN 1050
7040    IF N ">" 20 THEN 9010
7050    IF SQR(R9*8) / 4 "<" EXP(INT(Z) ) THEN 7070
7060
7070
7080
8010    REM EXAMPLES OF THE 'FOR' AND 'NEXT' STATEMENTS
8020
8030    FOR I = 1 TO 10
8040        REM (BODY OF THE LOOP)
8050    NEXT I
8060    FOR Z9 = 7 TO −5 STEP Z − 2.5
8070        REM (BODY OF THE LOOP)
8080
8090
8095
8096
9010    REM EXAMPLE OF THE 'RETURN' STATEMENT
9020
9030    RETURN
9040
9050
9060
9999    END
```

Figure 8.4 A "nonsense" program that incorporates all ten elementary BASIC statements.

Since spaces are ignored in all BASIC statements, use them freely to make LET statements more readable.

The variable at the left of an equal sign may also appear in the arithmetic expression on the right. This is possible because the equal sign is not the same equivalence operator as in algebra. It is a replacement, or assignment, operator. The system evaluates the entire arithmetic expression and then assigns the value to the named variable(s).

PRINT Statement

The PRINT statement elicits a printout of a program's results. Both variables and constants can be printed. Constants are used to annotate and label printed results. The PRINT statement contains a list of print elements that are separated by commas or semicolons. A print element may be any arithmetic expression, an alphanumeric expression, or a constant. If a text constant is used, it must appear in quotation marks.

Each line of the printing device (usually your terminal) is divided into zones, each fifteen spaces long. If the last zone contains fewer than twelve spaces, the system does not regard it as a zone for printing and ignores these spaces. Printing is done within zones, always starting with the leftmost zone on the line. A comma signals the printing device to advance to the next zone. Any quoted-text constant prints exactly as it appears, but without the quotation marks. At the end of the PRINT statement's list, the system starts a new line unless the PRINT statement ends with a comma. If the statement ends with a comma, the system advances to the next zone and remains there, waiting to resume printing on the same line when it encounters the next PRINT statement.

If the system executes a PRINT statement that has no print element list, the current line is ended and the next PRINT statement causes printing to begin in the first zone of the next line. If there is no current line, the printer skips a line. This is useful for vertical page formats.

A quoted-text constant may occupy more than one zone if it is longer than fifteen characters. The last used zone will be filled out with spaces until the next zone is reached. The quoted-text constant is never split between lines. If it extends beyond the last zone, some of it may be lost.

A packed form of output is available by using a semicolon instead of a comma. A comma tells the computer to move to the next zone for the next answer; a semicolon inhibits a skip to the next zone. Therefore, more than five numbers can be packed on a line if each number requires less than a full zone to print. If a semicolon appears after quoted text, the output device does not skip any spaces before printing the next item. Therefore, two quoted text items will print without space between them unless one or more spaces appear at the end of the first item or at the beginning of the second item. Similarly, when a variable follows quoted text, with or without a semicolon, it will print out with no space between it and the end of the quoted text (except that a blank appears in place of a plus sign for positive numbers). This feature may be used to align decimal points in lists of numbers that have different numbers of digits before the decimal point. The program must determine the number of leading digits and print quoted text that contains the correct number of spaces.

BASIC prints numbers in a format that is not under the user's direct control. However, use the following rules as a guide to interpret printed results: Numbers are always printed from the leftmost position in the zone; a negative number is printed preceded by a minus sign and a positive number is preceded by a space that implies a plus sign; if an exponent is printed, it always includes a sign just after the letter ''E.''

1. If the number is an integer, no decimal point is printed. If the integer contains more than (typically) ten significant digits, it is formatted as (a) the first digit, (b) a decimal point, (c) the next five digits (less trailing zeros), and (d) an ''E'' followed by the appropriate signed integer.
2. No more than six significant digits are printed for any decimal number. Leading zeros to the left of the decimal point and trailing zeros to the right are not printed.
3. Exponent notation is used for a number less than 0.1, unless the entire significant part of the number can be printed as a six-digit number. Therefore, 0.00123 means that the number is exactly .001230000000; 1.23E–3 means that the number has been rounded to .001230. The program in Figure 8.5 shows how different values may be printed out.

```
10   LET N = −4
20   PRINT 2↑(2*N),
30   LET N = N + 1
40   REM THE BASIC 'IF' STATEMENT
50   REM TESTS 'N'. IF 'N' IS LESS
60   REM THAN 20, CONTINUE PRINTING.
70   IF N < 20 THEN 20
80   END
```

3.90615E−1	.015625	.0625	.25	1
4	16	64	256	1024
4096	16384	65536	262144	1048567
4194304	16777216	67108864	268435456	1073741824
4294967296	1.71799E+10	6.87195E+10	2.74878E+11	

Figure 8.5   A short program to print out 19 numbers in the five 15-character wide zones of a common teletypewriter, with the printed output produced.

GO TO Statement

The GØ TØ statement causes an unconditional change in the flow of a program. Normally, upon completion of the operations specified, each statement relinquishes control to the next statement in sequence. The GØ TØ statement is one way to change that normal flow.

A GØ TØ statement contains the number of the line to which control is to be transferred. This line is called the *target line*. If the target line performs no action, such as a REMark statement or an empty line, the system performs the next statement that follows it.

Even though BASIC ignores spaces in statements, it is common practice to leave one space between the words "GØ" and "TØ" and before the statement number.

INPUT Statement

The INPUT statement is used to acquire the data to be operated upon by the program. Data for the INPUT statement is typed by the user at the terminal. If there is voluminous data, there are usually extensions to BASIC that permit data to be read from external data files. You may also want to investigate the pair of statements READ and DATA in your own BASIC system's manual.

An INPUT statement contains a list of variable names separated by commas. When BASIC encounters an INPUT statement, it prints a question mark on the terminal. You then should type the required values as numbers (in forms acceptable to BASIC). If more than one variable has been called for, you separate the numbers with commas. You must supply precisely the right quantity of numbers; too many or too few numbers will earn you a provocative error message from the BASIC system.

STOP Statement

If you want to terminate the program prematurely, most systems allow you to type "S" or "STØP" instead of data.

A program run ends when "STØP" is typed in response to an INPUT request or when execution reaches the END statement. The END statement may be reached by a GØ TØ, but in this case the END statement number must be known. This may not be practical in a large BASIC program.

The STØP statement acts as a GØ TØ to the END statement. It consists only of the word "STØP." The two program portions of Figure 8.6 are exactly equivalent in meaning. The STØP statement simplifies the distinction between any arbitrary GØ TØ and one that will terminate the program run.

```
223 GO TO 403        223 STOP

     . . .                . . .

323 GO TO 403        323 STOP

     . . .                . . .

403 END              403 END
```

Figure 8.6 Use of STØP statement as an alternative to the GØ TØ statement.

IF Statement

The IF statement directs that certain things be done under certain conditions. This statement directs the system to perform some special action if some assertion is true. If the assertion is false, the system takes no action, as though it never encountered the IF statement. In its simplest form, the IF statement is often referred to as a conditional GØ TØ.

In the conditional GØ TØ form of the IF statement, if the assertion is true, then the system goes to a statement, the number of which is supplied in the IF statement. The statement number is preceded by the word "THEN." If the assertion is false, the system performs the next statement after the IF.

In its simplest form, an assertion relates one expression to another. The operators used to show the relations are as follows:

Equal ($=$)
Greater than ($>$)
Less than ($<$)
Less than or equal ($=<$ or $<=$)
Greater than or equal ($=>$ or $>=$)
Not equal ($<>$ or $><$)

Limit testing is often performed with the IF statement. In this application some part of the program is performed only when the data being tested lies outside the given limits. Figure 8.7 contains a program to print the natural exponent of a series of numbers. Certain large numbers cannot be used successfully to compute the exponent. These cases are identified by a diagnostic message issued by the program.

```
10   INPUT A
20   IF A = > −709.78 THEN 40
30   GO TO 70
40   IF A > 709.089 THEN 70
50   PRINT EXP(A)
60   GO TO 10
70   PRINT "MAGNITUDE TOO LARGE", A
80   GO TO 10
99   END
```

Figure 8.7   Use of limit checking to validate data with the IF statement.

The IF statement is also used to construct loops. Only the simplest programs are written in a straight line in which every statement is followed by another statement to the END statement. Most programs perform a group of statements several times, usually varying one or more values each time. This is called *looping*.

Simple loops can be constructed with the GØ TØ statement. A program with this kind of loop might never stop. Figure 8.8 illustrates such a program. Although this program does not appear to have an end (statements 200, 210, and

220 will be performed over and over again), you could terminate it by typing "STOP" in response to the INPUT statement.

```
200  INPUT E, G, D
210  LET N = G − D
220  PRINT E, "NET PAY = ", N
230  GO TO 200
999  END
```

Figure 8.8   BASIC program with a simple endless loop.

Controlled looping is much more important than simple GØ TØ-type looping. In a controlled loop the system maintains a count of the number of times something is done (or is to be done). This implies knowing some starting number, ending number, and the size of steps to take from the first to the last. Figure 8.9 shows two similar programs. The first is written in linear form without looping. The second is written with a single loop. Both of these programs calculate the squares of a set of numbers. The first number is 10, the last is 13, and the step

```
10  PRINT 10, 10*10       10  LET N = 10
20  PRINT 11, 11*11       20  PRINT N, N*N
30  PRINT 12, 12*12       30  LET N = N + 1
40  PRINT 13, 13*13       40  IF N = < 13 THEN 20
50  END                   50  END
```

Figure 8.9   Two similar programs: with and without looping.

from one to the next is one. The advantage of a loop is that the same thing need not be written over and over again. For example, if the program were to compute the values from 10 through 1,000, instead of just 13, the linear form of the program would contain 991 PRINT statements. If a loop were used, only the constant value 13 on line 40 would be changed (to 1,000).

In the example above the four basic parts of every loop can be identified as follows:

1. Initialization of a counter (line 10)
2. Body of the loop consisting of one or more lines (line 20)
3. Modification of the counter (line 30)
4. Loop-end test of the counter (line 40)

Loops are so important that BASIC provides a pair of statements just to indicate them. These are the FØR and NEXT statements.

FOR Statement

The FØR statement identifies the beginning of a loop. It also provides three of the four required parts of a loop and the name of the variable to be used as the controlling parameter. The three parts of the loop given in the FØR statements are as follows:

1. Initialization
2. End-test
3. Modification

Figure 8.10 gives the informal names for the constituents of a FØR statement. A FØR-variable can be any common numeric symbolic name. The "from," "to," and "step-size" may be arithmetic expressions of any complexity. The step-size (with the word "STEP") is optional. If the step-size is not given, the system assumes the positive constant 1. None of the expressions in a FØR statement need

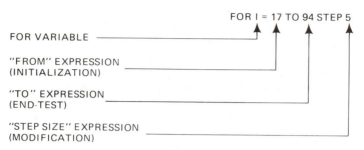

Figure 8.10 Names given to parts of a FØR statement.

be restricted to integer values. No FØR statement can mean anything without a companion NEXT statement.

NEXT Statement

The NEXT statement indicates the end of a FØR-loop. All of the statements that lie between the FØR statement and its associated NEXT statement constitute the body of the loop. The extent from the FØR through the associated NEXT statement is called the *range* of the FØR. Notice that the NEXT statement always contains the same symbolic name as its associated FØR statement. Figure 8.11 compares looping with an IF statement (as it was done in Figure 8.9) and looping with a FØR statement.

```
10  LET N = 10              10  FOR N = 10 TO 13 STEP 1
20  PRINT N, N*N            20      PRINT N, N*N
30  LET N = N + 1           30  NEXT N
40  IF N = < 13 THEN 20     40  END
50  END
```

                    (a)   (b)

Figure 8.11 Two similar looping programs, written with and without the FØR statement.

If the step-size in the FØR statement is positive (or absent, assumed to be +1), then the body of the loop will perform over and over again as long as the FØR-vari-

able is less than or equal to the value of the "to" expression. For a negative step-size, the loop will be performed as long as the FØR-variable is greater than or equal to the "to" expression's value.

Few programs are simple enough to require only one loop. It is simple, however, to write one FØR-loop within the body of another. The range of the inner loop must be entirely within the range of the outer loop. Any number of FØR-loops may be nested. Figure 8.12 shows valid and invalid forms of nesting.

```
        FOR J = 1 TO 10              FOR J = 1 TO 10
(a)         FOR I = 1 TO 3      (b)      FOR I = 1 TO 3
              . . .                        . . .
            NEXT I                     NEXT J
        NEXT J                             NEXT I


                    FOR J = 1 TO 10
                        FOR I = 1 TO 3
                            FOR H = 1 TO 2
                              . . .
                            NEXT H

                            . . .
(c)                         FOR H = 4 TO 2 STEP −1
                              . . .
                            NEXT H

                          . . .
                        NEXT I

                      . . .
                    NEXT J
```

Figure 8.12   Valid and invalid forms of nested FØR loops.

GOSUB Statement

The essential importance of *procedures* in programming language has been emphasized several times in this design course. In addition to being useful tools in the logical partitioning of a program into separable parts for separate consideration, programs arranged around comprehensive suites of procedures tend to be easier to implement and easier to test. The procedures can, for instance, be independently written and tested (within some limitations, such as using only certain assigned symbols to avoid conflicts with other independently written modules). And, of course, properly written procedures can be modified independently of other parts of the program.

BASIC provides for procedure invocation with the GØSUB statement. The actual entry point of the program is determined by the line number that appears in the GØSUB statement. It is a good idea to annotate the entry point of each procedure (i.e., subroutine) with REM statements to separate them from other parts of the main program.

The GØSUB statement is similar to the GØ TØ statement in format and operation, but GØSUB records the number of the line immediately following the GØSUB so that control can be returned there upon completion of the procedure's execution. Examples of two uses of the GØSUB statement are shown in Figure 8.13.

```
100   LET X = 20              100
110   LET Y = 40              110
120   GOSUB 5000             120
130   PRINT R              5000
140   LET X = 40           5010
150   GOSUB 5000           5020
160   PRINT R               130
170   STOP                  140
5000  REM PROCEDURE 'HYPOTENUSE'   150
5010  LET R = SQR(X*X + Y*Y)      5000
5020  RETURN               5010
9999  END                  5020
                            160
                            170
                           9999
          (a)               (b)
```

Figure 8.13 Examples of the use of a common subroutine with the GOSUB and RETURN statements, in (a), and a "trace" of the line numbers executed (b).

RETURN Statement

If there is no RETURN statement, a GØSUB is just like a GØ TØ. However, when GØSUB is executed, the number of the line following the GØSUB is recorded in a push-down (first-in, last-out) stack. When the RETURN statement is executed, the top line number is removed from the stack and execution resumes there. Figure 8.13(b) illustrates the controlled flow of statement sequencing that results from using the GØSUB and RETURN pair of statements.

Data Declarations

In BASIC you don't have to explicitly name every individual item or array that you intend to use in the program, even though it is a practice encouraged in the "pidgin" notation we introduced in earlier chapters. Individual variables (equivalent to *items*) can only have names consisting of a single letter or a letter followed by a digit. Whenever they are used, they are assumed to have been declared. And for arrays of up to ten elements, you don't even have to specify to BASIC what the array name is. Since array names are always one letter and followed by a parentheses (for the subscript), there is no confusion.

Whenever a symbolic name can be used in a BASIC program, a reference to an element of an array may also be used. This permits individual elements of an array to be used, among other places, in any arithmetic expression. The symbolic name used for the name of any array must not be confused with the same symbolic name used to represent a single value because both may be in the same program. The array name is always followed by a left parenthesis. The symbolic name standing for a single value is never followed immediately by a left parenthesis.

Figure 8.14 gives a sample of each symbolic name. In some BASIC systems array names are limited to a single letter.

```
110    LET K = 5
120    LET K(K) = 4
130    PRINT K(K)
140    END
```

Figure 8.14   Program which uses the same symbolic name for both an individual quantity and an array name.

Getting Access to Basic

Where can you get access to BASIC so that you can practice? Since BASIC is probably the most widely implemented language and also the most idiosyncratic language, you will find gaining access both easy and frustrating at the same time.

You can buy time on a time-sharing system, which is where BASIC really started. However, you probably won't want to sign up for service until you see that you are going to use the system enough to warrant. All of the major commercial time-sharing service vendors offer BASIC. The BASIC language processors on time-sharing systems all offer certain novel extensions to the language—each one different from all the others. But you will find that the common core of the language will be virtually the same in all cases.

You can probably obtain a BASIC compiler (or interpreter, as they are sometimes implemented and called) for a minicomputer, especially if it is one of the popular models. The service you get on the mini will be equivalent to the basic core of the BASIC language, but you can expect fewer super-power extensions than in the time-sharing mode. Frankly, while you are learning, you won't care much about these extensions anyway.

You can also obtain BASIC compilers that run under the popular operating systems of large-scale computers. However, many of these have restrictive sets of the language. And if your large-scale in-house computer doesn't support programming from a terminal, BASIC will be inconvenient to use.

You may also consider the many BASIC compilers that are available on microcomputers, but, you must be wary: Most of them are nonstandard and have some of the core of the language left out while extensions have been added. BASIC translators on micros are ideal, however, because there is little economic pressure to get off the high-priced computer that the other alternatives create.

The only way to learn BASIC is to write BASIC. Just as you learned the fine points of electronic design in the college lab, you can only learn the finer points of programming by actually programming. Find out where you can gain access to BASIC and try it out.

When an array is referred to, it is automatically defined as having the number of dimensions specified by the number of subscripts and the permitted range of each subscript is set to zero through ten. The upper bound (ten) is provided automatically, but it may be changed by the DIM statement discussed below. For programs that use small arrays, the user need not be concerned about the subscript bounds because of the automatic definition implied by the use of a subscripted symbolic name.

Each subscript represents one dimension of an array. The numerical value of the subscript is used to select a specific element of the array. A subscript may be written as any arbitrarily complicated arithmetic expression. Since an element of an array may appear in an arithmetic expression, subscripts may be calculated by using subscripted symbolic names. If the subscript is not an integer, the integer part of the numerical result is used and the fractional part is ignored. This is equivalent to using the INT(X) function. A subscript never may be negative. The maximum value of the subscript depends on the value of the upper bound on the dimension (ten, in the case of an implied dimension).

DIM

When the default dimensions of an array implied by use are not suitable, the DIM statement is used to supply the explicit dimensions. For subscripts of an implied array, the upper bound ten may be too small for some applications. Furthermore, small arrays of multiple dimensions can cause large areas of unused array space to be defined. The DIM statement contains a list of array names, followed by integers that specify the upper bound for each subscript. The upper bounds are enclosed in parentheses, like subscripts, and are separated by commas.

In the first example the DIM statement is not required because the array A will have these dimensions by default. The DIM statement may occur anywhere within a BASIC program, although it is customary to put it all at the very top. Examples of the DIM statement are illustrated in Figure 8.15.

```
1010   DIM A(25)
1020   DIM Z(2,18), B9(150), C(1024)
```

Figure 8.15 Some examples of the DIM statements that reserve memory space for arrays in BASIC.

Translating Designs to Programs

Your neat, complete designs written in some "pidgin" form—or even in the form of flow charts—can be converted into BASIC programs once you understand how to make the transition. These same steps can be used to translate your design into *any* computer language. The principle is simple: In the chosen programming language (in our case, BASIC) find one or more statements that will satisfy the implementation of each kind of construct used in your program design notation.

For example, in the program design notation introduced and used in earlier chapters we made frequent use of the **if-then-else** statement. In BASIC, as we have learned, there is an "IF" statement, but there the similarities end. BASIC doesn't provide for any complex group of statements following "THEN" (only a line number is permitted). Furthermore, BASIC doesn't have an "ELSE" clause. Even with these limitations, though, you can create a BASIC language equivalent to your original design. For example, look up the **if-then-else** structure in Figure 8.16. There you will find a group of BASIC statements that can perform the same work, although not in so structured or readable a fashion.

PIDGIN FORM	BASIC FORM	
a; b; c	1010	a
	1020	b
	1030	c
if a then b else c	2010	IF a THEN 2040
	2020	c
	2030	GO TO 2050
	2040	b
	2050	. . .
while a do b	3010	IF a THEN 3030
	3020	GO TO 3050
	3030	b
	3040	GO TO 3010
	3050	. . .
for i ← a to b do c	4010	FOR i = a TO b
	4020	c
	4030	NEXT i
procedure x; a;	5010	GOSUB 6010
.	5020	. . .
.	.	
.	.	
a;	.	
	6010	a
	6020	RETURN

NOTATIONS WITHOUT EQUIVALENTS
begin . . . end

Figure 8.16 Some equivalent forms between our procedural design notation and the core of the BASIC language.

Figure 8.16 is a translation guide from the "pidgin" notation to BASIC. It should not be followed slavishly, but it should serve as a guide to alert you to the particular kinds of statements you ought to be looking at to translate your program. Figure 8.17 is a similar guide for the data structures. BASIC is representative of an era in which data structures weren't treated with the importance they are today, as evidenced by the paucity of data description facilities. Those lacks make BASIC a language that is not terribly useful in certain complex classes of applications.

PIDGIN FORM	BASIC FORM
item a, b, c of real	(not required)
array a(0 . . . n) of real	1010 DIM a(n)
list a(0 . . . n) of real	2010 DIM a(n, 1)
	.
	.
	3010 FOR I = 0 TO n
	3020 LET a (I, 0) = I + 1
	3030 LET a (I, 1) = 0
	3040 NEXT I
	3050 LET a(I, n) = 0

NOTATIONS WITHOUT EQUIVALENTS
begin . . . end
type . . . of . . .

Figure 8.17 Some equivalent forms between the design notation's data description capabilities and BASIC's.

Getting Around Deficiencies

It is a truism that "you can implement any program in BASIC." This is true in *any* modern programming language. However, it is a matter of how convenient the implementation may be and how human-engineered the inputs and outputs can be made. BASIC is very convenient for numeric computations because this is the environment for which BASIC was designed, but BASIC is clumsy at "bit fiddling." But what if we have to "bit fiddle" (handle logical-and, -or and -invert functions on Boolean variables)? Since BASIC doesn't admit Boolean data types, how can the data be processed?

We can allocate an array to hold one bit per element, those values being restricted (by our program) to **0** and **1**. Obviously, we can then write procedures (subroutines) that process these values to yield appropriate results. Of course, we will also consume a lot of storage for each bit we need to process, and that will limit the size of Boolean bit-fiddling job we will want to do. We *said* it wouldn't be convenient. But it *can* be done.

So, instead of asking what a language lacks, we should ask the more relevant question: How do we make this language do what we want to do? Generally, there will be a way, but it may tend to be inelegant, inconvenient, and not a little inefficient.

9

Writing and Running
a
BASIC Program

The moment has come. It is time to specify, design, and implement a complete program for a unique task. Of course, we can't laboriously record all of the steps required even of such a simple program as we are about to elucidate. But if we record some of the major "milestones" in our progress, perhaps you will be better able to see how it can be done.

A Typical Problem

Did you ever have a polynomial that you were working with that you wished you could have had a "quick look" at? Especially with empirically determined formulas, a look at the shape often offers insight into the underlying phenomena. Even when you use a calculator, you have to work through several points before you can get a sense of the curve shape. But with a computer all you have to do is implement (or modify) a program. For our purposes, we will limit our consideration to polynomials that have up to three coefficients and only one independent variable. After you understand this program, you can easily expand the program to suit other needs.

This is a good example of the kind of programs that most designers write. Although it appears to be a computational problem, you will find that most of the program is devoted to controlling the output medium to draw the graph. Most computer-oriented solutions are characterized by a limited amount of actual "core" work surrounded by a lot of input/output peripheral device control.

The objective is to design and implement a program (in BASIC) to accept coefficients and values for an independent variable and then plot the resulting function as a graph on a printing device like a teletypewriter. As in any good software design, we should create a program that is readable and easy to change. For the purposes of our example, we will assume that the polynomial is the simple $ax^2 + bx + c$, although our "easily changeable program" rule will make modification of that formula simple.

The input to our program must consist of the coefficients (a, b, and c) and the lower and upper bounds of the independent variable.

Our intended output, of course, is a graph. A printing terminal can be treated as a sheet of quadrille paper; each "cell" is made up of one of the printing positions on a particular print-out line. Each printer has a specific line width that is measured by the number of printing positions. To limit the print-out size, we establish some fixed number of lines to be printed. If the printer can handle sixty (or more) print positions, and if we set a limit of fifty lines, our "graph paper" is fifty by sixty. We can draw the x-axis across the paper (and the y-axis up and down the page), or we can draw the y-axis across the page. Because we will want to print out each line of the graph sequentially, we want the independent variable to be our loop control variable. That means that the y-axis should be printed across the page. Since there is only one value per line to be plotted, we space the print head across the page until we find the appropriate point and we mark the point with an asterisk.

The y-axis is divided into a number of graduations limited only by the number of print positions on a line. The x-axis is fixed at some number (say fifty) for the number of lines we need to print in order to get enough resolution to be able to see the graphed function. The "domain" of each cell along the x-axis can be determined in advance: The difference between the largest and smallest x's (which are, of course, supplied as input) is divided by the number of lines to be printed. This computes the increment to be applied to each x in order to get to the next value to be computed with.

If we were to draw the graph by hand, we would probably compute all the values of the function, one for each point along the x-axis. Then, using the array, we would manually plot the points. In the computer we do the same thing. We compute all of the points first because we need to know the largest and smallest values computed; these limits are then used to divide the y-axis into appropriately sized cells. For any value for some "x," then, we need only divide the value by the increment along the y-axis to compute the number of spaces to print out before emitting the asterisk for the graphic point. The y-axis increment is, of course, ($y_{max} - y_{min}$) divided by the number of print positions across the line used for the y-axis.

Now, for each computed point (which is, of course, associated with some particular value of x along the x-axis), we print out one line. This line consists of many spaces followed by a properly positioned asterisk. Succeeding lines are printed until the entire list of computed points is exhausted. This results in a graph that can be taken off the terminal to be studied.

A narrative description of the program we have just outlined is presented in Figure 9.1. With very little additional guidance you should be able to easily understand how the program works. This would be a good form of documentation to use if you were designing a program for someone else to use.

VARIABLES

a, b, c	Coefficients of the polynomial
x_{min}, x_{max}	Lower and upper bounds on independent variable
n_x	Number of graduations along the X-axis
n_y	Number of graduations along the Y-axis
array y	The computed function values for each x

PROCEDURE

1. Set up n_x and n_y
2. Read in a, b, c, x_{min} and x_{max}
3. Compute x_{del}, the increment across the X-axis, as $(x_{max} - x_{min})/n_x$
4. For each x from x_{min} to x_{max}, in steps of x_{del}, compute each $y \leftarrow axx + bx + c$
5. Find minimum and maximum values computed for y
6. Compute y_{del}, the increment across the Y-axis, as $(y_{max} - y_{min})/n_y$
7. Draw the Y-axis
8. For each x from x_{min} to x_{max}, in steps of x_{del}, draw one line. On that line, for each related value of y, space over $(y - y_{min})/y_{del}$ spaces and print an asterisk.

Figure 9.1 A narrative description of the steps needed to implement the graph plotting program.

Formal Design Description

The next step is to design the entire program and to make some of the unclear things of Figure 9.1 explicit. The design, illustrated in Figure 9.2, is the result of several trial attempts over a few hours. Initially, some of the major separable features were partitioned into procedures for separate implementation. That resulted in three procedures: "read data" (to read all the input data), "plot" (to draw one line of the graph), and "draw axis" (to annotate the *y*-axis). Later, to make modification easier, a fourth procedure was added to contain the polynomial being graphed ("function").

The main program is, essentially, a cleaned-up and formalized version of the rough narrative in Figure 9.1. The specific detailed steps are included in Figure 9.2, so that a program can be written directly from the design.

To make things easier later, we chose to assume the existence of three magical procedures that act just like their BASIC counterparts. That is, "print" operates

```
begin
    item a, b, c of real;
    item x, x_min, x_max, x_del of real;
    item v, y_min, y_max, y_del of real;
    item i, n_x, n_y of integer;
    array y (1 .. 100) of real;

    procedure print (*see text*); stub;

    procedure input (*see text*); stub;

    procedure int (*see text*) of real; stub;

    procedure function of real;
        function ← a*x*x + b*x + c;

    procedure read data;
    begin
        print ("I plot polynomials of the form")
        print ("axx + bx + c, for", n_x, "values of x.");
        print ("What are the coefficients, a, b, and c?");
        input (a, b, c);
        print ("What are the lower and upper bounds of x?");
        input (x_min, x_max)
    end;

    procedure plot;
    begin
        item spaces, n of integer;
        print ("I");
        spaces ← int ((v - y_min)/y_del) - 1;
        for n ← 1 to spaces do
            print (" ");
        print ("*")
    end;
    procedure draw axis;
    begin
        item n of integer;
        print ("I will now plot", a; "xx +", b; "x +", c);
        print (" for x ranging from", x_min; "to", x_max);
        print (" and y ranging from", y_min; "to", y_max);
        print;
        for n ← 1 to int (n_y/10) do
            print ("I........");
        print ("I")
    end;

    n_x ← 50;
    n_y ← 60;
    read data;
    x_del ← (x_max - x_min)/n_x
    x ← x_min;
    y(1) ← function;
    y_min ← y(1);
    y_max ← y(1);
    for i ← 2 to n_x do
    begin
        x ← x + x_del;
        y(i) ← function;
        if y(i) < y_min then y_min ← y(i);
        if y(i) > y_max then y_max ← y(i)
    end;
    draw axis;
    y_del ← (y_max - y_min)/n_y;
    for i ← 1 to n_x do
    begin
        v ← y(i);
        plot
    end
end
```

Figure 9.2 A design for the graph-plotting program, suitable for implementation in any programming language.

on its operands like a BASIC PRINT statement, "input" acts like an INPUT statement, and "int" is identical to BASIC's INT function.

All of the variables used in the program are declared at the beginning of the design notation, and then the three magical procedures are defined as *stubs* (meaning that only the interface between the procedure and its user is specified, not the internal implementation).

The "function" procedure represents the polynomial that we will graph out by using this program. The "read data" procedure prints out guidelines to the user and then it accepts the five input data values we expect. The "plot" procedure prints a capital "I" in the left margin (our *x*-axis), and then it spaces over (*zero* or more times, as required) to allow a single asterisk to be printed. The procedure for "draw axis" prints out a single ten-character string enough times to be nearly as long as the *y*-axis; note the semicolon in the print list which, in BASIC, allows printing to continue on the same line. The last "I" prints at the end of the scale and terminates the printing line.

The main program for plotting establishes graduations for the *x*- and *y*-axes, and then it causes the input data to be read. The *x*-axis increment is calculated, and the first *y*-value is computed. To keep track of the lowest and highest *y*-values ever computed, we initialize "ymin" and "ymax." Then, for the rest of the values of *x*, we compute the related *y* and update "ymin" and "ymax." After all the computation is done, we draw the *y*-axis and compute the *y*-axis increment so that plotting can use the entire *y*-axis for maximum data variation across the line. Then, for each line, we select the computed *y*-value and plot it out.

You should study this design carefully. Ideally, you should understand it all before you proceed further in this discussion.

Converting a Design to BASIC

Throughout this design course we have emphasized the description of data structures before (or at least at the same time as) procedures. When a well-designed and annotated program is being converted to BASIC, the same principles are applied. However, here you are required to simultaneously take into account the restrictions imposed by the "real" language. For example, as you learned in Chapter 8, BASIC cannot accept fully spelled-out symbols; symbols are limited to a single letter or a letter followed by a digit. Therefore, a synonym list (Table 9.1) must be prepared. The design symbols are bound to equivalent BASIC symbols in the documentation (this table makes a good item for your working design manual). Then, during coding, when you encounter a symbol for which you don't immediately remember the BASIC synonym, you can look it up easily.

Next, the individual statements in the design are translated into equivalent forms in the chosen programming language. In BASIC the first statement that is executed is the first statement in the program (since there is no equivalent of the *procedure* statement to alert the BASIC system to skip the code to be invoked later). Therefore, we may choose to put the main procedure first and the sub-

TABLE 9.1 A typical equate table to show the correspondence between names in the software design and the equivalent names that conform to the rules of BASIC.

DESIGN NAME	BASIC NAME	DESCRIPTION
a	A	Coefficient a
b	B	Coefficient b
c	C	Coefficient c
x	X	Independent variable x
x_{min}	X0	Lowest value of x
x_{max}	X9	Highest value of x
x_{del}	X5	Increment between successive x's
v	V	A value of y(i)
y_{min}	Y0	Lowest value of y
y_{max}	Y9	Highest value of Y
y_{del}	Y5	Increment between successive y's
i	I	An index to the array, y
n_x	X1	Number of cells in x-axis
n_y	Y1	Number of cells in y-axis
y	Y	Array of nx values of the function
spaces		Number of spaces before plotted point
n	N	A loop counter

ordinate procedures last. Alternatively, we could maintain the same arrangement of procedures followed by the main program and then head the entire program with a single GO TO statement on the first line that transfers control to the first statement of the main procedure.

Figure 9.3 is a manual translation of part of the design (taken from Figure 9.2) into code in BASIC. Space has been freely used so that equivalent parts are adjacent. You can see how designs are clearly transliterated into programs by simple means.

Normally, you would manually translate the entire program to BASIC by handwriting onto a keypunch manuscript form. A keypunch operator or secretary would type the program onto cards, paper tape, or cassette tape, depending on the medium that your chosen computer would need. Then the program would be converted to machine-readable form, after which you would obtain an error-free listing (that is, with all of the typist's corrections removed) and desk-check it carefully. You might discover that you yourself have made some errors or you might find some typographical errors from the keying operation. The complete listing in Figure 9.4 is an example of a full BASIC program. CAUTION: There are two "bugs" in this program that will be discovered later.

Executing the Program

Your raw program (in source code form) is not enough to satisfy most computers. You aren't done yet! You will have to "tell" your computer that the programming language you are using is BASIC and how you want this particular

(a)

$n_x \leftarrow 50$;
$n_y \leftarrow 60$;

read data;

$x_{del} \leftarrow (x_{max} - x_{min})/n_x$

$x \leftarrow x_{min}$

$y(1) \leftarrow$ function;
$y_{min} \leftarrow y(1)$;
$y_{max} \leftarrow y(1)$;

<u>for</u> $i \leftarrow$ <u>2 to</u> n_x <u>do</u>
<u>begin</u> $x \leftarrow x + x_{del}$;
      $y(i) \leftarrow$ function;

      <u>if</u> $y(i) < y_{min}$
          <u>then</u> $y_{min} \leftarrow y(i)$
      <u>if</u> $y(i) > y_{max}$
          <u>then</u> $y_{max} \leftarrow y(i)$
<u>end</u>;

draw axis;

$y_{del} \leftarrow (y_{max} - y_{min})/n_y$;

<u>for</u> $i \leftarrow$ <u>1 to</u> n_x <u>do</u>
<u>begin</u> $v \leftarrow y(i)$;
      plot
<u>end</u>

(b)

```
1060   REM SET UP GRAPH HEIGHT AND WIDTH (NUMBER OF CELLS)
1070   LET X1 = 50
1080   LET Y1 = 60
1090   REM READ IN THE FACTORS OF THE POLYNOMIAL
1100   GOSUB 3000
1110   REM COMPUTE THE INCREMENT BETWEEN SUCCESSIVE X'S
1120   LET X5 = (X9 − X0)/X1
1130   REM SET UP FIRST VALUE AND INITIAL TRIAL VALUES FOR
1140   REM   YMIN AND YMAX
1150   LET X = X0
1160   LET I = 1
1170   GOSUB 2000
1180   LET Y0 = Y(1)
1190   LET Y9 = Y(1)
1200   REM NOW, FOR ALL X'S COMPUTE AND FIND YMIN AND YMAX
1210   FOR I = 2 TO X1
1220     LET X = X + X5
1230     GOSUB 2000
1240     REM FIND LOWEST AND HIGHEST VALUES YET COMPUTED
1250     IF Y(I) >= Y0 THEN 1270
1260       LET Y0 = Y(I)
1270     IF Y(I) <= Y9 THEN 1290
1280       LET Y9 = Y(I)
1290   NEXT I
1300   REM ALL Y'S COMPUTED. NOW DRAW THE Y-AXIS
1310   GOSUB 5000
1320   REM COMPUTE THE INCREMENT BETWEEN SUCCESSIVE Y CELLS
1330   LET Y5 = (Y9 − Y0)/Y1
1340   REM PLOT EACH LINE OF THE GRAPH, FOR NX VALUES OF X
1350   FOR I = 1 TO X1
1360     LET V = Y(I)
1370     GOSUB 4000
1380   NEXT I
```

Figure 9.3 The manual translation of the graph-plotter (a), into an equivalent BASIC program (b).

125

```
1000    REM THIS PROGRAM PLOTS FUNCTIONS OF A POLYNOMIAL
1010    REM    ON A SERIAL (CHARACTER-BY-CHARACTER) PRINTER.
1020    DIM Y[100]
1030    REM ★ ★ ★ ★ ★ ★ ★ ★ ★ ★
1040    REM (MAIN PROCEDURE)
1050    REM ★ ★ ★ ★ ★ ★ ★ ★ ★ ★
1060    REM SET UP GRAPH HEIGHT AND WIDTH (NUMBER OF CELLS)
1070    LET X1 = 50
1080    LET Y1 = 60
1090    REM READ IN THE FACTORS OF THE POLYNOMIAL
1100    GOSUB 3000
1110    REM COMPUTE THE INCREMENT BETWEEN SUCCESSIVE X'S
1120    LET X5 = (X9 − X0) / X1
1130    REM SET UP FIRST VALUE, AND INITIAL TRIAL VALUES FOR
1140    REM    YMIN AND YMAX
1150    LET X = X0
1160    LET I = 1
1170    GOSUB 2000
1180    LET Y0 = Y[1]
1190    LET Y9 = Y[1]
1200    REM NOW, FOR ALL X'S, COMPUTE AND FIND YMIN AND YMAX
1210    FOR I = 2 TO X1
1220      LET X = X + X5
1230      GOSUB 2000
1240      REM FIND LOWEST AND HIGHEST VALUES YET COMPUTED
1250      IF Y[I] > = Y0 THEN 1270
1260      LET Y0 = Y[I]
1270      IF Y[I] < = Y9 THEN 1290
1280      LET Y9 = Y [I]
1290    NEXT I
1300    REM ALL Y'S COMPUTED. NOW DRAW THE Y-AXIS
1310    GOSUB 5000
1320    REM COMPUTE THE INCREMENT BETWEEN SUCCESSIVE Y CELLS
1330    LET Y5 = (Y9 − Y0) / X1
1340    REM PLOT EACH LINE OF THE GRAPH, FOR NX VALUES OF X
1350    FOR I = 1 TO X1
1360      LET V = Y[I]
1370      GOSUB 4000
1380    NEXT I
1390    STOP
2000    REM ★ ★ ★ ★ ★ ★ ★ ★ ★ ★
2010    REM PROCEDURE FUNCTION
2020    REM ★ ★ ★ ★ ★ ★ ★ ★ ★ ★
2030    LET Y[I] = A ★ X ★ X + B ★ X + C
2040    RETURN
3000    REM ★ ★ ★ ★ ★ ★ ★ ★ ★ ★
3010    REM PROCEDURE READ DATA
3020    REM ★ ★ ★ ★ ★ ★ ★ ★ ★ ★
3030    PRINT "I PLOT POLYNOMIALS OF THE FORM"
3040    PRINT "AXX+BX+C, FOR ";X1;" VALUES OF X."
3050    PRINT "WHAT ARE THE COEFFICIENTS, A, B, AND C";
3060    INPUT A,B,C
3070    PRINT "WHAT ARE THE LOWER AND UPPER BOUNDS OF X";
3080    INPUT X0,X9
3090    RETURN
4000    REM ★ ★ ★ ★ ★ ★ ★ ★ ★ ★
4010    REM PROCEDURE PLOT
```

```
4020    REM ★ ★ ★ ★ ★ ★ ★ ★ ★ ★
4030    REM PRINT X-AXIS IN THE LEFT MARGIN
4040    PRINT "I"
4050    REM SPACE OVER TO THE POINT WHERE POINT IS TO BE PLOTTED
4060    FOR N = 1 TO INT ( (V − Y0) / Y5) − 1
4070       PRINT "  ";
4080    NEXT N
4090    PRINT "★"
4100    RETURN
5000    REM ★ ★ ★ ★ ★ ★ ★ ★ ★ ★
5010    REM PROCEDURE DRAW AXIS
5020    REM ★ ★ ★ ★ ★ ★ ★ ★ ★ ★
5030    REM ECHO INFORMATION BACK OUT FOR CONFIRMATION
5040    PRINT "I WILL NOW PLOT"; A; "XX +"; B; "X +"; C
5050    PRINT "   FOR X RANGING FROM"; X0; "TO"; X9
5060    PRINT "   AND Y RANGING FROM"; Y0; "TO"; Y9
5070    PRINT
5080    REM NOW, TYPE THE Y-AXIS
5090    FOR N = 1 TO INT (Y1 / 10)
5100       PRINT "I----.----";
5110    NEXT N
5120    PRINT "I"
5130    RETURN
9999    END
```

Figure 9.4   The program, as typed into the computer, derived from the design in Figure 9.2. CAUTION: there are two errors embedded in this program as it stands.

program treated. For convenience, you will want to give this program a name and store it away in the computer's files for future reference. All these orders are contained in the *job control language* or *command language* for the computer system you are using. If your use of the computer is on-line (that is, you are at a terminal and interacting with the computer), you will use one of the command languages. If you are using a batch-oriented system in which you create an entire sequence of commands and then submit the entire job to the computer (typically through a human operator), you will use a more complex job control language. In either case, you should find someone who is knowledgeable about your particular computer system and let him show you how to do it.

The basic steps you should follow are listed below:

1. Sign-on (or job identification)
2. Naming of your new program file
3. Transmission of the program for storage
4. Execution of the program under BASIC
5. Modification of the program to correct errors (repeating steps 4 and 5 as necessary)
6. Final saving of the debugged program
7. Sign-off

The sign-on and sign-off procedures are highly dependent on the various computer environments. On many minicomputers these procedures don't exist; you turn power on or off as required. If your system is extremely small, you might not be allowed to name your program file. In most cases, however, you have to if you want to be able to save it on tape or disc for later retrieval and use. If you are using BASIC on a microcomputer, you might not have the facility; carefully label your program tapes with version and revision levels (and dates), as described in Chapter 6.

Since BASIC was designed to be used in an interactive environment like a time-sharing system or a dedicated minicomputer, our examples for the remainder of this chapter will assume the use of some kind of terminal-oriented command language. The commands we will use are summarized in Table 9.2. They are commands that are representative of the genre, but they happen to be specific to the Hewlett-Packard 3000 Series BASIC system we used to generate these examples.

TABLE 9.2 Important user-interactive commands on the Hewlett-Packard 3000 BASIC System.

GET XYZ	The BASIC system "gets" the file named XYZ from the large disc storage and places it in main memory where you can operate on it.
TAPE	Used to alert the system that a program or data file on tape must be read into main memory, so the prompt characters shouldn't be issued out to the terminal.
KEY	Used to revert to keyboard input mode after TAPE.
RUN	Specifies to the system that you want to execute the BASIC program in main memory.
SAVE XYZ	The BASIC system "saves" the program you have in main memory in a file space named XYZ so you can GET it later by that name. If XYZ already exists, you type its name with an exclamation point (XYZ!) to notify the system that it's okay to replace the previous copy with this new version.

When you first use a BASIC system, you should have a competent and experienced user explain what is happening and what your options are for the next step in the process. Lacking such an experienced guide in person, the rest of this chapter is an annotated protocol taken from the teletypewriter terminal during an actual program development session. Read the notations carefully because they explain what is happening. Although the terminals don't do it, we have underlined all the things the operator typed into the computer.

In an interactive system like the H–P 3000 system we used for these examples, the operating system of the computer interacts with the user who is expected to be seated at a terminal. Whenever the system is ready for the user to issue a command [like RUN or SAVE (see Table 9.2)], it prints out a "prompt" character in the left margin; the H–P system uses ">." In Figure 9.5 you can clearly see when previous operations were completed; that is when the system issued the "greater than" character to prompt you to issue the next command.

In general, you tell the computer to do something by using the carriage return key on the terminal keyboard. When a line of text is composed (and, of course, already received character by character by the computer), you can tell the computer to act upon it by hitting the return key. The first few characters on each line are the command that will be interpreted.

If the first character on a line is a digit, the BASIC system assumes that you have typed in a new (or revised) line for your program; it takes the digit as the first part of the BASIC line number. If the number already exists in the program, the old line is deleted and this new one is inserted (if this new line contains no characters except the line number, the old line is deleted). If the number is new, this line is inserted into the program at the appropriate point.

If the first character on a line is not a digit, the word is looked up on a table inside the computer software system to decide what to do next.

Operation of the Program

In Figure 9.5 we first signed onto the system (using whatever procedure the particular system required; it is not germane to our discussion) and we received our first prompt character. This means that we can issue any command we want. Since we have our program on tape typed earlier by a qualified typist, we want to enter it into the main memory of the computer. We use the TAPE command. Then we load the tape and turn on the reader; the characters are sent to the computer and stored. Since each line begins with a number, the statements are all added to what was originally an empty program space. The program we entered in looks exactly like Figure 9.4.

At the end of the program entry process we type in KEY (and, of course, our ubiquitous carriage return) to get the system back into an interactive mode. It responds with a prompt character. We specify that we want to SAVE this program in a file named PLOTTER. Now is the time to save the program; if we lose the 'phone line between the terminal and the computer or if there is a power failure, we can recoup without having to reenter the entire program. Of course, the main reason for SAVE is that it allows us to use this program tommorrow, next week, next month, or next year.

Now we are ready to RUN the program. The first two or three lines of output, of course, come right from our own program. At the end of the third line we type in the required numbers and signal our completion with a carriage return. Our BASIC program resumes and types out the next line, to which we respond with more data. Now the plotting program goes to work. (By the way, the total elapsed time since we typed RUN has been less than 30 seconds)

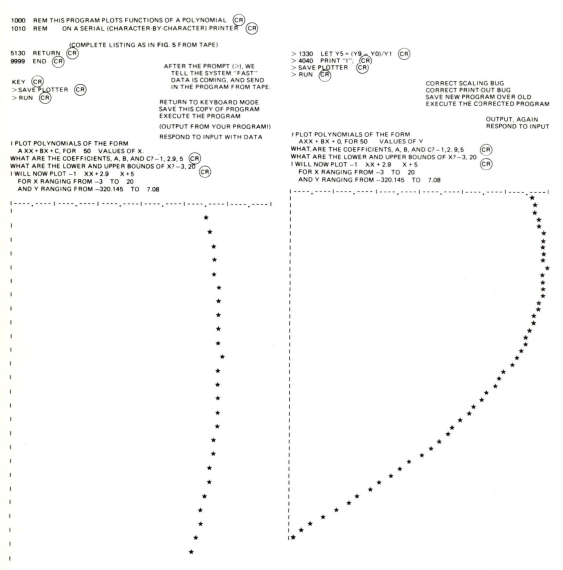

Figure 9.5 An annotated protocol (journal) from a run of the BASIC plotting program on the H–P 3000.

Our graph begins printing out. We immediately note an error: Each time a line is printed, the vertical line of I's that make up the *x*-axis get spaced down by one line. Look carefully. The initial "I" on the line is all by itself. The plotted point is printed on the *next* line. Something is wrong in one of our PRINT statements.

We note another error: The full horizontal (*y*-axis) width is not being used! Somehow we must have miscounted the number of positions to space over before plotting.

We find that there are two lines in our BASIC program that are in error (we will find out *how* to find the bugs in the next chapter). In computing "ydel," the increment across the *y*-axis, we accidentally divided by the number of graduations on the *x*-axis. Changing X1 to Y1 solves that problem. We also note that the print statement that issues the "I" for the *x*-axis prints a single "I" on a line. It should have been followed by a semicolon (probably a typo). We enter the two "editing" commands needed to change these two lines in the original program, and then re-save it over the top of the old version of the program in the disc files of the system.

Now we can run the program again. We used the same data inputs to the BASIC plotting progam and got the results we wanted.

The program ends with a prompt character to tell us that the program is done and to alert us to issue any new commands we may have. But we are done. We turn the terminal off and the system automatically takes care of the rest.

10

Testing
and
Debugging Techniques

Testing and debugging computer programs are so poorly understood as an academic discipline that they make many newcomers to programming wary. In fact, the methods involved in testing and debugging programs are little more than organized common sense. The subject is discussed in the literature so infrequently that one might assume that there is a conspiracy among those in the know! In fact, once you have learned the tricks and techniques of debugging in the course of implementing a few programs, you will see how simple it all is—and you will forget how concerned you may have been when you first began.

Program correctness and reliability are the goals we set for ourselves at the beginning of most projects. But to expect 100% foolproof operation of software is to underestimate the complexity of some of the systems we implement. In fact, much of the standard of performance we expect out of software may end up being subjective judgment. However, the one thing humans expect of their computers is *predictability*. When a progam behaves unpredictably, humans become suspicious of its inherent design integrity—and usually with justification. The purpose of testing is to assure predictable behavior, for if the behavior is satisfactory (which it must be before we will accept it into operational status), then the behavior will continue to be satisfactory. When a program doesn't behave according to our expectations, we engage in debugging, the methodology used to isolate and rehabilitate erroneous program segments. In the example used in Chapter 9 our BASIC program had two bugs that we detected by observing that the expected behavior did not match the expected behavior. Then, although the steps used were not described there, we isolated the problem to a probable cause, made the appropriate corrections, and retested the progam.

The better designed the progam is, which is generally correlated to how well the required program behavior is understood, the fewer iterations over the testing-debugging cycle have to be taken. The objective, of course, is one sequence of tests—and no debugging! Although this is virtually unattainable, it is the only target worth aiming at. The degree of confidence we eventually place in a program is directly related to the number of test-debug iterations we have to take. When we test a program and find no additional errors, our confidence is built (provided, of course, that our test cases are relevant). But if everytime we pose a new test, the new bug is caught, we might suspect that the more we test, the more bugs we will find. Eventually, of course, most programs reach a state in which we feel we have confidence in them, but if the early history were laden with bugs, our confidence would never be as great as it would have been had we found few errors.

Exhaustive testing is often proposed as one way to completely verify the correctness of a computer program. But a few moments' reflection will show why this is not practical. First of all, there are a tremendous number of "paths" through a program, each of which must be tested (see Figure 10.1). When there are two sequential decisions, there are four basic paths through the program. In

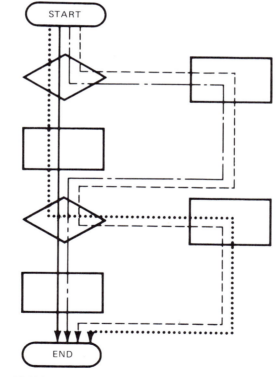

(a)

Figure 10.1(a) A simple sequential program with four paths.

the case of the example in Figure 10.1(b), there are still four paths; each additional binary decision doubles the number of potential paths in the program through the longest sequence of decisions. The total number of paths grows as 2^n, where n is the number of sequential decisions. Most programs are designed with n in the range of about 30 to a few hundred. If the number of decisions is a mere 50, the total number of paths may exceed 1,125,000,000,000,000! At the rate of one test case per microsecond, it would take over 35 years to run all the tests—*after* you have designed the 10^{15} test cases required and predicted the 10^{15} outputs you should expect.

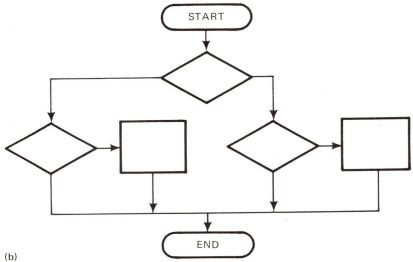

(b)

Figure 10.1(b)   A program with more decisions and therefore more paths that have to be tested.

Exhaustive testing is not practical. What we try to do is apply the principles of mathematical induction. If it works for beginning cases and it works for the end case, we can probably assume that the "middle" is safe. This kind of solution is tractable because we can declare "sets" of data to be within the range to elicit predictable behavior from the program, thus avoiding individual-value exhaustive testing.

Bugs Are Human

Computer programs are written by people, and people are still prone to making errors. In the software world these errors are called *bugs*. The process of finding and exterminating them is called *debugging*. The process of preventing them and of preventing their consequences when they do occur is called *defensive programming*, the principles of which have been embodied in the preceding chapters.

Before we can discuss how to catch and correct bugs, we ought to gain an understanding of the beast.

First, we must distinguish between mistakes and failures. Machines can have failures, but human beings make mistakes. Except for the occasional hardware glitch, most computers don't make "mistakes." Attributing the mistakes of the programmer to the computer is usually a sign of programmer immaturity.

A bug is called a bug only to preserve the sanity of the programmer. If all bugs were called what they really are—human blunders—the programmer's self-confidence would diminish to the vanishing point. Debugging really means self-criticizing because each bug can usually be traced to one or more "dumb" mistakes.

What Is a Bug?

In the loosest sense, a bug is any defect or imperfection that causes a program to exhibit undesirable behavior. In the dictionary sense, a bug is any defect or imperfection. Although the dictionary definition is globally acceptable, it is certainly not sufficient. Clearly, a misspelled comment in a program would not normally constitute what we call a bug in a computer program. Furthermore, a defect or imperfection in what? Should an erroneous paragraph in the user's documentation be considered a bug?

Bugs appear in computer programs (and in the data embodied in those programs). Therefore, if we define what a debugged computer program is, we define "bug" by implication. When a computer program that was previously declared to be debugged fails, what distinguishes this incident from prior incidents? Two possibilities exist: input data and environment. The environment includes the supporting software, the computer, and its input/output configuration. However, since these things change sufficiently infrequently, they are immediately suspect when a bug appears. The problem lies in the input data.

A debugged program, then, is one that has not yet been supplied with the input data or environment that will induce failure. This definition of a debugged program is not just an exercise in semantics; it can be extremely useful. The definition implies, for instance, that:

1. Software is untrustworthy (it might fail someday).
2. If input values are assured to lie within certain limits, then reliability can be assumed to be higher than if input validation doesn't exist.
3. If all else remains fixed (i.e., same program, same data), the environment must have changed.

The "debuggedness" of a program is often related to its specifications. That is, a program that meets all of its specifications is sometimes said to be debugged. However, since the specifications were written by an error-prone human, the specifications might also contain bugs.

The general rule about spending effort on design is important to bug reduction. You can't create tests for your software unless you are completely aware of the required behavior of the software—and you can't know that without complete and thorough design effort. That is why design flaws are so difficult to spot. The behavior of your program is not predictable because you don't know enough to predict it. Therefore, when bugs do occur, you are unequipped to find and exorcise them. Conversely, that is why implementation and coding errors are so easy to detect: the program's behavior doesn't match expectations (again, see Chapter 9).

Kinds of Bugs

Below are listed the five distinct kinds of bugs that can be identified:

1. Catastrophic
2. Major
3. Enhancement
4. Minor
5. Documentation

A catastrophic error makes the software virtually unusable. Most bugs that exist early in the program's life will be of this kind. Until the catastrophic errors are all corrected, the software is usually not released out of the programmer's hands.

A major error means that the software is usable, but in some degraded mode of operation. For example, some desirable feature may induce untoward side effects by corrupting data in memory. Until the error is corrected, this feature should be avoided. Major errors are usually found during the initial development stage, although a few may be found in field trials or other initial use by the customers.

A major enhancement is not really a bug, except in the end-user's mind. This kind of change to the software would so dramatically improve the behavior of the program that it should be incorporated. A major enhancement is usually the consequence of insufficient front-end design or is the result of initial experience with the new system on the part of the end-users.

Minor enhancements or error corrections are usually cosmetic in nature. Wording in printouts might be changed or minor inconveniences might be eliminated, but the system is completely usable as it stands. These are almost always the result of end-user comments on how they would change the system to improve its utility.

Documentation bugs are not of any lower priority than program bugs, but they don't require any modification in the programs themselves. The bug should be repaired especially if the documentation is used by newcomers to the software who may be misled in the future.

Testing Your Program

Choosing test cases can sometimes be as difficult as designing the program you are to test. But the problem is even further complicated by the fact that you need two distinct and different kinds of test cases. You need to create test cases that will exercise the various parts of a program during the design and implementation phase so that you can build confidence in the correctness of your program. And, before final delivery you need a separate set of user-oriented functional tests.

To test the program for correctness, you should start with a simple test case and build additional test cases to exercise various program paths. Design of these tests requires detailed knowledge of the interior design of the program. An example is useful: In Chapter 9 we operated upon coefficients and an independent variable of a polynomial. The proper choice of initial input data values to exercise the *least* part of the program might have led to the input dialog of Figure 10.2.

WHAT ARE THE COEFFICIENTS A, B AND C?   <u>0, 1, 0</u>

WHAT ARE THE LOWER AND UPPER BOUNDS OF X?   <u>1, 10</u>

Figure 10.2   Very simple test cases should be tried first to verify the main program flow.

We have supplied the coefficients and range of the variable so that our equation is linear:

$$y = 0x^2 + 1x + 0 = y = x$$

This purely linear equation will cause a single (approximately) straight line to be drawn diagonally across the graph. This simple test verifies the main flow of the program, that it computes different values of y that are dependent on x, and that an appropriate range of values of x and y are plotted.

There are limits to how simple the initial test case may be. In our example, for instance, it is not permissible to set the polynomial to a constant by providing values of zero for both a and b coefficients because it would result in an infinitely small graduation scale on the y-axis. And the upper and lower bounds of x may not be equal because of the same problem. If we had tried that simple case, our computer system would have reported that we attempted division by zero, which is not allowed. (Follow the program logic of Figure 9.4 to see why division by zero would have been attempted.)

Sometimes it is useful to restrict the program that is being tested. If the volume of output data is too large to cope with, you might want to change the important variables' values to limit the amount you will have to look at. The number of cells along the x- and y-axes are good examples of this kind of restriction. Changing the values of **X1** and **Y1** (number of cells on the x- and y-axes, respectively) from 50 and 60 to 5 and 5 would allow you a "quick peek" at your program's operation. Later, after the basic things are working, you can remove the restriction and resume normal operation. Be sure to conduct *some* testing with the restrictions removed just to be sure.

After the main flow of the program has been debugged, you can move on to more complicated things. Although the example we used in Chapter 9 doesn't have any other paths to check, most programs do. Using a master listing of the program and colored pencil or pen, draw a vertical line down the page next to all the statements your main-flow tests exercised. The unmarked statements will need separate verification. The untested statement sequences will always be headed by some conditional statement; you need merely select a test case that will cause flow to be thrown to the untested group. As you complete each test, mark your listing.

Each and every test case must be made under the premise that you know what the outcome will be. If you can't completely predict your program's behavior, how can you be certain that it is operating correctly? Sometimes the sheer amount of data makes manual computation of test case results impractical. If it does, you can usually find a way to automate the process. If you are writing a program to process large numeric matrices (say, to solve systems of simultaneous equations), you may find the effort required to work through (say, invert) a 300 by 300 matrix too much to contemplate. Nevertheless, there are things you *can* do: You can verify that the program works for matrices of ranks 1, 2, and 3, for these *can* be easily sorted out manually. You can also use the standard test matrices available from sources like the Association for Computing Machinery. If your program inverts a large matrix, you can reinvert the results to see how it compares with the original data; you could even print out a difference matrix if and only if the differences exceed some given tolerance. You could multiply the inverse by the original matrix to see that you get the identity matrix.

After you have tested main flow and alternate flow, you must verify your algorithms—is what you are computing correct? In each algorithm there are typically turning points. In the approximation of trigonometric functions, for example, factors of pi are often involved. Your test cases should not necessarily be evenly distributed. You should exploit the algorithm. Your test cases should have lots of "density" around zero, $\pi/8, \pi/4,$ and $\pi/12$, or whatever other factors your program uses.

The boundaries should also be checked. What happens if extremely small or large numbers are used as input data? And what happens if absolute "garbage" is supplied as data? The grossly erroneous data filtering should have been handled when alternate flow paths were checked, since bad data would have exercised another path. But the boundaries represent another problem. If your program uses calendar dates, you should verify that the program won't accept over 31 days in any month, that it won't accept over 30 days in "September, April, June and November," and that leap year is accounted for in February. Your test cases should include values near the boundary (but valid), just at the boundary (both valid and invalid sides), and beyond the boundary (in this case, also be sure to test for a calendar date less than 1).

Performance Testing

To push the program to its limits, another kind of test is often required, especially if the program is to be used in a real-time environment. If lists are used in your program, you should create a test case so wild that it will exhaust the list space. Then, you can verify that your program behaves reliably when all space is consumed in memory. This test case often requires nothing more than the same input data repeated over and over until the program becomes saturated. Sometimes you can't afford to create this test data because it is complex and voluminous. In these cases, the procedure that you use for accepting input data can be temporarily replaced by another subroutine that synthesizes the data according to some rules. Of course, you must be sure that your synthetic input data producer is debugged, and for that reason the producer program should be as simple as you can make it.

If your software accepts inputs in real-time, you should snythesize some way of generating more inputs than you ever expect to have to accept and then driving the program into saturation. Sometimes you have to program another computer to generate this data. This procedure is called *stimulation testing*. You can verify that your intended actions take place (say, ignoring excessive inputs and completely processing accepted inputs before taking in any more). If your program "gives up," you lose!

How Much Testing Is Enough?

The ultimate measure of how much testing is enough is rooted in the end-user's confidence in the program. If you cannot gain the user's confidence, your program will never be used. Elegant theories are beginning to appear in the technical literature, but nobody is sure yet how one decides to stop testing.

The converse, however, is well understood. Divide your program into "pages" of about fifty lines each. If you detect more than an average of one bug per page, you should probably throw the program out and start over because it is symptomatic of a poorly understood and therefore poorly written program. Rewriting with the benefit of hindsight will result in a better program and less risk (since you have no idea how many additional bugs may be lurking within the original poor code).

Remember, testing can only show the *presence* of bugs, not their *absence*.

Functional Testing

The testing (around the borders and into saturation) that we have discussed so far brush against the requirements for functional testing that must be done independently of the tests you conducted to make the software work. Functional tests should be conducted by someone who is more familiar with the application than the programmer is but who is less familiar with the internal program organization.

These tests should probably be "worst case." It is almost a game: The test designer should try to outwit the programmer and find faults *before* the program is placed into production use. You, as programmer, should not fear these tests, unless you did only a few trivial program tests of your own. For your own sake, it is better to test your program and then let the end-user perform the functional tests. If your program is robust, the end-user will have vast confidence in your program (and, by implication, in you for having written such a fine program).

Bug Diagnosis

Diagnosis of a bug depends exclusively on information. Theoretically, debugging can proceed with nothing more than a listing of the complete program and some data. In practice, the programmer lets the computer do some of the work. The input data is handled by the program, and if the outputs and recorded side effects are acceptable, a lot of desk checking can be avoided. However, when the results of the execution are unacceptable and a bug is detected, then the programmer engages in diagnosis.

The first step is to confirm that a problem actually exists. If you wrongly predicted the outcome of a test, the expected behavior of the program will not obtain —because of your error in output prediction, not because of a bug in the program. Before you invest hours in tracking down a bug, you should demonstrate to your satisfaction that it does exist.

The amount of information needed to isolate a problem is astonishingly small. In most cases, a bug is reflected in a few bits, bytes, or words of incorrect data values. Unfortunately, if you haven't the foggiest idea of which data items will be most useful in bug isolation, you will be tempted to display any data values that might be remotely involved with the problem. Debugging is a cerebral exercise, and some thought as to the nature of the problem will save hours of unnecessary work spent chasing elusive trends of logic induced by vast amounts of print out.

As soon as you find a troublesome test case, *save it*. During the diagnostic process, especially if the bug is elusive, you may simplify your test cases in order to get closer to the problem, but the original test case that exposed the bug should be rerun after you have fixed the program. If the reduction of the input data makes the bug disappear, you have new positive information about the nature of the problem.

Diagnosis Strategies

Isolating the place where a fault exists in a program is the major part of diagnosis. Once we know where to look, we can usually spot the necessary corrections easily. However, when we are faced with a few thousand lines of unfamiliar code, the basic debugging diagnosis strategies need to be invoked.

The *deductive* approach uses measurements to isolate the problem area. Picking some data point near the middle of the flow we verify the correctness of the data. If it is correct (and we have measured the right thing, of course) then our problem is further down the flow. In the plotting program of Chapter 9 we might have examined the contents of the Y-array to determine whether the values stored there "looked" reasonable. If not, the problem is before that point.

The *inductive* approach hacks away at the problem from both ends: The initial entry conditions for a piece of code are examined, and the exit values are checked. If the produced values don't "square" with the inputs, we have isolated the problem. We then continue the inductive approach, isolating the problem step by step, by looking at ever-smaller pieces of the program.

In most cases, we will use both techniques alternately. We might start with a simple midpoint test and isolate the faulty region and then apply the inductive approach until we narrow down the scope of the problem. Usually, when we get to within a single page of the hypothesized problem area, we should find the bug manually by desk checking our code. We are given the opportunity to review the robustness of the design and we should take it.

Debugging Decisions

Each small step in diagnosis is a decision that is based on some data about the behavior of the program. If the data exists, then some concrete decision ("well, it's not in there") can be made. If the progam's behavior under the conditions of interest is not known, two courses of action are left:

1. Ignore the decision.
2. Make the decision anyway.

The process involves dividing the program into two parts: the part that potentially involves the bug and the part that does not. Hopefully, successive iterations will make the first part smaller and the second part larger.

If you don't have enough data to make a concrete decision, you can either instrument your program to collect that data or you can perform a manual simu-

Program Instrumentation

Software, like hardware, can have *test points*. But in software the test points are usually removed (or disabled) when the program is used in production. During the debugging phase, however, instrumentation can be invaluable.

The simplest kind of instrumentation of a program is the addition of judiciously selected PRINT statements. This is especially useful if your program fails without producing significant output so that you can track down the problem. You can add PRINT statements to your program to print out important values for later analysis. Since much of what you print out may be valueless (the values are generally valid), you should consider using IF statements to select invalid data that is to be printed.

Good programmers instrument their programs liberally, and they use a variable (typically named DBUG) to switch the instrumentation on and off. By changing the value of DBUG (either by modifying the source code, reading in some special input sequence, or patching a location in memory), they can turn on the extra printouts as required. The instrumentation stays in the program forever.

The residual instrumentation has hero-producing potential as well. If a bug crops up in field trials or functional tests, you can easily enable the debugging instrumentation to help find the problem. If the features of the software are such that you need more execution time or memory space, you can reach into your program and remove the redundant instrumentation—instant hero!

lation of the program and trace each statement from some given starting data. If the suspected part of the program is very large, you will probably want to use instrumentation.

Manual simulation of a program commonly gets novices into trouble because they are tempted to take shortcuts that produce misleading results. The preferable strategy is to rerun the program with necessary instrumentation. However, this may not lead to the debugging dichotomizing decision either, since the new diagnostic statements added to the program will have to be debugged. In a real-time system mere addition of instrumentation may cause the time-dependent problem to disappear.

Every decision made in diagnosis is tentative. This statement ought to be framed on your wall. Every decision is tentative. Every decision is subject to reconsideration in light of paradox. Each time you are faced with a paradoxical situation ("That just can't happen in this program!"), then the set of decisions made while arriving at that point must be reconsidered. If all those decisions can be justified, no paradox exists.

To assist in deciding which particular decisions were made, it is useful to make notes directly on the program listing. If a quick scan and review of the decisions don't yield a solution, you ought to go back to the top—or some other place where you are *absolutely* confident that everything works. Then follow the flow of the program until you come to the place where the paradox exists. In order to avoid skipping over some program areas that seem to be "obviously correct," it is sometimes a good idea to go through these steps with someone else. While you are reading your program aloud and explaining what is going on, you will often find the problem.

Bug Isolation

Isolating a bug, although it appears easy, is not a trivial task. Unfortunately, the bug is not necessarily in the obvious place. The first place to look, of course, is at any changes that have been made recently. Usually, minor changes to programs induce side effects that show up as other bugs. Always look to the recent changes first.

Change only one thing at a time. If you change too many things at once, a new bug may appear.

In most cases, a subroutine or other program unit can be pinpointed as the culprit. The clue is usually some unusual input or output data. Each procedure in your program can be tested and debugged by verifying that the inputs are always valid, that the outputs produced are always valid, and that the appropriate side effects are the only ones that occur.

If an offending procedure *is* located, the search should not stop because there might be two or more bad procedures.

Kinds of Errors

After you have located the site of the problem, look for obvious programming errors. The valid range of input values, the proper sequence of statements, or the syntax of the statements themselves may lead to changes that will make it necessary for you to correct the program.

All data values should be initialized prior to use. When you analyze a procedure, be sure that every argument supplied to the procedure has been initialized with a valid value prior to the procedure invocation. Similarly, for the independent variables inside the procedure, be sure that values are set before they are fetched for use. And be sure that output values being passed back up to the calling procedure are all getting set validly.

Next, make sure that you are dealing with the correct data. If an array contains subscripts that range from 0 to 99 and if the procedure that operates upon this array assumes subscripts ranging from 1 to 100, you will get some strange results. Each loop should be checked that both the first and last iterations are performed with valid values for the induction variable. Check to see that you haven't misspelled any of the symbols in your program. Good programming practice calls for similarly named variables for similar kinds of objects. The bug we found in Chapter 9 that caused limited use of the *y*-axis was induced because we typed in X1 instead of Y1.

Has data been executed or are your instructions being used as data? On Princeton class computers that have common store for both programs and data, some instructions can treat other instructions as data, modifying them and thus causing very strange flow paths that are outside those you might expect. You should not execute data and you should not modify instructions. These practices are especially problematical in microcomputers in which programs are often stored in ROM's or PROM's: The program works fine from RAM during debugging, even though it modifies itself, but when the program is stored in read-only memory, it no longer works. Most programmers begin by suspecting the PROM's or the PROM programming equipment instead of the true problem.

Interfaces are another rich source of bugs, especially the interfaces between procedures. Unless they are adequately documented at the outset (and rigorously applied), minor changes in interface specifications between procedures and their dependent programs can cause huge bugs. You must confirm that all the input data required is supplied to the procedure and that the procedure supplies all of the required outputs. For example, if the address of a variable is to be supplied to a procedure, and if the calling program assumes that the variable is never modified, you might pass the address of a constant (say, 3.14159). Now, if because the interface specifications weren't settled and the procedure *does* modify the variable, the rest of your program that depends on the value of pi will exhibit pathological behavior.

Diagnostic Environment

Your tools for program diagnosis range from the source listing to some rather sophisticated software aids (and for real-time problems, even the new Logic Analyzers). The language translators (compilers and assemblers) can provide much useful information, most of which is useful in your desk-checking phase. The assembly listings of actual object code from compilers are valuable when you are trying to relate some suspicious memory contents back to your original source program.

Language translators can offer useful cross-reference listings, but they are usually provided only on the larger computers. The names of all the variables in a program are listed alphabetically, and some identification of the statements that use these variables are printed out. If you suspect that a particular variable is being modified erroneously, this list can help you find all the places that set values into that space.

Breakpoints are usually provided by a debugging monitor program. A breakpoint enables you to "plant a trap" in your program. When execution reaches that point it is interrupted. If you are at a terminal, you can examine various memory locations in order to isolate the problem; this is the main advantage of programming at a terminal. If you are remote from the computer itself, you may have to use the breakpoint for *snapshots* of memory contents.

A snapshot of memory is a quick display of a few selected registers or memory locations. You can use them to trace the changes in values from iteration to iteration. On large computers where you do not have the luxury of being on-line, snapshots are not very useful because you don't know what data to examine and you can't change your strategy during program execution. On large computers you usually just get a *dump* of memory. A dump is a printout of your entire memory contents, usually in octal or hex, from which you are expected to obtain your information.

But even a dump (in the absence of anything better) can be useful. Use it like a map. If you look from the dump to your program, you are lost. But if you look from your program to the dump (to verify that certain values are as you anticipated them to be), you are doing diagnosis.

Review Your Progress

You may eventually realize that the level of detail to which you have descended is not getting you anywhere. Here the experienced programmer begins to question his own debugging process. Each decision point is mentally reviewed, and each one is subjected to new quality tests to be certain that some other likely avenues haven't been left unchecked.

11

Other Programming Languages

Although BASIC is a very popular language, especially among casual users of computers, it is not the only language. There are hundreds of programming languages, each with a different set of features, each enjoying a different sized corps of dedicated users. Some companies even develop special-purpose languages just for their own needs; government agencies frequently do.

Hope springs eternal in the breast of management that someday there might be just one computer programming language. There are many advantages, including program portability among competing computer products, the survival through multiple generations of computer innovation, standardized texts and training for staff, and higher reliability of resulting software. However, all attempts in the first 30 years of computers have met with failure. It is not yet possible to standardize on one single programming language, although it can be done in limited contexts.

The federal government, led by the Department of Defense, tried to standardize on COBOL exclusively a few years back. But that language's name (*Co*mmon *B*usiness-*O*riented *L*anguage) hints at the problem: The language is suited for conventional kinds of commercial data processing applications common to management, but it doesn't have the facilities one would like to have for efficient scientific computations, or detailed bit-by-bit control needed in process control, or very sophisticated communications capabilities required in latter-day applications.

The "standard" list of "approved" languages now includes seven, most of which will be reviewed in this chapter. But why should you know about all these language? Will you have to learn to program in each of them? No, you won't learn how to program in every language, although serious programmers know a dozen or more languages well enough to be productive. You must know which languages are available so that you can choose the best tool among those available. Think of programming languages as logic families: You are used to selecting among TTL, DTL, CMOS, and ECL; now think in terms of BASIC, FORTRAN, COBOL, and APL.

You really can't choose the *wrong* language. You can only choose an inconvenient one. You can solve any of the interesting problems you are likely to find in any of these languages. The issue is one of convenience. If you must spend lots of time writing statements to compensate for some lack in the language, you could have chosen a better language. For example, given the problem of inverting a matrix, the FORTRAN or COBOL programmer would set out to write a matrix-inverting routine. The experienced BASIC programmer would know that the language *has* matrix inversion built-in. The programmer with knowledge of both would be able to choose at the appropriate time.

More BASIC

Before we examine the other languages you might run into, you ought to learn more about BASIC. In Chapter 8 we introduced a ten-statement subset of the entire language. Many of the more powerful features were suppressed in that discussion in order to avoid obscuring the essential basis of the language and techniques for its use. Now, without being exhaustive, we will expose the feature-laden side of BASIC.

There are many fundamental capabilities of BASIC that we ignored earlier. We said that BASIC was limited to dealing with the set of floating-point numbers, which was true in the original version of the language. However, when BASIC began to be used outside the classroom, this restriction was too severe. Therefore, the ability to handle the data type made up of "strings" of ASCII characters was added. An example of *string* expressions compared with conventional arithmetic assignments is shown in Figure 11.1. Note that the variables that contain strings are unique in that they include a dollar sign at the end. When the string variable

```
1000   LET A = 6                          1000   LET A$ = "STRING"
1010   LET B = 9                          1010   LET B$ = "THIS IS A"
1020   PRINT A + B                        1020   PRINT B$; " "; A$
1030   REM                                1030   REM
1040   REM    NOW, ADD NUMBERS            1040   REM NOW, CONCATENATE STRINGS
1050   REM                                1050   REM
1060   LET Z = A + 4 + B                  1060   LET Z$ = B$ & "NOTHER  " & A$
1070   PRINT Z                            1070   PRINT Z$
1080   END                                1080   END

         (a)                                        (b)
```

Figure 11.1 (a) A simple BASIC program for handling numbers, compared with (b), a similar program that deals with character strings of text. The "&" operator joins two strings of characters together (concatenation).

appears in a print statement, it is printed out character by character. Since you can modify string contents during execution, you can actually process textual data.

One use of strings is to describe the way you want data formatted for printing. When you provide a PRINT statement with a USING clause (see Figure 11.2), the string that follows the word USING is used to specify how numbers are to be formatted and printed out. In this particular example, A will be printed out as a five-digit integer, B will be printed in dollars and cents, and C$ will be printed as ten successive characters. The specific rules for the string that describes the data formatting can be found in any good book on BASIC. They are too complex to introduce here.

```
2000   LET Z$ = "  #####   $##,###.##   ##########"
2010   .
       .
       .
2800   PRINT USING Z$, A, B, C$
2810   .
       .
       .
```

Figure 11.2 A brief example of controlled-formatting of data on BASIC, especially valuable for getting columns of data printed out.

If you had to type in all of the data required by your programs every time you used them, you would probably have lots of errors (and sore fingers). Worse, you would limit the scope of the problems you were willing to tackle. Most contemporary BASIC translators offer the ability to read and write data stored in tape or disc files.

In the simplest kind of file-oriented input/output the INPUT and PRINT statements are augmented with names of files that exist on some storage medium. In the BASIC system implemented at Dartmouth College (considered among BASIC buffs to be the origin of the language), files are assigned both names and numbers (see Figure 11.3). The INPUT and PRINT statements use these numbers

```
1000   REM
1010   REM        DECLARE ALL OF THE FILES WE'LL NEED
1020   REM
1030   FILE # 1: "APPLES"
1040   FILE # 2: "ORANGES"
1050   REM
1060   REM READ IN THE NEXT RECORD
1070   REM
1080   INPUT # 1: A, B, C, D$
1090   REM
1100   REM WRITE OUT A COPY OF THE RECORD
1110   PRINT # 2: USING "### ### ### #####", A, B, C, D$
1120   GO TO 1080
1130   END
```

Figure 11.3 A simple little data-copying program in BASIC that deals with two files named APPLES and ORANGES.

to refer to the files. There must be some complex operating systems software (see Chapter 13) that can find files by name on the disc or tape backing store.

Often random-access file capabilities are also included in BASIC. These statements allow individual records in a file to be read and written without having to "pass" all of the records in a sequential file. This means, for instance, that you can accept INPUT from the terminal in any order and update master file records in that order instead of insisting that the operator precisely order all of the input data first.

One of the nicest features of BASIC is its inherent inclusion of statements that will manipulate matrices. If you frequently deal with linear networks or simultaneous equations, you will appreciate these features. You can add or subtract two like-shaped matrices, which you can use instead of having to write detailed loop-control statements. But BASIC also provides for true matrix multiplication and matrix inversion. Several examples of BASIC matrix statements are shown in Figure 11.4. And in most BASICs you can also store and retrieve matrices of strings.

```
1010    DIM A (50, 50), B (50, 50), C (50, 50)
1020    REM
1030    REM MAKE A AN IDENTITY MATRIX, 30 BY 40
1040    REM
1050    MAT A = IDN
1060    REM
1070    REM READ IN CONTENTS FOR THE B MATRIX
1080    REM
1090    MAT INPUT B (30, 40)
1100    REM
1110    REM TRANSPOSE B
1120    REM
1130    MAT A = TRN(B)
1140    REM
1150    REM DOUBLE VALUES OF ENTRIES IN B MATRIX
1160    REM
1170    MAT B = B + B
1180    REM
1190    REM MULTIPLY THE TWO MATRICES
1200    REM
1210    MAT C = A*B
1220    REM
1230    REM INVERT THE C MATRIX
1240    REM
1250    MAT A = INV(C)
1260    REM
1270    REM PRINT OUT THE RESULT
1280    REM
1290    MAT PRINT A
1300    END
```

Figure 11.4   A nonsense program to demonstrate the features of matrix arithmetic in BASIC.

Why Select BASIC?

BASIC is a good language to use if your needs are casual and if you don't have to have primitive control over input/output devices. Because of the nature of the language, it is seldom used for large programs over about 1,000 lines of code. It is usually provided on small computers, and it is becoming popular on microcomputer systems.

The language suffers mostly from the fact that every implementer feels that BASIC is fair game for language improvements. Many of the powerful features of BASIC are significantly different from translator to translator. The minicomputer companies have done a more rational job of sticking to the model laid down by Dartmouth College. Most of the micro-based BASIC interpreters are written by small software houses that have limited compiler-writing experience; thus, the quality varies drastically.

The best reference on BASIC will be found in Stephen V. F. Waite and Diane G. Mather's *BASIC*.[1] Written by one of the author's of Dartmouth's BASIC system, this is the best book for learning the language. For formal specifications, see the proposed ANSI standard definition of BASIC.[2]

Fortran IV

BASIC was developed because FORTRAN was too difficult to teach. Although the language is more powerful than FORTRAN, many of the concepts are difficult for novices to grasp. If you have to deal with very precise numbers or with complex arithmetic, FORTRAN may be the best language to choose.

FORTRAN comes in numbered varieties. FORTRAN I (the first FORmula TRANslator) was developed at IBM to prove the point that a compiler that generated efficient code *could* be developed. Many pundits of the late 1950's scoffed at the idea. But the research tool proved so valuable that it became the *de facto* language for large scientific and engineering programming establishments. A few years later FORTRAN II was developed to delete unused language features and to add the important concept of subroutines, which had been excluded from the first effort. Later FORTRAN IV came along (nobody seems to know what happened to FORTRAN III). Today, FORTRAN II is known as ANSI Basic FORTRAN (which confuses some people) and ANSI FORTRAN. The basic version of FORTRAN has many restrictions, but it is generally a subset of the full FORTRAN language. The standards (available from the American National Standards Institute in New York City) describe the features of what constitute valid statements in the FORTRAN language(s).

---

[1] (Hanover, N.H.: University Press of New England, 1972.)

[2] Available from Computer and Business Equipment Manufacturer's Association, 1828 L. Street N.W., Washington, D.C.

Much of FORTRAN looks a lot like BASIC (see Figure 11.5) because BASIC was modeled on FORTRAN. But the complex details of, for instance, FORMAT statements, confuse novices. The FORMAT statements, which describe input and output data, are certainly more powerful than BASIC's USING clause, but they also demand much more careful attention.

```
C
C    THIS IS A SIMPLE FORTRAN PROGRAM TO
C        READ IN DATA, SEARCH FOR A VALUE
C        AND REPORT WHETHER IT WAS FOUND.
C
         DIMENSION ARRAY (1000)
C    READ INPUT DATA
         READ (10, 701) N, (ARRAY(I), I = 1, N)
    701  FORMAT (I 5, 150 (8/8F10.2) )
C    READ IN THE ARGUMENT
         READ (5, 702)  ARG
    702  FORMAT(F10.2)
C    SEARCH FOR THE ARGUMENT IN THE LIST
         DO 100 I = 1, N
             IF (ARG .EQ. ARRAY(I) ) GO TO 250
    100  CONTINUE
C    DIDN'T FIND IT
         PRINT 703, ARG, N
    703  FORMAT (14H COULDN'T FIND ,F10.2,  4H IN  ,I3,  7H ITEMS.)
         STOP
C    FOUND IT
    250  PRINT 704, ARG, I
    704  FORMAT  (6H FOUND ,F10.2,19H IN ELEMENT NUMBER ,I3)
         END
```

Figure 11.5 A simple FORTRAN program, illustrating the additional complexity required over BASIC.

The FORTRAN statements do not have to be numbered (and, obviously, lines that start with "C" are comments). The DIMENSION statement is like BASIC's DIM, except that spelled-out names may be used instead of letters and single digits. In this example, ARRAY is the name of a 1,000-element array of real numbers (floating-point). Other variables used in this example are ARG, N, and I. Any symbol that starts with I, J, K, L, M, or N is automatically assumed to be an interger; all others are floating-point numbers. In addition to the DIMENSION declaration, you can name a datum and assign it the type COMPLEX for handling the imaginary part. For highly precise numbers, you can declare that twice as many bits are to be used to store the value. A recent addition to the standard also allows the CHARACTER data type to be declared so that strings can be easily handled.

FORTRAN has a powerful subroutine invocation scheme that permits the creation of separate subprograms that are merged later during a system integration phase. Each subroutine is generally compiled separately from the main program and then the subroutines are all linked together by part of the systems software called a *linking loader* (see Chapter 13). Each subroutine may have arguments declared (see Figure 11.6). When the subroutine is invoked, these values are effectively replaced by the values supplied in the calling program. This powerful feature is also capable of being severely abused and it causes numerous subtle program bugs during testing.

```
C
C    THE MAIN PROGRAM
C
         A = 5.3
         B = 7.0
         CALL SUM (C, A, B)
      10 CALL SUM (C, C, B)
C    CONTINUE UNTIL C IS NO LONGER LESS THAN 100
         IF (C .LT. 100.0) GO TO 10
         PRINT 709, C
     709 FORMAT (8H SUM IS , F4.1)
         END
C
C    THE "SUM" PROCEDURE
C
         SUBROUTINE SUM (RESULT, X, Y)
            RESULT = X + Y
            RETURN
         END
```

Figure 11.6   The arguments of the subroutine in FORTRAN are effectively replaced by the values supplied when the subroutine is invoked.

Many of the restrictions that exist in FORTRAN were induced by history. On the computer used to implement the first FORTRAN compiler, for example, there was no character on the printer for the quotation mark (ASCII hadn't been invented yet). Therefore, the designers defined *Hollerith constants,* which begin with a number and are followed by the letter "H" and then the number of characters specified by the leading number (e.g., 5HABCDE). Not only is this difficult to read and write, but it is prone to errors. Many FORTRAN compilers permit quotation marks around strings, but many still do not. Other more severe restrictions will be discovered as you begin to study that language.

Why Select FORTRAN?

FORTRAN is often the only language taught in engineering schools. For many professional programmers, it may be the only language with which they have had any real experience. FORTRAN is used daily in thousands of installations to implement very small and very large programs. Even entire compilers (one for FORTRAN) have been written in the language. Program sizes over 100,000 lines of code written by large teams are not uncommon.

Since FORTRAN is almost always compiled, it is usually provided only on the large computers (although at least one FORTRAN exists for the 8080). Most minicomputers offer FORTRAN, but you may have to use a larger configuration to gain access to its facilities. The compilers for FORTRAN are complex because of some difficulties with the language that are too complex to discuss here. Because of the vast array of features provided in the language, the compilers must be able to handle all of them and therefore they are generally twice the size of comparable BASIC compilers (which, in turn, are larger than comparable interpreters in most cases).

Despite claims for other languages, FORTRAN allows the highest portability among computers. If you write your programs in accordance with the standard, you are almost guaranteed of being able to compile it on whatever computer you may select (provided, of course, that it has a FORTRAN translator). The tendency to embellish the language that burdens BASIC is not apparent in FORTRAN. If the underlying computer has some unique capability, the vendor often adds a few statements to the FORTRAN language to exploit it, but use of these statements is optional. Many FORTRAN programmers, especially engineers and designers, maintain personal libraries of finished and tested programs in portable form. They get carried from project to project and from job to job.

Once you become proficient in FORTRAN, you can write highly complex programs almost as easily as you can write equivalent software in BASIC, but getting there is part of the problem. Probably the best introduction in recent years is R.C. Holt and J. N. P. Hume's *Fundamentals of Structured Programming Using FORTRAN.*[3] The FORTRAN standards are ANSI X3.9 (the main language) and ANSI X3.10 (Basic FORTRAN).

COBOL

COBOL grew out of early Department of Defense efforts to develop one standardized language for all applications so that the DOD could remain independent of particular computer models and makers. It hasn't worked out that way, but the advantages in personnel training and long-term maintenance of large, complex software systems have justified the effort. Today, many commercial establishments (banks and insurance firms) virtually prohibit the use of any other language. You may find that the standard of your own employer's EDP department may prohibit the use of other languages. You should not be roped into COBOL, however, unless your applications can be successfully written on it.

COBOL is especially good at handling lots of small pieces of similar kinds of data, as are typically found in commercial and industrial data files. COBOL is oriented toward the reading and writing of complicated data records and arranging them in storage for easy processing. The processing capabilities are relatively meager, and subroutines are an obvious afterthought in the design. A typical COBOL program is shown in Figure 11.7.

[3](Reston, Va.: Reston Publishing Company, 1976.)

```
IDENTIFICATION DIVISION.
     PROGRAM-ID.   SEARCHER.
ENVIRONMENT DIVISION.
     CONFIGURATION SECTION.
     SOURCE-COMPUTER.     IBM 360.
     OBJECT-COMPUTER.     IBM 360.
     FILE CONTROL.
          SELECT INPUT-DATA ASSIGN TO TAPE-1.
          SELECT TERMINAL ASSIGN TO CRT-1.
DATA DIVISION.
FILE SECTION
FD   INPUT-DATA
     LABEL RECORDS ARE OMITTED.
01   SIZE-RECORD.
     02    N                PICTURE 99999.
01   DATA-BLOCK.
     02    DATA-VALUE       PICTURE 9(8)V2
                    OCCURS 5 TIMES.
FD   TERMINAL
     LABEL RECORDS ARE OMITTED.
01   ARGUMENT.
     02    ARG              PICTURE 9(8)V2.
WORKING-STORAGE SECTION.
77   I                     PICTURE 999.
77   M                     PICTURE 999.
01   DATA-LIST.
     02    ARRAY            PICTURE 9(8)V2
               OCCURS 1000 TIMES.
PROCEDURE DIVISION.
START-UP.
     OPEN INPUT INPUT-DATA, TERMINAL.
READ-INPUT-DATA.
     READ SIZE-RECORD.
     MOVE 6 TO M.
     PERFORM READ-TABLE-ITEM
               VARYING I FROM 1 BY 1
                    UNTIL I GREATER THAN N.
     READ ARGUMENT.
SEARCH-TABLE.
     MOVE 1 TO I.
     SEARCH DATA-LIST VARYING I
          WHEN I EXCEEDS N, NEXT SENTENCE
          WHEN ARG EQUALS ARRAY (I) GO TO FOUND.
     DISPLAY "CAN'T FIND",ARG,"IN",N,"ITEMS".
     STOP RUN.
FOUND.
     DISPLAY "FOUND",ARG,"AT ELEMENT NUMBER",I.
     STOP RUN.
READ-TABLE-ITEM.
     IF M GREATER THAN 5
          READ DATA-BLOCK THEN
          MOVE 1 TO M.
     MOVE DATA-VALUE (M) TO ARRAY (I).
```

Figure 11.7 Although COBOL programs are lengthy, they are also easy to read—especially the PROCEDURE DIVISION entries.

A COBOL program is broken up into DIVISIONS. The first division (ENVIRONMENT) describes the computer, the second (DATA) describes *all* the data, and the last (PROCEDURE) describes the actual program. The entire program is generally written as a unit, typically up to a few thousand lines. Because of all the data descriptions, small COBOL programs don't exist. COBOL is definitely *not* for use if you are writing "quickie" programs that you don't intend to keep around for a long time.

COBOL offers many more options in the description of commercially oriented data. The descriptions themselves are necessarily more complicated and lengthy. After the data is described, the PROCEDURE division can almost be read. In this particular example no special care was taken to add a lot of the "noise" words that make the programs even more readable. Although there is a comment capability in the language, it is seldom used for that reason.

Subroutines are invoked by the PERFORM verb, which may pass no arguments. In fact, since all of the data in the program is declared in one place (the DATA division), all the data is global to the program. This often induces subtle bugs because one subroutine's side effects cannot be insulated from another's.

Files are handled by naming them and then describing all of the different kinds of records they may have. Files must be OPEN'd before they are used for READ or WRITE operations, and then they must be CLOSE'd at the end. Data can be DISPLAY'd on a computer terminal or the computer's console.

The power of COBOL is in its ability to cast large, complex, and common activities into a single verb in the language. In other languages searching involves writing complex loops of code, especially if the items being compared are in any way complicated. In COBOL the SEARCH verb (see Figure 11.7) is provided as a means of performing a table search. Similarly, huge data bases can be resorted into a completely different order with a single sentence that begins with the SORT verb.

Why Select COBOL?

If your program will have to manipulate several data files but perform rather simple-minded processing on each record, COBOL may be the best language for the job. If the data files are complicated and are used by many other jobs for other purposes, it is almost certainly a COBOL job. But the cost for producing COBOL code is significantly higher than for producing more compact notations, and long development times are not uncommon. The kinds of problems COBOL is applied to also influence lengthening schedules because these problems are often fraught with unforeseen complications.

If you have to handle large amounts of floating-point computations, COBOL is not your best language. If your problem is so ill-defined that you expect to make many iterations over the program to improve it, COBOL will be difficult to use because the program's structure is so difficult to ferret out from all the COBOL verbiage.

COBOL isn't COBOL either. The ANSI standard X3.23 for COBOL was dated 1961 and 1968. The latter became the standard of the 1970's, and it is what most manufacturers supply with their computers. In 1974 ANSI approved revisions and made a new COBOL: 1974. Unlike the current FORTRAN proposed standard upgrades, COBOL 1974 makes many COBOL 1968 programs subject to change. Many of the older programs won't be able to be processed with new translators. And COBOL will probably be revised *again* in 1979. The developer of long-lived software should be wary.

COBOL translators are almost always compilers because the customers want efficient object programs that are going to be used for hours and hours each day. Almost any large mainframe computer company that intends to sell computers must provide COBOL today. The minicomputer companies have begun to offer COBOL compilers, and several small software houses offer COBOL for popular minis. COBOL has even been implemented for compiling 8080 microprocessor programs on a minicomputer (although we can't imagine what you would use it for).

In an attempt to define well-structured subsets of the language, the COBOL standard establishes several different configurations of verbs and data descriptions. Unfortunately, the number of valid configurations means that many COBOL translators are mutually incompatible. The COBOL for the microprocessors is a variant. It is not COBOL at all.

If COBOL is your choice, you might start with reading Claude J. DeRossi's *Learning COBOL Fast.*[4] It treats the most common subset of the language and it is applicable to both COBOL 1968 and 1974. We don't recommend obtaining the standard, but if you are a masochist, order X3.28–1974 from CBEMA.

APL

APL is derived from the title of IBM-er Kenneth Iverson's book, *A Programming Language.*[5] The book describes what is essentially a single coherent notation for describing mathematics, sequential computer operations, and other diverse operations. It is extremely compact, but once you get the "hang of it," it is easy to write. Most of APL is based on concepts that bear little resemblance to the structure of this design course.

APL programmer/users are encouraged to sit at their terminals and compose "throw-away" programs as required instead of implementing large complexes of specialized programs. As APL "functions" (functional equivalent to our subroutines or procedures) are created to fulfill needs, they are filed away in such a

[4](Reston, Va.: Reston Publishing Company, 1975.)
[5](New York, NY: John Wiley & Sons, Inc., 1966.)

manner as to provide an instant extension to the language. Except that the system's functions are symbols and your functions are spelled-out words, the functions are all treated the same.

Anything typed in between the inverted triangles is a *definition* (i.e., a subroutine to be defined but not yet executed). When you type in a line that refers to your own or the system's functional definitions, your program gets executed and invokes functions as necessary. You will notice (in Figure 11.8) the total absence of input/output statements. Anything that can have a value but is not directed to be stored somewhere (with the left-pointing arrow, for example) will be directed to the terminal for printing. The data is usually entered with the function invocation, although most systems also provide for access to data files.

```
        ∇A  IN  B
[1]     R←B ι A
[2]     →5 × ι R>ρB
[3]     'FOUND',B,' IN ELEMENT NUMBER',R
[4]     →0
[5.]    'CAN''T FIND',B,' IN',ρB,' ITEMS'
        ∇

        ∇SEARCH ARG
[1]     'DATAVALUES' FTIE 1
[2]     N←FREAD 1,1
[3]     I←1
[4]     ARRAY←ARRAY,FREAD 1,I
[5]     I←I+5
[6]     →4 × ι I≤N
[7]     FUNTIE 1
[8]     ARG IN ARRAY
        ∇


        SEARCH 75
```

Figure 11.8 An APL program is laden with special symbols and a unique set of operations that can be performed. You should not be expected to be able to read this program and understand it.

APL is a computation language. Although it can handle alphanumeric strings of characters and although it has other strong features, it is weakest in the area of files and data management. Good applications for APL might include reference to data files, but in ways in which most requests are not well structured and require some special-purpose programming for analysis. For example, statistical data bases are more commonly used with APL than inventory records.

APL is a big-machine language. Since it deals almost exclusively with large arrays, the details of which are concealed from the user, large memories are a necessity. And because so many things depend on prior execution (such as the sizes of arrays or the total number of them), an APL translator must be an interpreter. For special one-shot programs, this is fine; for fast, production processing of bulk data, APL can be outdone. At least one APL has been implemented on a microprocessor, but without very large arrays and without file access capability.

Why Select APL?

For frequent casual needs for computation power, APL is your best choice. If you want to create programs for others to use, (or process a large data base in a production kind of job), use something else.

The notation is difficult to learn. Not only are the concepts contrary to contemporary programming practice, but the large suite of special symbols that must be remembered makes the problem even more severe.

Since APL needs a big machine, you will need a terminal to your employer's computer or one of the commercial APL time-sharing services. These programs are not very portable. Although other makers are slowly implementing APL interpreters, the field is now dominated by IBM.

APL is best used as a trial balloon tester. You can quickly implement a small subset of an intended computer application in APL and test the algorithm before you commit yourself to a large, risky project.

To get started, you should read Leonard Gilman and Allen J. Rose's *APL/360*.[6]

You've Got An Edge

By following this design course you have gained an edge over most "professional" programmers who have learned programming in more conventional ways.

You are an "amateur" programmer because writing programs is not the primary goal of your job. "Professional" programmers differ from you because they are employed to write programs; they are not necessarily more competent than you (but probably more experienced at this point).

Most "professional" programmers are limited to one—or at most, two—languages. Since they know these languages well, you should consult them if you are in trouble. But they don't have the background in design-before-coding that you have. They tend to "think" in the language in which they will eventually program. This is unfortunate because the language that they are committed to might be the wrong one for the job. Yet they continue to use it because they know no other way to express their designs.

You, however, have a nice language-independent notation (Chapters 3, 4, and 5) in which you can design. Now you can select the right language and learn how to exploit it.

Just because you are an "amateur" programmer doesn't mean that you can't produce good software. You might even produce better software.

[6](New York: John Wiley and Sons, 1971.)

PASCAL

The last of the high-level languages that we will consider in this chapter is PASCAL, a new development from academia that is gaining in popularity. Many computer science graduates are getting their training in PASCAL. The language is relatively new, but the design incorporates most of the modern thinking on good programming techniques. Unlike the other languages, it is as powerful in its ability to describe data as it is in its procedural ability to process that data. Unfortunately, PASCAL remains relatively undeveloped in the area of input/output.

PASCAL was developed by Niklaus Wirth of ETH, a University in Zurich. PASCAL reflects the strong opinions of one of the better practitioners of the programmer's art. And because it has been designed by (essentially) one person, it maintains a coherent structure that committee-designed languages lack.

If the sample program in Figure 11.9 seems to resemble the "pidgin" notation we used in earlier chapters, it is because both "pidgin" and PASCAL are based on the same formal ideas. The difference, of course, is that PASCAL has a real implementation as a compiler that exists on available computers. All the program's variables are defined in the VAR statement, and the entire procedure is the basic block bounded by BEGIN and END. Some predefined procedures (RESET, READ, and WRITELN) exist for handling input/output operations. The rest of

```
(*PROGRAM TO FIND AN ELEMENT IN A LIST*)
PROGRAM SEARCH (INPUT, OUTPUT, DATAFILE);
VAR       DATA: ARRAY [1 .. 1000] OF REAL;
          ARG: REAL;
          N, I: INTEGER;
BEGIN
          RESET(DATAFILE);
          READ(DATAFILE, N);
          (*NOW READ IN THE ARRAY-FULL OF DATA*)
          I:=1;
          WHILE I < = N DO
          BEGIN
              READ(DATAFILE,ARRAY[I]);
              I := I+1
          END;
          READ(ARG);
          FOR I := 1 TO N DO
              IF ARRAY[I] = ARG
              THEN BEGIN
                      WRITELN(' FOUND',ARG:10:2,
                          ' IN ELEMENT NUMBER',I:3);
                      GO TO 9999
                  END;
              WRITELN(' CAN 'T FIND',ARG:10:2,' IN',N:3,'ITEMS')
              9999:
END.
```

Figure 11.9 A PASCAL program looks a lot like our pidgin notation; the informal form has been based on the same principles as PASCAL, but is not identical.

the statements should be familiar, although the assignment operator is : = because most key-punch and terminal equipment lacks the left-pointing arrow.

Why Select PASCAL?

So far, PASCAL is a large-computer language, although one compiler for a minicomputer has been announced. Because there is little manufacturer support for the language, its general acceptance may be delayed. Most of the available PASCAL compilers have come from colleges and universities and have been implemented as research projects, not for creating production tools. Therefore, each PASCAL translator offers slightly different interpretations of the reference language.

Since PASCAL has not been subjected to any standardization, and since anyone may use the name, some PASCAL compilers are not, in fact, full PASCAL.

Nevertheless, PASCAL, or some language very much like it, will likely become the future language in which serious programs will be written. It will take some manufacturer and government support before that happens, but the desirable benefits of PASCAL-like languages warrant the effort.

A good beginning text is Richard Conway, David Gries, and E. Carl Zimmerman's *A Primer on PASCAL.*[7] The "official" work, *PASCAL User Manual and Report,* was written by Kathleen Jensen and Niklaus Wirth.[8]

Assembly Language

Assembly language is a computer-oriented language, but it is different from the procedure-oriented language (or problem-oriented languages) discussed so far. In assembly language the programmer is responsible for describing each individual piece of the steps in the program. Figure 11.10 shows what a typical assembly program looks like, although only about 20% of the complete program is illustrated. This particular assembly language program is written for the Intel 8080 microprocessor. The details of operation are contained in the commentary of the program and are self-explanatory.

Why Select Assembly Language?

Assembly language translators (assemblers) exist for every commercial computer, from microprocessor to supercomputer. Therefore, if you have no other option, you can always use the assembly language. Since you have complete control over the quality and quantity of code produced, there is *no* economic incentive to write practical programs in the absolute binary, octal, or hexadecimal notation of the base computer.

[7] (Cambridge, Mass.: Winthrop Publishers, Inc., 1976).
[8] (New York, N.Y.: Springer-Verlag, 1974).

```
; THIS PROGRAM SEARCHES AN ARRAY
;    AFTER READING IT INTO STORAGE
SEARCH:   LXI    H,ARRAY    ;POINT TO SPACE IN RAM
          CALL   RDINT      ;READ INTEGER INTO (D,E)
          PUSH   D          ;SAVE ARRAY SIZE FOR LATER
LOOP1:    CALL   NEWIN      ;READ IN THE NEXT RECORD
          MVI    C,5        ;(THERE ARE UP TO 5 NRS IN IT)
LOOP2:    CALL   RDNUM      ;READ REAL NUMBER INTO @(H,L)
          DCX    D          ;COUNT NUMBER OF ITEMS READ IN
          JZ     COMPR      ;THEY'RE ALL IN.
          DCR    C          ;TIME FOR A NEW RECORD?
          JNZ    LOOP2      ;NOT YET.
          JMP    LOOP1      ;YES.
;ALL DATA IS IN. NOW, READ ARGUMENT AND COMPARE
COMPR:    POP    B          ;GET ARRAY SIZE BACK
          LXI    H,ARG      ;GO READ IN ARG
          CALL   RDNUM
          LXI    H,ARRAY-1
;THIS IS THE THREE-BYTE COMPARE LOOP FOR REAL NUMBERS
LOOP3:    LXI    D,ARG-1    ;POINT TO ARGUMENT (AGAIN)
          CALL   CMP        ;COMPARE FIRST BYTE
          JNZ    NOHIT      ;(IF NOT EQUAL, CAN'T BE THIS ONE)
          CALL   CMP        ;COMPARE SECOND BYTE
          JNZ    NOHIT
          CALL   CMP        ;COMPARE LAST BYTE
          JZ     FOUND      ;ALL EQUAL. FOUND MATCH.
NOHIT:    DCX    B          ;DONE 'EM ALL YET?
          JNZ    LOOP3      ;NOPE.
          CALL   MSG1       ;YES. GO PRINT OUT "CAN'T FIND"
          JMP    0          ;RETURN TO MONITOR
FOUND:    CALL   MSG2       ;GO PRINT OUT "FOUND" MESSAGE
          JMP    0          ;RETURN TO MONITOR
```

Figure 11.10 Part of a complete assembly language listing for a simple searching program, written for the 8080A microprocessor.

Assembly languages are difficult to use and make the humans who use them error-prone. The cost per statement of assembly language may be easily twice the cost of each statement in a more tractable language—and there are many more statements. In most cases, you should avoid assembly language unless you have no other alternative. Even then you might consider using assembly language only for that portion of your job for which it is absolutely required and resorting to some available higher-level language for the majority of the program.

If you *must* implement a very efficient (very small and/or very fast) program, you may have to use assembly language throughout. In microcomputer applications, for example, where production volumes can be in the hundreds or thousands, using one less ROM per unit is important. By writing in assembly language you will spend more development money, but you will save the cost of hundreds or thousands of additional custom ROM's to store the program.

Generally, assembly languages are unique to your computer and you are stuck with whatever the manufacturer provides. On microcomputers, however, it is

To Compile or Not to Compile

Language translators can be classified as assemblers, compilers, or interpreters. Assemblers differ from compilers and interpreters in that the programmer is responsible (in an assembly language) for the allocation of all resources, right down to each individual register of the computer. If you want to add two numbers in a program written in assembly language, you must be sure that data you may want later is preserved from the accumulator register, that the proper data values are loaded, and that the addition instruction is executed. In a compiler or interpreter you are relieved of this burdensome responsibility, but you can't reap any of the potential efficiency benefits.

Compilers and interpreters are used to translate "high-level" languages into a form the computer can execute. When a high-level translator "cracks" an arithmetic expression (like LET $C = A + B$), all the necessary instructions are created to do that function correctly. In an interpreter, as soon as the statement is decomposed and analyzed, it is executed; the addition of A and B values takes place, and the sum is stored in the memory location named C. Then the next statement in sequence is fetched and executed. In a compiler, when the statement is analyzed, the instructions that will cause A and B to be added and the sum to be stored are not executed. They are written into memory (or out to tape or disc) for *future* execution. And since this translated program can be saved and used over and over without retranslation, the resulting compiled program will tend to run faster than an interpreter.

Any language can be interpreted. Any language can be compiled. Because of their intended application domains, however, various language translators tend to be implemented as either interpreters or as compilers. The COBOL language is almost never interpreted; the APL language is almost never compiled. About half of the BASIC translators are interpreters and about half are compilers. Most FORTRAN translators are compilers.

In the scale of execution efficiency, assembly language offers the greatest potential, compilers next, and interpreters least of all. Although the potential for superior assembly language exists, most compilers can outperform mediocre programmers. In many cases, compilers can actually produce smaller and faster programs than programmers can produce, unless the programmer really hones that code carefully. The programs executed by interpreters tend to be very small (but you must then add the size of the interpreter because it must coexist with your own program), and they about fifteen times slower on the average than compiled code. Interpreters offer the advantage that you can interact with your program during execution and make changes that will be reflected in future execution. This is important during debugging.

The ideal translator would provide both interpreting and compiling capability, with the linguistic ability to descend into assembly language whenever absolutely necessary. No such languages exist at this time.

popular for small software and systems houses to sell different assemblers to different markets. Some of these assemblers are very, very primitive, but a few outperform the semiconductor firm's own. You should find out what is available before you select one.

There are no really good books on assembly language programming, except those devoted to a particular computer's notation. Generally, the manufacturer's computer system reference manual is sufficient. Standardization among assemblers is impractical without standardizing the instructions and word sizes and register complements of all computers.

12

Real-time Programming

It is in the implementation of complex real-time software and abstract systems software (see Chapter 13) that programmers test their mettle. All of the techniques described in the preceding must be refined to a high art before you can hope to successfully implement reliable real-time software. Yet, today's applications demand that processes occur in synchronism with the outside world, and that synchronism is the essence of real-time. If your first application with your new programming skill must cope with real-time, you have a real challenge facing you. This chapter is designed to get you over the rough spots without burdening you with too much sophistication.

All the easy applications have already been done (Chapter 1). The easy, take-your-time jobs have become programming clichés. The problems we face today are more often intimately involved with the direct control of some process than with information processing. When the software must process a paycheck in a payroll system, it matters little if the process takes a few seconds or a couple of minutes. When you have to control a chemical experiment with explosive potential, milliseconds may be extremely important. Few computer pioneers imagined the inexpensive availability of computer power that could be applied to chemical processes in the early years. Payroll was one of the first commercial applications.

A *real-time* system must maintain responses to stimuli that are in the world outside the system itself. If responses from the computer are keyed to individual stimuli—if each stimulus evokes a response from the computer before the next stimulus is acknowledged—we have a real-time system. In practice, purely sequential recognition of stimuli and generation of responses are too limiting. Some overlap is possible. But in real-time systems it is almost always true that the sum of all possible stimuli would saturate the system's resources. In essence, managing real-time software is the management of resource allocation to minimize delays in responses computed to stimuli.

Real-time Systems Support

If you are implementing real-time software on a microcomputer, you will find that you can write all your own software. It can be very compact and easy to test because you will have the opportunity to design it to do just what you need (and no more). However, if your environment is at the opposite end of the spectrum and you must use a small part of a large-scale computer, you must interface with layers and layers of systems software that you will have to understand in order to make use of it. Generally, this software will be more cumbersome and complicated (with more loopholes and ambiguities) than the underlying hardware.

In the middle domain (the world of minicomputers in which much of the real-time programming is done) you may have sophisticated software at your disposal, you may have primitive real-time support, or you might have to (or be able to) do it all yourself. Most minicomputer makers supply real-time software that allows you to use the same software that the rest of the operating system uses. Instead of writing your own interrupt servicing routines and schedulers, you may interface to those already provided in the software system.

Unfortunately, much of this prepared software will be too large for efficient use in many applications. You must trade off the advantages of not having to write it all yourself against the additional program size and time you have to accept as penalties and the added complexities of having to interface with the unique real-time software system.

The manuals for most available real-time software are models of obfuscation. Since there is little standardization of design techniques, each maker writes manuals using a unique vocabulary. The interface conventions are all different, too, making comparisons among competing systems almost impossible.

Whether you have to use an ''inherited'' real-time software system or you have to ''roll your own,'' you will have to know the basic techniques used. In the discussion that follows only the simplest possible scheme is presented. There are so many different schemes used in different systems that it takes books to describe them all. A good starting place would be Yourdon's *Design of On-Line Systems.* [1]

Recognizing Stimuli

Events that happen in real-time generally must be recognized quickly in order to leave sufficient processing time for computation of the response. Whether the event is an incoming character from a communications channel, a changing status

---

[1] Edward Yourdon, *Design of On-Line Systems* (Englewood Cliffs, N.J.: Prentice-Hall, Inc., 1974).

of some remote water-level sensor, or a significant contact closure, some way of recognizing that event is important. The two possible ways of handling event recognition are *interrupts* and *polling.*

In a polling system the important input signals are read and analyzed cyclically, whether anything important has changed or not. In an interrupt system normal data processing continues until the hardware senses that something important has happened. Generally, polling systems are simpler and are easier to make reliable, while interrupt systems are more efficient and induce less jitter into the stimuli-response cycle.

Polling requires that the controlling software in the computer regain control sufficiently often to guarantee that no significant input data changes are lost. This can impose some unreasonable demands on the cooperating software. Each subroutine in the system may have to be subordinate to a special program called a *scheduler,* and each subroutine may have to be limited to some maximum execution time by design. The important input signals can be scanned for significant changes between scheduler calls on the subordinate subroutines.

Polling can be done on any computer, but it requires careful software design so that there will be no degradation of performance. An errant program that occasionally consumes more than its allotted time may cause sporadic errors. These errors are extremely difficult to track down because the cause (a bug in some subroutine) and effect (the missing of significant inputs) are apparently unrelated.

Polling systems can be easy to debug if the entire program is small. Polling is frequently used as the real-time interface means in microprocessor applications, occasionally with minis, and almost never with large-scale computers.

Interrupts and Servicing

Most computers have interrupt electronics built in. If your computer doesn't, there isn't much you can do (unless you want to add the new electronics) except poll inputs. In an interrupt system, normal low-priority software is executed until something significant occurs. At that point, the low-priority software is interrupted and some higher-priority software is allowed to execute. If neither of these two programs affects one another (except, perhaps, through a shared common communications region in memory), interrupts make a single computer act like two or more.

Normally, an interrupt is sensed just prior to the fetching of an instruction by the computer. If the interrupt input to the computer is active (Figure 12.1), the instruction that was about to be fetched doesn't get addressed. Instead, some other instruction (one in an *interrupt service routine*) gets fetched. So that the interrupted program can be resumed in the future, it is necessary to save all of the registers of the CPU. that affect the execution of the interrupted program. Later,

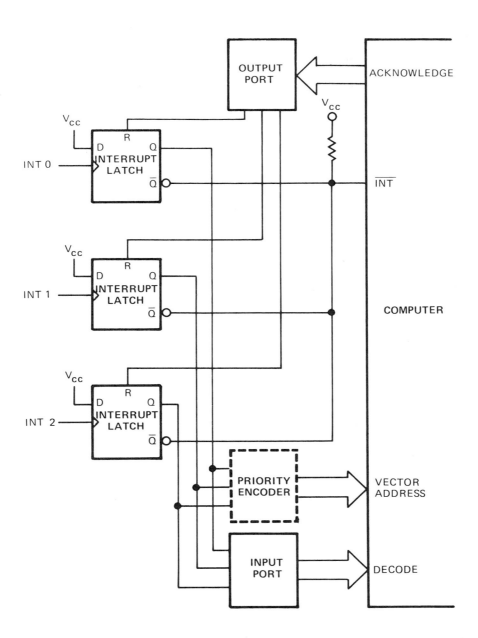

Figure 12.1 Interrupt system for a small computer, which might even be part of the CPU assembly. Interrupts are sent to the control section of the computer, decoded, and then acknowledged.

after the interrupt has been serviced, the register contents can be restored and execution resumed as if nothing had occurred.

In the simple interrupt scheme shown in Figure 12.1 some arbitrary number of interrupts are latched. If any one of them is active, then the INT input to the computer is pulled low. When the next instruction is about to be fetched, the computer reacts to the interrupt signal by (typically):

1. Preserving the program counter of the interrupted program in another register on some push-down stack
2. Loading the program counter with a fixed address designed into this computer to which all interrupts are referred

Then the instruction fetch proceeds normally. The computer usually has a flip-flop internally that inhibits the sensing of an interrupt until a special instruction is issued that reenables the interrupt scheme.

The inputs to the computer can be read in and decoded by the software to determine which particular interrupt(s) occurred. The output port of the computer connected to the interrupt logic allows individual interrupts in the latches to be acknowledged and cleared under software control.

In a sophisticated variation, instead of setting a single address into the program counter and requiring software to *poll* the interrupt latches to find the offending source, the interrupt latches can be decoded and used as part of the address. Eight interrupt sources can be fed into a priority encoder that generates a single three-bit value that is representative of one of the interrupt sources. These three bits are used in the computation of the actual subroutine address, causing *vectoring* to one of eight different locations. There must be as many interrupt service routines as there are potential interrupts connected to the priority encoder, but each interrupt service routine will gain control significantly faster than the simpler scheme allows.

Interrupts, especially vectored interrupts, are potentially difficult to cope with. Unless the software is written very carefully, very strange side effects and hard-to-find bugs may crop up. As a general rule, the interrupt service software should do just as little as possible to maintain real-time. Instead of recognizing a stimulus and then creating an immediate response, it may be better to recognize the stimulus and then schedule some other more complex software for execution outside the real-time portion of the software. The ways to schedule software will be discussed later in this chapter.

In general, the smaller the software, the less there is to go wrong (go wrong, go wrong, go wrong). If something does go wrong, it will be easier to comprehend. As a general guideline, 100,000 bits is about the amount of information one programmer can know intimately. If your real-time software is larger than 12.5K bytes, you can be certain that no one person knows it all and there may be bugs lurking within. Another general guideline is important: Most real-time bugs will happen just often enough to be troublesome, but not often enough to get caught.

Interrupt Software

Handling asynchronous interrupts, which may strike at any time, requires that some programming rules be observed throughout the program. If cooperation between the real-time interrupt servicing software and the background (nonreal-time) software isn't complete, havoc can reign.

Each interrupt procedure must have private data space in which it can hold important variables without worrying about having them disturbed by other routines. There must also be shared variables through which real-time and nonreal-time segments communicate.

When an interrupt strikes, it is important for the interrupt servicing software to preserve the state of the CPU for the interrupted program. By recording all of the relevant register contents (the *state word*), and then restoring them later, the interrupted program can proceed without apparently having been interrupted. A schema for the interrupt servicing software is given in Figure 12.2. Since the interrupts are automatically disabled while an interrupt is being serviced, only a limited amount of data storage space is required to hold the saved-register contents. Some change must be made in the body of the interrupt servicing procedure, either to an output port or to some memory location, so that the interrupt can be responded to. In many cases, the interrupt response is to schedule some nonreal-time procedure for execution as soon as practical. After the interrupt is serviced, the register contents that were saved upon entry to the routine are restored, interrupts are reenabled, and the interrupted program is resumed.

If interrupt servicing routines are not written very carefully, they can cause severe problems. Imagine what would happen if—occasionally—all of the registers of the interrupted program didn't get restored properly. It would be almost impossible to debug this corrupted program. Similarly, if the interrupt servicing and interrupting programs don't cooperate completely, the result may be a long-delayed but eventually catastrophic side effect. Figure 12.3 shows what can happen.

In this example a nonreal-time program generates data in a buffer (one it obtains from a free-space allocation routine), and then it appends the full buffer to the end of the list of buffers awaiting transmission out on some (slow) transmission channel. In addition to the buffers that are shared between the real-time and nonreal-time parts of the system, there is a counter of the number of buffers that exist in the chain to be transmitted. The supplier of the buffer increments the pointer when a buffer is appended to the list; the consumer decrements it when a buffer is released back to the free-space chain.

A race condition can very easily be created in this situation. If a new buffer is appended to the end of the list and if the supplier of this buffer is about to increment the counter, the following situation may occur:

1. The nonreal-time program fetches the counter from memory into a CPU register preparatory to incrementing it (from 3 to 4).
2. An interrupt strikes and the interrupt service routine sends the last character

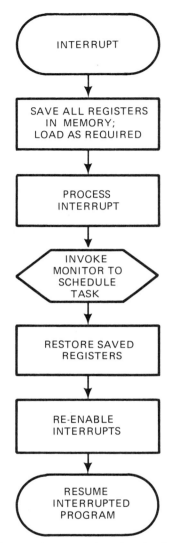

Figure 12.2 Interrupts are services by simple sequences of instructions that are used to schedule more complex subroutines to accomplish the actual work much later in time.

in a buffer, releases the buffer to the free-space pool, fetches the counter, and decrements it (from 3 to 2).

3. When the interruptable program resumes, it increments the CPU register (from 3 to 4) and stores this new value back into the counter.

4. As a consequence, the real-time software has only three buffers, but it indicates that there are four.

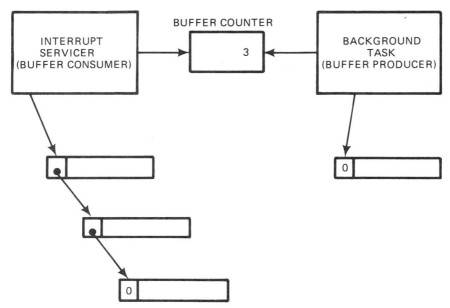

Figure 12.3 The set-up for disaster, unless the two software elements cooperate completely and avoid modifying the Buffer Counter simultaneously.

This problem is so common that it has two broad solutions. First, no communication between real-time and nonreal-time routines may take place in the interruptable state. In other words, the use of the intercommunication region must take place under real-time conditions. Second, no real-time program should *assume* anything. There must be some redundancy that can be used to implement some recovery plan. In this case, the redundancy is in the list-element pointers; there are only three buffers in the list, regardless of the number that may exist in the counter. But, to the software, which is correct? Did the counter get corrupted or did one of the buffer pointers get corrupted? By "auditing" all of the buffers, we can account for each and every one of them to see if a buffer is "lost" to the system. If a buffer is "lost," it can be restored to the free-space list. If all buffers are accounted for, then the counter must have been in error and its value can be corrected.

This defensive approach in recovery software is called *firewalling* of the system components. It must be the first duty of any real-time system to protect itself from corruption, for if it becomes corrupted, none of its other goals can be assured. If the error-detecting software finds an error, some recovery strategy must be implemented. In general, it is better to lose some data than it is to let the entire system fail. Of course, if data is lost, some notification of that fact can be made. Either entire software sequences can be reexecuted to reconstruct the partially corrupted data or some other "logging" action can be taken to notify interested parties of the systems actions.

Queuing

When an interrupt service routine schedules (or, more correctly, appeals to a monitor for the scheduling of) a routine for nonreal-time procedure, some queuing of all these requests must be performed. A queue is nothing more than a list or an array of all of the nonreal-time procedures that must be executed, along with some indication of the data that is to be operated on.

The simplest queue is the *round-robin,* or first-come-first-served, queue (Figure 12.4). Schematically, things to be scheduled are added to the queue [Figure 12.4(a)] and a processor takes the oldest item, initiates the execution of that procedure, and then initiates the next. A small table in memory [Figure 12.4(b)] is usually managed by a software *monitor* that considers the queue its private property. The

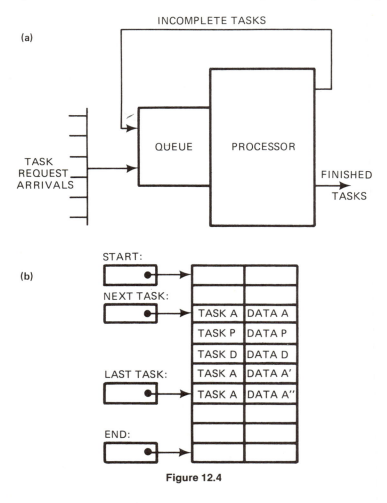

Figure 12.4

monitor consists of a set of routines that can add new requirements to the table, select the oldest for execution, and has some provisions for handling the unique case in which the entries in the queue come faster than the software can be executed to clear them.

This queue doesn't have any provisions for different priorities for different activities, however. Sometimes it is necessary to implement multiple queues, each in a separate table. The monitor must then have a priority selection algorithm as part of its logic. The simplest might merely require that all entries in queue n be cleared before any items in queue $n + 1$ are examined.

Queues are usually implemented as circular tables (Figure 12.5). These tables are

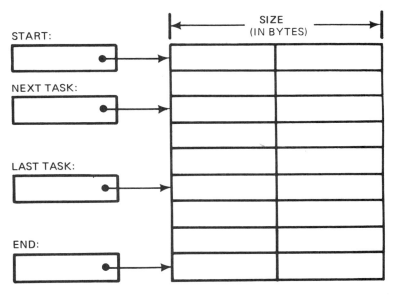

```
procedure task done;
begin
        next task ← next task + size;
        if next task > end
        then next task ← start
end;

procedure new task;
begin
        last task ← last task + size;
        if last task > end
        then last task ← start
end
```

Figure 12.5 A linear array of cells can be made into a circular buffer through suitable procedures to handle the "wrap around."

operated on to give the appearance of an inexhaustible supply of memory locations, although if inputs are presented more rapidly than outputs are taken, the table may fill up. If the table becomes full, either some queueing requests must be denied or an entire table full of queued items is lost when the next-free-space pointer "wraps around." If the queued items are maintained as a list (Figure 12.6), the only way items are lost is if the free-space from which list items are removed becomes exhausted. Since already queued items are "safe" in the queue (out of free-space), wholesale loss of items will not occur.

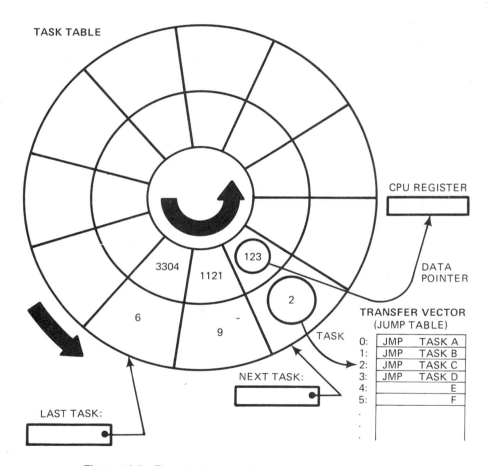

Figure 12.6 The circular task table contains data pointers which get loaded into a common CPU register, and indices to tables where the actual address of the required subroutine can be found.

Managing the Task Table

The enqueued entries are called the *tasks* of the system. Each task is character- ized by the address of some subroutine to be executed and the address of some place in memory where relevant data is stored. The circular table, whether imple- mented as a list or an array, can be represented schematically as in Figure 12.6.

Since the scheduling of tasks is dynamic, entries are constantly being made and removed throughout the operation. The time sequence of task table contents may become very complex. In the simple example that follows we implement only the simplest queue and show its step-by-step operation. Conceptually, the distinction between the "high-water mark" (oldest entry) and the "low-water mark" (the newest) is easy.

Entries in the table are in the form of pairs of addresses or integers that can be translated into addresses. The identification of the task to be performed (sub- routine to be called) is usually maintained as a small integer so that the identifica- tion number remains the same for a given task throughout the life of the system, regardless of the actual address at which the subroutine begins. This simplifies the maintenance of the system and the decoding of the task table contents during debugging. It is easier to remember that "task 52" means some particular function than it is to have to look up the name of the subroutine referred to by location. Since the data usually resides in different locations at different times, the data portion of the entry is usually a simple address. It may point to an array or a list that contains all of the information that the subroutine will require for execu- tion. Usually, since the data area consists of only a word or two, it might even be included in the task table.

Operations on the Task Table

The contents of a task table may be changed in one of the following four basic ways:

1. Successful completion of a task
2. Addition of a new task from the interrupt servicing or polling software
3. Unsuccessful completion of a task (delay)
4. Addition of a task scheduled from within another task

The tasks themselves are all designed to be interruptable. The monitor that controls the task table is generally interruptable, but it can be invoked from the interrupted state of the CPU to schedule activities on behalf of interrupt service software. Sometimes this table is called the *background task schedule*.

Starting with a small sequence of tasks in a table [Figure 12.7(a)], we can now show how different activities take place. This task table, at the time the "snapshot" was taken, contained entries for three tasks, the oldest of which calls for task 2. That entry is pointed to by the "Next Task" pointer. The most recent entry has scheduled task 6; that entry is pointed to by the "Last Task" pointer. If "Last Task" ever equals "Current Task," we can declare that the task table is empty.

If we assume that the monitor is in control at this juncture, we can now transfer control to the subroutine that is associated with task 2 (through the transfer table shown in Figure 12.6). Before we invoke that routine, however, we load the address of the data space into some "standard" CPU register where all subroutines called from the monitor expect to receive their data references. This entire process is interruptable, as is the task to which we have transferred control. It is the responsibility of the called subroutine to return control to the monitor at the end of its required time. Furthermore, the subroutine must be written to use only the assigned data areas it "owns," and it may not execute indefinitely lest it prevent other real-time events from being responded to.

When the called task returns control, the monitor increments the "Next Task," thus clearing it from further consideration (and freeing the space for some future task to be queued). Incidentally, if the "Next Task" points to the same space as the "Last Task," the monitor sits in a "wait loop" until there is something to do.

But in our case [Figure 12.7(b)] there are two more tasks that have not been initiated yet. Therefore, the monitor transfers control to the subroutine for task 9.

Now, while that software is executing along, imagine that an important interrupt is sensed and processed. While the interrupt is being serviced, the monitor is invoked to schedule a new task (in this case, task 21). The interrupt servicing software then returns control to the interrupted subroutine of task 9; the task table has been changed [Figure 12.7(c)].

Now, imagine that task 9 has decided that it cannot proceed. Perhaps it requires access to some resource that is not available, or perhaps the task is designed to wait until a certain time period has passed as reflected in some memory contents updated for the real-time clock hardware (by the task associated with the interrupt associated with that hardware). In any event, since task 9 cannot continue, it must be rescheduled. Thus, task 9 appeals to the monitor to reschedule task 9 and use the very same data area. Now when the monitor regains control, the original task 9 will have been passed, but it will have been rescheduled by "leapfrogging" over the other entries in the table [Figure 12.7(d)]. In the same way, a long task can be partitioned into different subtasks, each one scheduling its successor for completion. In fact, the entire purpose of one task might be to schedule several other tasks so that they can proceed in an arbitrary order; there is usually one final task that completes (does not reschedule itself) only after all of the predecessor tasks have completed their work. In this fashion, you can implement an arbitrary number of arbitrarily complex but independent processes, the completion of which is then reported by this last task.

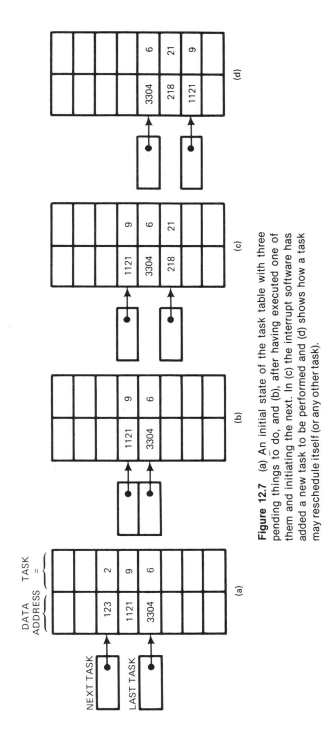

Figure 12.7 (a) An initial state of the task table with three pending things to do, and (b), after having executed one of them and initiating the next. In (c) the interrupt software has added a new task to be performed and (d) shows how a task may reschedule itself (or any other task).

Maintaining History

One of the major problems in real-time software is debugging it in the environment of delayed effects. Often, some early event will cause a subtle change in memory contents that won't be detected until sometime later in the execution cycle. The best thing you can do is add some permanent instrumentation that records the major points in the execution history in a circular table.

If the major software is implemented as a finite-state machine (FSM), then each time the FSM changes state, the prior state can be recorded in the circular table. When a failure is detected, the recent history leading up to the error can be reconstructed. The circular table might also contain one or two bytes of key data related to that state change to enhance the value of the history table.

In general, software instrumentation in real-time systems should never be removed. Even in execution of a system that is in production, subtle errors that require in-the-field debugging can creep in. Here the history table will prove immensely valuable.

If the software is not constructed as an FSM, the scheduler tables can be used to reconstruct the history of the operation, especially if the tables are large enough to prevent premature overwriting. If neither FSM states nor scheduler indices are available, you can record major subroutine calls as elements of recent history.

13

Systems Software

Much of electronic and systems engineering involves interfacing standard subassemblies, usually with some unique interposing hardware. In software the same condition prevails. In each case, large and powerful capabilities can be tapped, but at some cost in terms of relative inefficiency or learning effort. In the world of programmers, we call the subassemblies *systems programs* and the collection of them *systems software*. There are even systems programmers, the elite cadre of programmers who have sufficient experience and skill to develop that software.

Systems software includes the compilers, interpreters, and assemblers described in Chapter 10, as well as the monitors referred to in Chapter 11. There are also systems software: operating systems, relocating linking loaders, text editors, and utility programs. Knowing what these are and how they can be used can save you much effort.

Monitors and Supervisors

A single program that performs a single oversight kind of activity is usually called a *monitor*. For example, a program in memory that allows you to load in an entire program and execute it (with the provision that the monitor also allows you to terminate the job somehow) might be called a monitor. Monitors, as raw programs, are usually only provided on the smallest computers.

Monitors are sometimes augmented with generalized input/output software so that individual programs do not have to have special software written by the programmer. The Input/Output Control System (IOCS) is the software that mates with the connected peripheral devices and permits using programs to deal with, say, a line printer without having to rewrite all the detailed control software. When we add this capability to a monitor, we create a *supervisory system* (Figure 13.1). This systems software usually has a special program component (called the *command processor*) that resides in memory at all times. This program is designed to accept specially formatted *job control statements* and act on them. The monitor's more primitive features are usually included as part of the command processor in the supervisor.

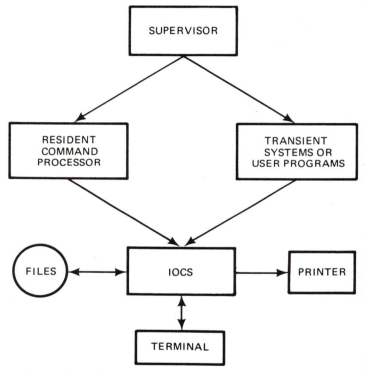

Figure 13.1 Model of a small supervisor, incorporating an Input/Output Control System (IOCS).

Supervisors usually allow the storage and retrieval of programs, both in source and object form. The supervisor, through the job control language, may allow access to compilers and assemblers that are brought into storage as required. The individually translated object programs are stored on the same disc (or occasionally tape) medium. After all the required programs are translated, they are loaded into memory and executed. At the end of the job more commands are accepted from the same or a different user, thus avoiding "dead" time between jobs.

A typical sequence of supervisor commands and the supervisor's responses is shown in Figure 13.2. If these commands are issued one at a time, and if each response must be elicited before the next command may be issued, the user is said to be *on-line* to the system. If all the commands and relevant programs and data are grouped together and submitted as a unit, the system is said to be *batch oriented*. If the batch system can be accessed from a remotely located terminal, the system is said to offer *remote job* (or batch) *entry*. Supervisors of the most elementary kind are usually offered on the larger configurations of microcomputers and on minicomputers. Some minis even offer remote job capability, although this is almost always reserved for the larger systems.

//ACCOUNT	CAROL OGDIN, 7039-1121	Name and account number for charge allocation
77.06.05	11:21	System supplies time and data
//COPY	INPUT, FILE = "PROGRAM"	Invoke a utility program to copy the following cards into a file named PROGRAM
(Data Cards)		
//EOF		(End-of-file at end of data cards)
	COPIED 632 RECORDS TO "PROGRAM"	System tells us what happened
//FORTRAN	INPUT = "PROGRAM", OBJECT = "OBJ"	Compile the FORTRAN program named "PROGRAM", put object file on "OBJ"
	(System prints FORTRAN listing here)	
//EDIT	INPUT = "OBJ", "FORTLIB", GO	Link-edit the "OBJ" program and the necessary subroutines FORTRAN programs require from "FORTLIB", and then execute the program
//DATA		
(Data Cards required by FORTRAN program)		
//EOF		(End-of-file at end of data cards)

Figure 13.2   A simplified sequence of job control statements to control compiling, translation, and execution of a FORTRAN program.

Operating systems offer all this and more. First, the IOCS is revised so that a common control structure exists and the interfaces are made independent of the devices. Thus, configurations can be changed (so long as the operating system is changed at the same time) without affecting the applications programs. Second, multiple programs are allowed to coexist in memory and interleave their execution for maximum computer utilization. As soon as one of the programs requests some service that is likely to take some time to complete (say, the reading of a record from some external device), the operation is initiated (or scheduled), the requesting program is placed in a suspended state, and some other program is initiated. Since all the programs (user and systems) must cooperate in such a system, every program is obliged to conform to the operating system's rules. If it doesn't, the operating system will throw the offending program out of memory and issue a nasty message on the printed output or the user's terminal. Usually, in these large systems memory-protection hardware is installed so that an errant program can't corrupt the operating system or another suspended program.

On systems that have operating systems you may be required to use the facilities of the system whether you want to or not. Interfacing special real-time electronics to a sophisticated operating system that was not designed with those devices in mind can be virtually impossible.

Environment

The larger the system, the more likely you are to have broad software support. Microprocessors and microcomputers are often supplied with little more than a monitor suitable for loading in very small programs. At the other end of the scale, on large-scale centralized computing facilities it is not uncommon to see 128,000 bytes allocated to the resident part of the operating system and to see access to literally hundreds of different systems software packages.

Microcomputer development systems are being modeled after the successful minicomputer systems which, in turn, have been modeled on the largest operating systems. Unfortunately, the manufacturers do not have a good reputation for turning out the best in systems software. Often, other sources provide better, more efficient, and more reliable software. Large parts of operating systems are often provided by vendors other than the original manufacturer. This is especially true of communications control software and data base management systems that efficiently store and retrieve large volumes of data. These large additional software systems can be fully as large as the operating system itself, and, thus, the resident memory requirements are doubled.

Operating System Use

Whether your operating system or supervisor is large or small, in the beginning there will probably be only a few things that you will ever use it for. The highly sophisticated uses should be left to the experts. For the most part, you will need the ability to translate your program, load it into memory, execute it, monitor the execution so that you can get enough information to debug the program, and then relinquish the computer to someone else. Once your program is in production, all you have to do is load and execute your program (and relinquish the computer at the end, unless your application requires the entire computer all the time, as is the case with most microcomputer applications).

The remainder of this chapter will be devoted to describing the different software tools at your disposal in different environments and what kind of performance you can expect from them.

Language Translators

All the language translators have basic operational characteristics of which you should be aware. Most of the translators operate on a two-pass basis: The program you submit to the computer is read once to collect information on the entire program and compact that information into arrays and lists in memory. Then the program is read a second time and each statement is translated into the object program. The collected information is used to control the process. There are subtle differences on different computers that have different objectives, but this basic plan is the most popular.

On a large-scale computer your FORTRAN or BASIC program is read in from the source medium. As each statement is recognized, the essential information on it is stored as an entry in a table somewhere in memory. The statement is written out to a disc file. After all statements have been processed, the disc file is "reset" to the starting point and the second reading of the code begins. Using the internal form of the program, the details of the code are rearranged to *optimize* your program. Things that can be computed at compiling time instead of being delayed until execution time are computed. Code that may have been written inside a loop that never changes is moved to an equivalent point outside the loop. Unnecessary instructions are detected and eliminated. The result of this optimization process is a reorganized internal form of the program, but one that is fully equivalent to your original program.

The reorganized program in memory is used, along with the disc copy of your original program, to finally produce the object program you require. While each statement is read in, it is printed out—often along with the object code that was generated by the compiler so that you can see what has happened. As the object program gets created, it is written back onto the disc. This object program will be used later by the *loader*.

On very small computers that do not have external storage media (like microcomputers and small minis), while the internal tables are being created no copy of your program is written back out to disc. Therefore, after the program has been read in completely, you have to rewind your program input medium and get it ready to be read in a second time. Because of the limited storage capacity, compilers do not usually offer any significant optimization features.

Compilers on minicomputers tend to be more like the large-scale compilers, although optimization is seldom provided. In fact, the quality of code may be downright poor because the small computer size limits the practical complexity of the part of the compiler that produces the object code.

Assemblers work very much like compilers except that they, of course, don't have any optimization capability. Assemblers also produce the object code in a form acceptable to a *loader* so that it can be copied into memory for execution at a later time.

The real effect that your translator will have on your work depends on how reliable it is and how helpful it is when it detects an error in your program. Since your source program in a high-level language bears little resemblance to the final program stored in memory for execution, you are virtually at the mercy of the reliability of the compiler. If it generates erroneous code, you may have to spend days tracking down bugs that you didn't cause. If the compiler is new, or if a new version has been announced, suspect it. Try to avoid some of the offending statements to see if that will cure the problem. Don't try to deduce from the object code how the compiler works because it is too abstruse and it apparently depends on nonsensical conventions. However, before you go off screaming at the systems programmers remember, because of the utter dependence programmers must place in compilers, designers make them some of the highest quality software written. Eliminate all your own errors before challenging the correctness of the compiler, lest you be labeled a troublesome novice.

You should also find out (preferably before you begin coding) whether the compiler you intend to use is going to help or hinder you. In the earliest days of compilers when you made a simple mistake, the compiler stopped and issued the noninformative message "SYNTAX ERROR." Today, an error should not terminate compilation. But the error diagnostics should be concise and they should appear right under or adjacent to the line that contains the error. A good trick here is to read the appendix of your translator's reference manual that reproduces the error messages and the causes for each. If this part of the manual is easy to read, you will have no trouble deciphering your translator's error messages. If you see incomprehensible error messages and the explanation (or non-explanation) "Self-explanatory," you know that you are going to have trouble. Perhaps you should investigate the other languages available on this computer.

Forms of Object Programs

The programs that you generate from a translator are called *object programs,* and different object programs require more or less sophisticated *loaders* to read them into memory for execution. The simplest object program, and one that requires only the simplest loader, is an *absolute object program.* In this program each and every instruction in the object file is assumed to have a fixed and final memory location. All the loader need do is read the object code line [see Figure 13.3(a)] and store the successive words away in successive locations in memory. Of course, this program does not dare occupy the same space as the loader, lest the loading process be corrupted. This loader is often included as part of the monitor used with micros and it is often provided as an optional ROM-based program on minis. Absolute loaders are seldom used on larger computers.

In most cases, the larger the computer, the more likely it is that the specific memory locations to be assigned to the program are now known at translation time. In large systems that permit multiple simultaneous programs, the actual locations in memory may change from day to day as the "job mix" changes. Obviously, absolute object programs would have to be retranslated each time they were to be executed, but adding the property of *relocatability* saves the day.

Relocatable object programs [Figure 13.3(b)] are always assembled or compiled as if the first location to be assigned were zero. Every instruction that refers to an address in memory is marked so that it can be adjusted when the program gets loaded. The *relocatable loader* starts with knowledge of the address at which the

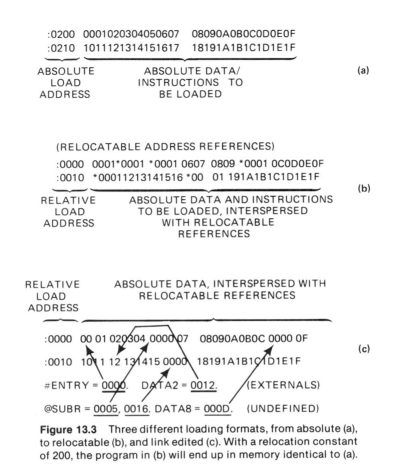

:0200 0001020304050607 08090A0B0C0D0E0F
:0210 1011121314151617 18191A1B1C1D1E1F

| ABSOLUTE LOAD ADDRESS | ABSOLUTE DATA/ INSTRUCTIONS TO BE LOADED | (a) |

(RELOCATABLE ADDRESS REFERENCES)

:0000 0001*0001 *0001 0607 0809 *0001 0C0D0E0F
:0010 *00011213141516 *00 01 191A1B1C1D1E1F

RELATIVE LOAD ADDRESS   ABSOLUTE DATA AND INSTRUCTIONS TO BE LOADED, INTERSPERSED WITH RELOCATABLE REFERENCES   (b)

RELATIVE LOAD ADDRESS   ABSOLUTE DATA, INTERSPERSED WITH RELOCATABLE REFERENCES

:0000 00 01 020304 0000 07 08090A0B0C 0000 0F   (c)

:0010 10 1 12 13 14 15 0000 18191A1B1C 1D1E1F

#ENTRY = 0000.   DATA2 = 0012.   (EXTERNALS)

@SUBR = 0005, 0016. DATA8 = 000D.   (UNDEFINED)

Figure 13.3 Three different loading formats, from absolute (a), to relocatable (b), and link edited (c). With a relocation constant of 200, the program in (b) will end up in memory identical to (a).

program is to be loaded; this address is added as an "offset" to every one of the marked addresses. When the entire program has been loaded, all of the addresses will have been adjusted to reflect the now established memory locations of interest (Figure 13.4).

Relocatable programs allow the same program to be deposited at different locations at different times without having to recompile or reassemble. A different complication occurs when there are two different areas of memory to consider. In microcomputers, for example, the relocatable program may be "burned" into PROM, but the data storage memory may have to be at other addresses altogether. In this case, separate relocation constants (offsets) may have to be established for RAM and PROM, and the loader may have to distinguish between the two kinds of references in the relocatable code.

Another advantage that the relocatable loader provides is the ability to take two or more separate pieces of program and load them into contiguous places in

185

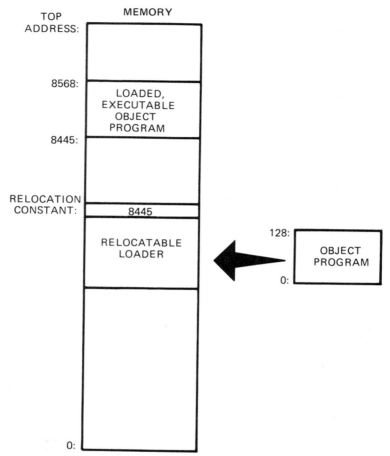

Figure 13.4 The relocatable loader is a program that accepts an object program and then changes all address references so that execution can proceed unimpeded.

memory. The first segment is loaded at the starting address given; the second is loaded at the address starting just after the end of the first, and so on. Thus, a composite program can be "pieced" together in order to avoid the necessity of recompiling the whole program if a small error is found. The various software modules can be translated independently and then loaded to form the final unit.

The difficulty with this is that programs that call one another, or refer to relocatable data areas, all have to "learn" where things are located before execution can start. This is often accomplished by implementing a *transfer vector* that is always loaded starting from some fixed location. Since each subroutine is called via the transfer vector, each subroutine knows how to refer to its neighbors. The actual jump addresses in the transfer vector are entered into memory (manually) after the entire program is loaded and the target addresses are known.

Since this operation can be very lengthy and error-prone, *linkage editors* have been constructed to relieve the burden. In a linkage editor each program module has all of its important symbols defined in tables by symbolic name. All of the points in the module that might be referred to from another module are named and given relative addresses inside the module. All of the names to which this module refers but which do not appear within the module (symbols that in more conventional assemblers or compilers would have been rejected as "undefined") are also listed. They point to all the places in the program from which the references are made. These two lists compose the *dictionary* of the module.

The linkage editor reads in all of the object program text and performs all of the relocation required. The two dictionary parts are read and converted into entries in two separate tables in memory. All of the definitions of symbols appear in one table and have their equivalent absolute addresses associated. All of the references to other symbols appear in another table and have the equivalent absolute addresses of places that need to have corrected addresses installed associated.

After all modules are in memory, the list of items that requires correction is processed, one at a time. For each item, the symbol is looked up in the table of definitions and an equivalent absolute address is established. This address is then stored at the place in memory specified by the reference table, thus correcting the incomplete code. When the entire reference table has been processed, an entire relocated and automatically linked program exists in memory. This program may be executed or it may be copied out to tape or disc as an absolute program. In some cases, linkage editors do the linking but leave the program in a totally relocatable state (as a single module) so that the edited program can be relocatably loaded as required.

Obviously, because of the storage requirements of the additional tables (which must reside in memory with the object program) and the larger editor program, the linkage editor usually appears only on the largest of computer systems. Larger minicomputer configurations sometimes offer linkage editors, but they are seldom provided on the smaller configurations or on microcomputers.

Execution Monitoring

Once the object program is in an executable state in memory, the execution time support ranges from sophisticated to nonexistent. Again, the level of software support is highly correlated to the size of the computer being used. The microcomputers, for instance, have only the barest minimum of execution time support, perhaps little more than a monitor program that permits execution to be stopped and memory contents displayed.

Systems that support operating systems usually support a wide array of debugging software. Often compatible with the selected programming languages, these tools permit monitoring ongoing executing during program checkout by issuing commands in the native language (or a notation very close to the language). Debug monitors are usually very powerful and allow you to set up "trap" conditions that are invoked only if things go wrong. Debug monitors are also very complex. When you don't need them, there is little incentive to learn how to use them. When you do need them, there never seems to be time to use them. You should find out what debugging aids exist and then decide whether you should learn how to use them or just rely on your own software instrumentation.

Every system provides a way of "dumping" memory out on a printer or terminal so that you can analyze what has gone wrong. Dumps usually are produced when the operating system finds the program offensive, although dumps can be called for explicitly. Dumps are of limited utility, especially if you are programming in a higher-level language. You might use the dump to confirm an hypothesis that you have about your program (e.g., "Well, if this happened, then my symbol IJK should be about 22. Let's look IJK's location up in the dump."). If, however, you scan the dump and look for "strange" things, you will waste much time. Use your program as a map to the terrain of the dump: As pilots know, if you look from the map to the ground, you are navigating; if you look from the ground to the map, you are lost.

The best debugging systems let you suspend execution, examine and change discrete variables, and then resume execution. Many of the BASIC systems allow you to do this by providing commands that are, in essence, BASIC without line numbers. Thus, "PRINT I" issued without a line number will cause the current value of **I** to be printed out. A command like "RESUME" allows execution resumption. These interactive systems are most often found on minicomputers.

Utilities

In addition to the wide variety of languages, loaders, and debug monitors, most software systems provide utility programs in the suite of systems programs. In a microcomputer monitor they might be little more than commands that convert decimal numbers to hex. But on systems supported by operating systems that can retrieve programs from backing store, the array of utility programs is usually complete. There are media-copying routines that allow you to copy tape to disc or tape to printer so that you don't have to write special software for these simple tasks. Two common utilities are the sorting systems and the text editors.

If you have much data to sort into a different order, standard software for sorting (or merging, if you have two or more files in the same order to be merged together) can be used. All you have to supply are some records (e.g., cards) that describe the files you want sorted, which data in each record is to be used as the "key" for the sort, and how the output files should be formatted. Notice that you have described the sorting process but without describing the process; that is already embodied in the utility sort program. This is an example of a nonprocedural language that you will no doubt be seeing more of in the future for specific and well-defined applications like sorting.

The text editor is a software system that permits you to retain your programs on the computer and modify them by specifying the changes. The resulting program is then replaced on the storage medium, ready for translation and execution again. Text editors range from the simple to the sophisticated. Some editors operate only on records (or lines) of the source code; you can add, delete, or change entire lines. Other editors allow you to specify individual characters on a line and how to modify them. Still others allow you to make sweeping changes to the entire text, like replacing all occurences of "INT" with "ABC." But these editors are both powerful and dangerous. Although you can change all occurences of "INT" to "ABC," you will also change "PRINT" to "PRABC," whether you want to or not. Most of these "string" editors are language insensitive.

Learning Systems Programming

Systems programs are almost always models of good programming. Even if you have no intention of ever writing a systems program, you can learn a lot from reading good systems programs because they are usually written by the most experienced and the best trained programmers on that computer. But you should never read "early generation" software that was written while the programmers were still gaining experience with the new architecture.

If your computer is "mature," then there are probably many good examples. Pick one of the available systems programs and read the source code listing (or at least part of it). You will begin to see how other programmers work and you will pick up many hints on how to exploit your particular computer if you are writing in assembly language. Since most systems programs are written in assembly language, they won't be of much help if you are limited to high-level language. But limiting yourself to a high-level language is like limiting yourself to digital logic design without descending into the electrical volts-and-amps problems of clever circuitry.

Index

ABS function, 103
Absolute object program, 184
Actions, 56
Algorithm design, 50-66
   binding time, 61-62
   designing the program, 63-66
   environment, 53-56
   formalization of requirements, 56-58
   program objectives, 58-61
   ready-made programs, 62-63
   requirements, 50-53
Algorithms:
   defined, 15
   design of, *see* Algorithm design
   verification of, 138
Alteration, 43-45
American National Standard, 76
American Standard Code for Information Interchange (ASCII), 21-23
American Standard for Use of Communication Characters, 83
APL, 156-158
APL/360 (Gilman and Rose), 158
Applications programs, 2
Arguments, 42
Arithmetic expressions, 101-103
Arrays, 33-35, 38, 61, 62

Art of Computer Programming (Knuth), 63
ASCII (American Standard Code for Information Interchange), 21-23
Assemblers, 6, 18, 144, 160, 162, 183
Assembly languages, 17-18, 96, 160-163
Assignment statement, 39
Association for Computing Machinery, 63, 138

Background task schedule, 175
Backus-Naur Form (BNF), 56, 80
BASIC, 17-18, 96-131
   advantages and disadvantages of, 150
   data declarations, 114-116
   deficiencies, handling, 118
   DIM statement, 116
   elements of, 99-100
   features of, 147-149
   FOR statement, 111-112
   getting access to, 115
   GOSUB statement, 113-114
   GO TO statement, 108-109
   IF statement, 110-111
   INPUT statement, 109, 148-149
   intraprogram documentation, 105
   LET statement, 105-107
   look of, 96-97

BASIC *(cont.)*:
NEXT statement, 112-113
PRINT statement, 107-108, 142, 148-149
RETURN statement, 114
statement structure, 98-99
STOP statement, 109
translating designs to programs, 116-118
variables, 99-105
writing and running programs, 119-131
converting designs to basic, 123-124
formal design description, 121-123
program execution, 124-129
program operation, 129-131
typical program, 119-121
BASIC (Waite and Mather), 150
Basic block, 43-44, 46, 49
Batch oriented system, 181
Begin-end pair, 29, 30, 42, 43, 45, 46, 49
Bench programming, 16
Binary language, 16, 17
Binding time, 61-62
Body of the procedure, 49
Boehm, Barry W., 85*n*
Bottom-up design, 60
Boundaries, testing, 138-139
Breakpoints, 145
Bugs:
defined, 135
diagnosis of, 140-141
isolation of, 143
kinds of, 136
testing for, 6, 18, 132-134, 137-140
see also Debugging

Catastrophic errors, 136
Circular tables, 173-174
COBOL, 26, 76, 146, 153-156
Coding, 6-8, 16-18
Collected Algorithms, 63
Command language, 127-128
Command processor, 180
Communications of the ACM, 63
Communique, 89
Compilers, 6, 18, 115, 144, 162, 183-184
Complex data structures, 29-31
Component identification, 94
Computers, 1
large scale, 4

Computers *(cont.)*:
microcomputers, 2, 3, 4, 17, 54, 55, 128, 182
minicomputers, 3, 4, 53, 54, 55, 128
uses of, 4-5
Concurrent incremental documentation, 85-86
Conditions, 56
Configuration control, 93-95
Contributions, WDM, 89-90
Controlled looping, 111
Control registers, 39
Conway, Richard, 160
COS function, 103
Cyclic Redundancy Check (CRC), 52

Data manipulation, 40-41
Data registers, 39
Data sequence charts, 82-83
Data structures, 21-38
arrays, 33-35, 38, 61, 62
complex, 29-31
data description, 25-38
data type, 21-23, 26-33, 38
dynamic, 34-37
global, 47
interfaced with procedure structures, 46-49
items, 31-33, 38
lists, 34-38, 61, 62
local, 47
numbers, 24-25
translation between data and information, 21-23
DBUG statement, 142
Deblunderizing, *see* Debugging
Debugged program, 135
Debugging, 6, 18-19, 58, 132-145
bugs:
defined, 135
diagnosis of, 140-141
isolation of, 143
kinds of, 136
testing for, 6, 18, 132-134, 137-140
decisions, 141-143
defined, 134
diagnostic environment, 144-145
kinds of errors, 143-144
monitors, 187-188

Debugging *(cont.)*:
  progress review, 145
  real-time software, 178
Decision tables, 56-58
Deductive diagnosis strategy, 141
Defensive programming, 134
Definition, 157
DeRossi, Claud J., 156
Design-in-the-whole vs. partial implementa-
    tion, 55
Designs of On-Line Systems (Yourdon), 165
Design team membership, WDM, 87-88
Dictionary of the module, 187
DIM statement, 116
Distribution list, WDM, 87
Documentation, 2, 3, 85-95
  amount of, 92
  bugs, 136
  concurrent, incremental, 85-86
  configuration control, 93-95
  intraprogram, 93
  working design manual (WDM), 86-92
    identifying contributions, 89-90
    items to document, 90-92
    revisions, 90
    structure, 86-89
Dodes, Irving Allen, 25*n*
Dumps, 145, 188
Dynamic data structures, 34-37

Editor program, 97
English as design notation, 68-69
Enhancements, 136
Entry, 56
Execution monitoring, 187-188
Exit point, 43
EXP function, 104
EX post facto flowcharts, 76

Finite-state machines (FSM), 56, 77-80, 178
Firewalling, 171
Firm documents, 90
Floating-point data, 25
Flow, controlling, 43-46
Flowcharts, 69-77
Flow lines, 71
For statement, 46

FOR statement, 111-112
FORTRAN, 17-18, 76, 150-153
Functional notation, 41-43
Functional testing, 140
Fundamental Algorithms (Knuth), 63
*Fundamentals of Structured Programming
    Using FORTRAN* (Holt and Hume),
    153

Generating polynomial, 52
Gilman, Leonard, 158
Global data, 47
GOSUB statement, 113-114
GO TO-less programming, 77
GO TO statement, 108-109
Greitzer, Samuel L., 25*n*
Gries, David, 160

Hardware, 1
Hwelett-Packard 3000 BASIC System, 128-
    129
Higher-level language, 96
Hollerith constants, 152
Holt, R. C., 153
Hume, J. N. P., 153

IF statement, 110-111
If-then-else statements, 44-45, 46
Incremental documentation, 85-86
Inductive diagnosis strategy, 141
Information, 21
Initialization of the variable, 46
In-line procedure, 44, 46
Input data description, 53-56
Input/Output Control System (IOCS), 179-
    180
INPUT statement, 109, 148-149
Interpreters, 162
Interrupts, 166-168
INT function, 104
Intraprogram documentation, 93
Items, 31-33, 38
Iteration, 43, 45-46
Iverson, Kenneth, 156

Jensen, Kathleen, 160
Job control language, 127-128
Job control statements, 180

Kemeny, John, 98
Key words, in BASIC program, 97
Knuth, Donald E., 25n, 63
Kurtz, Thomas, 98

Language translators, 144, 162, 182-184
Learning COBOL Fast (De Rossi), 156
LET statement, 105-107
Life-cycle costing, 35
Linear search technique, 13
Linguistic notations, 80-82
Linkage editors, 187
Linking loaders, 152
Lists, 34-38, 61, 62
Literals, 28
Loaders, 152, 183, 184-187
Local data, 47
LOG function, 104
Logic Analyzers, 144
Looping, 110-111

Major enhancements, 136
Major errors, 136
Mather, Dane G., 150
Media abbreviations, 94
Media-copying routines, 188
Microcomputers, 2, 3, 4, 17, 54, 55, 128, 182
Minicomputers, 2, 3, 4, 53, 54, 55, 128
Minor enhancements, 136
Monitors, 172-173, 179-180, 187-188
Multiple-precision capability, 23

NEXT statement, 112-113
Nonterminal symbols, 80
Numbers, 24-25

Object programs, 16, 18, 184-187
On-line user, 181
Operands, 99, 101-102
Operating systems, 3
Operators, 40-41, 99, 101-103
Out-of-line procedure, 44, 46
Output data description, 53-56

Packing of data, 23
Partial implementation vs. design-in-the-whole, 55
PASCAL, 159-160

PASCAL User Manual and Report (Jensen and Wirth), 160
Performance testing, 139
Peripheral device control, 73
Pidgin programming, 26
PL/M, 17-18
Polling, 166
Prewritten (canned) programs, 5, 62-63
Primer on PASCAL, A (Conway, Gries, and Zimmerman), 160
PRINT statement, 107-108, 142, 148-149
Probable contributions, 90
Problems:
  growing complexity of, 7
  specification of, 6, 13-15
Procedure, 11, 42
Procedure-oriented language, 96
Procedure structures, 39-49
  controlling flow, 43-46
  data manipulation, 40-41
  functional notation, 41-43
  procedural elements, 39-40
  program structure, 46-49
Programming:
  basics, 5-8
  bench, 16
  defensive, 134
  pidgin, 26
  real-time, *see* Real-time programming
  structured (top-down design), 60, 77
Programming Language, A (Iverson), 156
Programming languages, 6, 16-18, 146-163
  APL, 156-158
  assembly, 17-18, 96, 160-163
  BASIC, *see* BASIC
  binary, 16, 17
  choosing, 146-147
  COBOL, 26, 76, 146, 153-156
  FORTRAN, 17-18, 76, 150-153
  PASCAL, 159-160
  PL/M, 17-18
  procedure-oriented, 96
Program notations, 67-84
  data sequence charts, 82-83
  English, 68-69
  finite-state machines (FSM), 77-80
  flowcharts, 69-77
  linguistic notations, 80-82

Program notations *(cont.):*
  mixing, 84
  structured programming, 60, 77
Programs:
  analogy of, 9-13
  applications, 2
  coding, 6-8, 16-18
  debugged, 135
  debugging, *see* Debugging
  defined, 9
  design, 6, 15; *See also* Algorithm design
  editors, 97
  life cycle, 20
  object, 16, 18, 184-187
  prewritten (canned), 5, 62-63
  problem specification, 6, 13-15
  reading, 64
  source, 18
  structure, 46-49
  systems, 2, 4, 6, 179
  testing, 6, 18, 132-134, 137-140
  translation, 6, 16, 18
  use and maintenance, 19-20
  utility, 188-189

Queuing, 172-174
Quoted text, 100

Reading programs, 64
Read-write memory, 11
Ready-made programs, 5, 62-63
Real-time programming, 164-178
  interrupts, 166-168
  interrupt software, 169-171
  maintaining history, 178
  queuing, 172-174
  recognizing stimuli, 165-166
  systems support, 165
  task tables, 175-177
Relocatable loader, 184-186
Remark statement, 105
Remote job (or batch) entry, 181
Requirements, 50-53
  formalization of, 56-58
RETURN statement, 114
RND function, 104
Rose, Allen J., 158
Round-robin queue, 172

Royce, W. W., 85*n*
Rules, 56

Scheduler, 166
Semantics, rule of, 98
Seminumerical Algorithms (Knuth), 63
Sequential execution, 43
SIN function, 103
Snapshot of memory, 145
Software:
  defined, 1
  environments, 3-4
  kinds of, 2-3
  programming basics, 5-8
  systems, *see* Systems software
  uses of computers, 4-5
Sorting and Searching (Knuth), 63
Source program, 18
Special characters, 101
Specifications, 6, 13-15
SQR function, 102-105
State word, 169
Stimulation testing, 139
STOP statement, 109
String expressions, 147-148
Structured programming (top-down design),
    60, 77
Subexpression, 101
Subject index, WDM, 88-89
Supervisors, 180-182
Supervisor system, 180
Symbolic names, BASIC, 99
Syntax, rules of, 98
Systematic programming, 77
Systems programs, 2, 4, 6, 179
Systems software, 179-189
  environment, 182
  execution monitoring, 187-188
  language translators, 182-184
  learning systems programming, 189
  monitors, 178-180
  object programs, 184-187
  operating system use, 182
  supervisors, 180-182
  utilities, 188-189

TAN function, 103
Target line, 109

Task tables, 175-177
Tausworthe, Robert C., 85*n*
Tentative contributions, 90
Terminal symbol, 80
Testing, 6, 18, 132-134, 137-140
   See also Debugging
Test points, 142
Text editors, 189
Top-down design, 60, 77
Transactions on Mathematical Software, 63
Transfer vector, 186-187
Translation, 6, 16, 18
Translators, 144, 160, 182-184

User's Groups, 63
Utility programs, 188-189

Variables, 99-105
Vectored interrupts, 168

Waite, Stephen V. F., 150
WDM, *see* Working design manual
While-do statements, 45-46
Wirth, Niklaus, 159, 160
Working design manual (WDM), 86-92
   identifying contributions, 89-90
   items to document, 90-92
   revisions, 90
   structure, 86-89

Yourdon, Edward, 165

Zimmerman, E. Carl, 160